ABOUT THE AUTHOR

Nigel Richardson is a British journalist and author of five previous books who has
worked at the top level for more than 25 years (13 of them on the staff of the *Daily
Telegraph* in London). He writes about history, archaeology, landscapes, culture
and wildlife conservation and has won numerous awards and commendations
(UK Travel Journalist of the Year, *Sunday Times* Children's Book of the Week,
BBC Radio 4 Pick of the Week etc). Previous books include the travelogues *Break-
fast in Brighton: Adventures on the Edge* ⌐
Wilson) *Britain's Best Drives: Journeys*

T0054337

The
Accidental
Detectorist

The
Accidental
Detectorist

Uncovering an
Underground Obsession

NIGEL RICHARDSON

First published in Great Britain in 2022 by Cassell,
an imprint of Octopus Publishing Group Ltd
Carmelite House
50 Victoria Embankment
London EC4Y 0DZ
www.octopusbooks.co.uk

An Hachette UK Company
www.hachette.co.uk

First published in paperback in 2023

ISBN 978-1-78840-372-6

A CIP catalogue record for this book is available from the British Library.

Printed and bound in the UK.

13 5 7 9 10 8 6 4 2

Typeset in 11.75/19pt Heldane Text by Jouve (UK), Milton Keynes

Publisher: Trevor Davies
Senior Editor: Leanne Bryan
Design Director: Mel Four
Production Manager: Caroline Alberti
Photographer: David Mossman

This FSC® label means that materials used for
the product have been responsibly sourced

A note on the text
Some details of people and places have been changed in order to preserve
the anonymity of individuals and disguise the location of metal-detecting sites.

'The air is full of sounds; the sky, of tokens; the ground is all memoranda and signatures, and every object covered over with hints which speak to the intelligent.'

Ralph Waldo Emerson

CONTENTS

INTRODUCTION

He was sitting on the stubbled margin of a field near my cottage in Hampshire, tucked inside a big green fishing umbrella. As I approached with my terrier Bertie, I wondered what he could be doing, apparently camped out in this nondescript place of mud and wind. Spotting the metal detector lying on its side, I took it at first to be a bit of agricultural kit – a turnip extractor, maybe? – and the man an employee of the local farm estate. Then a bleep went off in my head. He had to be one of those boring fools who tramp across fields in headphones and gumboots, looking for something they never find.

This was my first sighting of a detectorist up close, but I'd observed plenty of his anorak-wearing cousins, furtively haunting the ends of railway station platforms with spiral notebooks and stubby pencils.

'Morning,' I said, feeling an inner smirk coming on.

Next to the detector was a military-style knapsack, a Thermos and an open Tupperware box containing a round of sandwiches made of white pulpy bread.

'Afternoon,' said the man, mid-munch, from the gloom of his umbrella nest.

I looked at my watch. It was 12.10pm. The man was a stickler.

'Found anything?' He shook his head. I persisted: 'Any particular reason you're looking here?' Then I remembered something and without waiting for him to reply supplied my own answer. 'Battle of Cheriton by any chance?'

The village of Cheriton lies three miles to the west of where we were. In March 1644, it was the site of a small but significant battle of the English Civil War in which Parliamentarian forces under Sir William Waller routed a Royalist army commanded by his close friend Ralph Hopton (the previous year, in a letter to Hopton, Waller had written: 'We are both upon the stage and must act such parts as are assigned us in this tragedy. Let us do it in a way of honour, and without personal animosities').

Apparently the farmer who worked the fields around Cheriton still ploughed up cannonballs and musket balls and other objects. An old oak tree near where we were now talking was reputedly where Sir Benjamin Tichborne, one of the fleeing Royalist officers, had hidden on the night after the battle. I had a mental flash of a haggard man in high boots and a floppy hat, scurrying across the field in front of us. A coin fell from his pocket, a button from his ripped jacket. Were they now zipped in a pocket of my new friend's knapsack? Would he tell me if they were?

The detectorist looked up at me blankly. Then his inscrutable features twisted in rage.

'Bloody hell,' he exclaimed. 'Get off! *Off!*'

He rocked forward and tried to swipe Bertie's head. Too late. While I was rambling on in know-all fashion, the dog had managed to strain far enough forward on his leash to filch the man's remaining sandwich from its box and was now desperately trying to gobble it down before it was somehow redeemed from him.

This incident gold-plated the encounter with a great punchline. The detectorist became just a prop and a sap in my store of tales of a life lived smugly. Five years later, when I came to meet my second detectorist, there was far less to be smug about. Bertie the artful little dodger had died. And the moving parts of my life as a travel writer for newspapers and magazines had been jammed up by a spanner called Covid-19.

Brexit – or at least the vote to bring about the UK's withdrawal from the EU – had already cast a shadow. But even as my country tore itself apart over its place in the world, I had continued to look and travel outwards. Then all our horizons were shrunk by a zoonotic virus that had probably started in a 'wet' market in China.

Unable to count on travelling abroad, I started writing a monthly newspaper column about Britain. It was an opportunity to make a point. It seemed to me that readers had stopped being the main audience of much travel journalism. The avalanche of glossy supplements was signalling behind their backs to advertisers and the corporate travel industry. The prism through which readers saw the world was being reduced to guff about secret hideaways and designer bedsheets.

There was, I felt, a more individual, grounded way of travelling. Memorable experiences, rooted in landscape and history, could be had in objectively unremarkable places – on the A1, a road I know well, for example. This loose idea was given a run-out in my first newspaper column of the Covid era. I then had to come up with ideas for subsequent columns. At this point I remembered my Hampshire detectorist.

During lockdown, I had taken to going on long solitary rambles, with binoculars round my neck to scope the sky for the buzzards and red kites that wheeled above the chalk downland where I lived. But my gaze was drawn down as well as upward. The fields and woods I trod were linked by sunken trackways overarched with canopies of hazel and hawthorn. The effect was one of walking through green tunnels, my boots often crowded into a narrow groove down the centre that had been worn in the chalk and flint by centuries of tramping feet.

I started to wonder about all the people who had gone before me on this web of trackways. And as I speculated, I started to 'feel' these spectral figures through the soles of my boots and see them in the corner of my eye.

The experience was like a jolt of earth energy, light bending from a long-dead place. I was within touching distance of John Masefield's ... 'souls unseen/ Who knew the interest in me, and were keen/ That man alive should understand man dead' (from 'Biography'). One of these souls looked familiar: the fleeing Cavalier I half-glimpsed when Bertie and I met the detectorist whose sandwich he snaffled.

Though my world had suffered a general deficit of light since that time, in one respect it had been enriched. A comedy series about metal detecting had proved an unlikely hit on TV and caused me to revise my snobby view of detectorists as, essentially, trainspotters in wellies. *Detectorists,* written by Mackenzie Crook, was gentle, bucolic and in its way profound. If Andy and Lance, played by Crook and Toby Jones, were anything to go by, the hobbyists who scoured our greensward in search of tokens of the past were citizen-philosophers with big hearts and a warm sense of place.

At its worst, the Brexit debate had poked a manure heap of xenophobia, among the English in particular. But Andy and Lance channelled a different sense of Englishness, one that didn't define itself by the exclusion of others. In one episode, Lance speculates on all the people that have passed here before us as he digs up his latest find:

> '. . . *there's nowhere we could tread that hasn't been trodden on a thousand times before by Celts, Druids, the Romans . . .*'
>   '*What you got?*' *[says Andy]*
>   '*A scaffold clamp . . . Saxons, the Vikings . . .*'

At the end of the episode, these ancestors are brought back to life in a time-lapse sequence that transfigures the Suffolk field the detectorists have been searching in. The trees shrink, the seasons change and figures from deep history appear and dissolve. The soundtrack to these mystical moments, a song called 'Magpie' sung by the traditional Northumbrian folk singers The Unthanks, has its roots in Old English song and lore. That Cavalier I kept seeing came from the same place. Not just the imagination but the earth itself.

Watching a rerun of this episode gave me an idea for the next column. The National Council for Metal Detecting (NCMD), the hobby's 'official voice', put me in touch with a detectorist called Kris Rodgers, who posts videos on a YouTube channel entitled 'Addicted to Bleeps'. A bearded, jovial dude (one of his words) with the catchphrase 'Greetings, bleepers, how the devil are you?', Kris has 120,000 subscribers, in Canada and the

US as well as the UK. The far south-east corner of England is his patch. He agreed to take me out and we arranged to meet one Thursday, in the post-lockdown weeks of high summer, in the car park of a Brewers Fayre pub on the outskirts of Dover.

The name (streamlined of its apostrophe) of this chain of 'family friendly pub restaurants' evokes an imagined past of cheery landlords, foaming pints and no-nonsense grub with gravy (other chains in the genre include Harvester, Chef & Brewer and Toby Carvery). But there is nothing phoney about the historic pedigree of this part of the English coast.

Mainland Europe is in your face, just over 20 miles south across the Dover Strait and visible as a spectral line or dusting of lights in clear weather. Romans and Vikings conducted raids and invasions on the Kentish coast. Dover and her White Cliffs have always been a front line and a faultline in the national psyche – not just the point of easiest entry for invaders and refugees but a big white barrier against any perceived dilution of our national identity and plunder of our riches by those same foreigners.

In the Battle of Britain, which was fought in these skies in the summer of 1940, the narrative of resistance to invasion found its defining moment. Like many boys of the post-war baby boomer generation I had grown up on a diet of war comics and aeroplane models celebrating the gallantry of those 'few' Hurricane and Spitfire pilots whom Churchill immortalised in his famous speech.

The day I met Kris was just two weeks before the 80th anniversary of the Battle of Britain and as we truffled for treasure in a Kentish field a Spitfire flew over, like a logo in the blue. At the same time, out in the Channel, another 'invasion' (the word is loaded but some people used it) was under way. The people came not in Nazi warplanes or Roman triremes but in barely seaworthy dinghies. And their intent was not to conquer but to escape war and poverty. More than three hundred men, women and children were picked up by Coastguard vessels or Border Force patrols on the day I went to Kent to try my hand at metal detecting.

In this lodestone of national identity and time of self-distancing, Kris and I clinked the elbows of our checked shirts. In real life the dial was turned down a notch from his ebullient on-screen persona. As he gave me a quick metal-detecting tutorial, shaking out the contents of his knapsack (all detectorists have them) on the asphalt of the Brewers Fayre car park, I warmed immediately to this green man of Kent.

'This'll give you an idea of the kind of stuff we turn up,' he said.

A pile of dusty objects lay before us. It looked like the contents of a vacuum cleaner bag. He sifted through.

'Half an R2-D2,' he said, tossing aside an old *Star Wars* figurine. 'Ye olde catapult. What I call "coins of nothingness". Oh, *that's* good.' He lifted to the light a small silver disc dated 1561: a hammered Elizabethan sixpence. Then something small and functional. 'Know what that is? Tricky one, *I* didn't know.'

I had no idea.

'Candle snuffer. Roman.'

The inventory continued. A spur. A 'rove', which is a copper washer used in boatbuilding apparently. Concluding, he said: 'But if I was to sum up metal detecting, it would be with these three things.' He prodded them into a line: 'Bullet. Musket ball. Coin.'

The warm-up over, I followed Kris's car north-east along the coast. Between a village and the fringes of a small town, we turned left on to a country road. A ridge rose on our left, the seaward side, with a windmill on the top. Inland stood a copse. We parked at the edge of a field below the windmill. This was part of Kris's 'land', the various fields and meadows that he had permission from the owners to detect on. Our field had just been cut for hay. The stubble was dry, the ground even.

We shouldered our machines – he was lending me his everyday model, an XP Gold Maxx Power, while he road tested a new detector for his YouTube channel – and headed off in the direction of the windmill.

'Talking of treasure,' he said, 'this is the real treasure, my friend.'

He opened his arms to a world that in that moment was just for us: the grass-fragrant field; the copse and ridge and English Channel; distant bungalows and static caravans scattered like white-and-beige pebbles; and above (never forget to look up), a cloudless sky sprinkled with buzzards.

'A lot of detectorists miss this,' said Kris. 'They're in it for gain. They miss the bigger picture of what it can give you.'

At the top of the ridge he demonstrated how to operate the detector, the importance of keeping the search coil (the halo-like head) parallel to the ground as you sweep it back and forth.

'A slow, relaxed motion,' he said. 'This is the tai chi part of it. Repeating these movements until your mind finally shuts up and you go to that zone where you become nothing and no one. And it's lovely.'

He smiled and rolled his shoulders, gently feathering the coil over the fresh-cut stalks and flinty earth. And I wondered what dins went off in his head that he felt the need to silence them.

'See?'

He invited me to have a go.

So far, I had carried my detector as if it were a dumb tree branch or a bag of tent poles. Now we powered up its intelligence and I set it to work, gripping the handle and sweeping the coil at hover level above the soil. Unlike, say, fly fishing, there appeared to be no arcane technique to metal detecting. It seemed as accessibly easy as a hip-swaying walk in the park.

'I listen for what I call "happy bleeps",' he went on, placing a coin in the ground and playing the coil over the top of it. The electronic signal was high-pitched and urgent. There were also *un*happy bleeps, low grunts caused by iron junk like horseshoes. The ground, Kris said, is talking to you. 'You've got to listen carefully to what it says.'

Spaced several yards apart, we swept slowly towards the copse at the northern end of the ridge. Kris talked about how he got started. He'd been a youth worker and played bass guitar in pub bands. When the kids he looked after were offered a day out with a metal detectorist, he went along and was hooked.

'It's a lovely thing and I'm so glad I found it,' he said. 'It goes way deeper than just digging up cool stuff. It's hard to suffer from anxiety or feel pressure when you're in a place like this. Hang on—.'

He had bleeps. He ran the coil back across the spot, as if rewinding a tape. The bleeps were halfway between happy and grumpy. Worth a dig. With a tough-looking spade, he levered up a plug of earth and squatted to examine it. Now he refined the search with an orange 'pinpointer', an electronic wand like the ones used for airport security checks.

The object was in the earthen plug. He split it apart as if he were breaking bread, saying, 'I think there's something proactively spiritual about putting your hands in mud.' He probed again with the pointer.

The object was now in the left-hand piece of the earthen loaf. 'Prepare yourself . . .' he said – and extricated a ring pull from a drinks can.

His most spectacular find, he said, had come just a few months before – a hoard of Bronze Age axe heads and other objects that he reported to the Portable Antiquities Scheme (PAS), the voluntary recording programme run by the British Museum, as potential treasure under the Treasure Act (1996). Experts from the BM were still assessing it. 'It's pretty massive in archaeology terms,' he said, 'but I prefer the more personal objects that tell a story.'

His favourite piece was the early fourteenth-century 'papal bulla' he found on the other side of Folkestone. A papal bulla is a lead seal that was attached to papal documents to prove their authenticity. Who was carrying the one Kris found? Had he just come off a ship? Was he bound for Canterbury? 'It has a rip in it, as if it was torn away from the holder,' he said. Kris's fantasy was that this man on a medieval Pope's business had been mugged – or murdered.

As we walked and talked, the Spitfire flew over. Gazing up at the roundels on the underside of the wings, I remarked on the deep and pure parochialism of where we were and what we were doing – sifting, probing, interrogating the very soil we had come from. I told him it was one of the things I liked about *Detectorists*: 'It didn't make a big deal of it, but it was partly about who we are.'

The soil spoke to us again, this time with happy bleeps. Kris dug, then probed with the pointer.

'Ah, look at that my friend.'

It was small and finely wrought – copper alloy with a green patina of oxidisation. He turned it over in his gloved hand.

'We've got ourselves a buckle. That's got some age to it.'

He reckoned it was Tudor (and the next day confirmed the fact). The buckle was D-shaped, single-loop and was attached to the clothing of some peasant or herdsman when Henry VIII sat on the English throne.

Kris handed it to me, saying, 'You're the first person to touch that for five hundred years' – then, correcting himself: 'Second person.'

As I took it, I felt something. Something like time becoming circular. In all my years of travelling the world – from Pyongyang to Pitcairn Island – the most faraway place of all had been hiding right here, in plain sight. Offering its memoranda and signatures in the most random and thrilling ways, from just an inch or two down in my home soil.

The buckle's phantom owner joined the fleeing Cavalier in my crew of unseen souls. The worry, in his time, would have been of Catholic invasion from Continental Europe. This paranoia reached its height in 1538 when Pope Paul III excommunicated Henry VIII following Henry's annulment of his marriage to the devoutly Catholic Catherine of Aragon. Henry had ordered fortifications along the South Coast to be beefed up and the following year visited Dover Castle to see for himself how the work was going. There was no rolling news then, but word travelled fast when it came to outside threat. Did our buckled friend once stand on this spot, scanning the sea for the masts of French or Spanish warships?

Kris also found a farthing – a plump and jaunty-tailed wren was seeing the sky again after 60 years – and I had a find of my own. My very first. It was so small that I couldn't actually see it in the lump of earth I held in my hand and Kris had to guide me to it, his pinpointer jittering crazily across my fingers. 'There,' he said, shaking and smoothing the soil off it and holding it up to my eyes. It was about the size of a pea and bluntly conical.

'Er, what is it?' I said.

A dress pin or fastener, reckoned Kris on quick examination. He aged it back to Tudor times, like our buckle. We found it not far from the buckle. Maybe our peasant, squinting out to sea, pulled his cloak tighter around him against the onshore breeze and the fear of invasion – and as he did so this little pin pinged off on to the ground. Feeling a ridiculous burst of pride – I was no slouch at this detecting game, I had just found a Tudor dress pin! – I placed it in the top pocket of my shirt.

After a couple of hours, Kris had to rush off to post a review of the new detector he was road testing on his YouTube channel. His parting words were, 'If you need any help getting started, give us a bell.' I hadn't actually said I was planning to take up metal detecting. My line had been that I was looking for just enough material for one 800-word column.

Once Kris had driven off, I sat in the car and poured myself a cup of tea from my Thermos. Drinking it, I pondered Kris's offer and found myself tapping my shirt pocket. Then I started the car and drove home through dissolving landscapes.

1

SECRETS OF THE ORCHARD

My machine turned up behind the wheelie bins one morning, dropped off by a phantom DHL driver. On its box was an image of the detector superimposed on a range of mountains – the rugged outdoors was now mine to dig holes and find scaffold clamps in!

I made a cup of coffee and carried the box into the living room. These days, bits of kit designed for middle-aged hobbyists are impressively idiot-proof – I'm a technical halfwit but within a few sips of coffee I had managed to slide, clip and tighten the rigid plastic parts into place.

The orange-and-black device that lay before me on the sofa looked, even down to the colour scheme, like the garden strimmer that had appeared behind the wheelie bins the week before. The week before that, I had taken delivery of a bright yellow, high-pressure patio cleaner. What did these colourful but atypical acquisitions tell me about the direction my life was taking all of a sudden? Did I even care? I cared just enough to check that no one was peering through the living-room window. Then I gripped my new toy and swept the John Lewis rug for treasure.

The detector and other tools were a case of late-onset maturity, brought about by the Covid-19 pandemic and the consequent requirement to 'stay home'. Luckily for me, home was an old cottage in the Hampshire countryside that I shared with my partner. We had owned it for nearly 30 years but had never spent so much uninterrupted time here.

As we grew into this strange interlude, we felt history stirring in the corners of our new world. The landscape of life was turning upside down, other realities were appearing. Part of this revelation had occurred on my outing with Kris in Kent. Who knew such things as the buckle and the dress pin had been lying in that field for five hundred years, waiting to be found? What did that say for the fields surrounding the cottage – a largely undisturbed corner of Hampshire that has been in human occupation for thousands of years?

The metal detector was to be my companion on journeys to destinations that had been here all along, places far too obvious for me to have noticed before: the ones in front of my eyes and beneath my feet.

Standing in my front room that morning, I felt certain that the ancestors were already lined up, awaiting their turn to touch the future. But metal detecting is science, not an act of faith. I didn't have a clue how to use the thing I was holding. In the early hours after unpacking the detector, I pored over the online instruction manual and studied video tutorials with an increasing sense of frustration.

All the information available online assumed a basic level of knowledge that I didn't have. It was like reading a cookbook and not knowing what 'peel' or 'boil' meant. Down in Kent I had detected dumbly, relying on Kris to set my machine and interpret its responses. He had offered to be on phone standby, but I needed someone on the doorstep. When I swept the internet for a likely local contact, Pete Welch popped up like a shiny coin.

Pete set up a group called Weekend Wanderers more than 30 years ago and has 'permissions' (i.e. agreements with farmers to detect on their land) across several southern English counties. In 2014, in a field near Buckingham, someone on a Weekend Wanderers rally found a hoard of more than five thousand eleventh-century coins (many from the reigns of Kings Aethelred the Unready and Cnut the Great) that was subsequently valued at £1.35 million and is now on display at the Discover Bucks Museum in Aylesbury.

On a bright day in early summer, Pete and I met in the garden of a pub next to a heritage railway line. The garden was rigged up with a giant TV screen and red-and-white bunting for the forthcoming European Football Championship and every so often a hooting steam train puffed by in a spasm of cream-and-maroon nostalgia.

For ease of recognition, Pete wore his Weekend Wanderers baseball cap, the logo devised so that the WW appeared either side of the image of an antique coin to make the word 'WOW'. When I admired the niftiness of the logo, he pointed out that 'Wow!' was the word most commonly exclaimed on 'digs' (a term, incidentally, that archaeologists don't approve of when applied to the activities of detectorists), along with 'Found much?'

Pete was exactly my age, a compact, twinkly bloke both warm and wily – a characteristic of serious-minded detectorists. His opening declaration was this: 'If I said to you, "Go and find some Roman coins 20 minutes' drive from here" you wouldn't know where to start looking, it'd be random. But I could take you to a place and you'd go, "Oh, a Roman coin." Coz I know where to look. But there's lots of places I *don't* know where to look. Because what you've really got here is a largely unexplored country.'

The idea of Britain being still 'largely unexplored' in a metal-detecting sense came as a relief. I suffer from a variant of Impostor Syndrome, the feeling that whatever I am associated with its best days are behind it. Cases in point include all the sports teams I played in, and the profession I fell into (journalism – already on the skids when I started out). I had been worrying that I was arriving late at this party too.

Since I had tuned into the idea of becoming a detectorist, scarcely a week seemed to have passed without some revelation of an unassuming hobbyist making a stellar find, often in an incongruous location. These stories tended to pop up at the end of TV news bulletins as feel-good fillers, but they made me anxious. Leave some stuff in the ground for me!

Pete's comment conjured a more reassuring scenario, of old Britain lying there like a tramp in a ditch, just waiting for me to rifle its raggedy breeches. As I would learn, this is a mugger's way of regarding our common heritage. But metal detecting was to be nothing if not a process of growing up.

Over prawn-and-avocado baguettes, Pete riffed on some metal-detecting essentials, from use of maps (check 'em out first, from old Ordnance Survey to Google Earth) and psychology (chatting up farmers for permissions) to turf wars and the kind of people he referred to coyly as 'A-holes'.

On the subject of getting started, he was clear: 'Any new machine that I buy, I bench-test it,' he said, raising and lowering his baguette for emphasis. 'I put it on to a wooden table and I pass across the coil bits of iron, silver, gold, small things, large things. Write down what response you get. That's the biggest problem new people have. They don't bench-test it enough.'

The day after meeting Pete Welch, I laid my detector – a beginner-to-intermediate model fairly new to the market called a Quest Q30 – on the wooden table in the garden and assembled around it various metal objects I had managed to cobble together. Detectorists post videos on YouTube going through exactly this bench-test (or air-test) process. But they have real finds to use as their test specimens, things they want to find more of.

I had to make do with a hotchpotch: an iron ring I found on the Thames foreshore at Rotherhithe, in the spot where boatbuilding and boatbreaking took place; a gold Spanish eight-escudos piece dated 1802, from the reign of Carlos IV; a modern Norwegian one-krone piece; a pair of brass nutcrackers in the suggestive form of shapely female legs; and a head-and-shoulders figurine made of spelter (a zinc–lead alloy like bronze) that I had found while working in the garden a decade before.

The idea was to note the tones and record the 'target ID' number (from 1 to 99, on my machine) that appeared on the detector's display panel as I swept each object back and forth across, but not touching, the 'search coil'. This is the circuitry at the end of the shaft, resembling a spoked wheel or closed horseshoe, where the clever stuff happens. The coil transmits an electromagnetic field into the ground and any metal within that field will respond by generating its own electromagnetic field that the machine then picks up and interprets as both an ID number and a language of bleeps and tones.

The response depends on the conductivity of the object. Bits of old iron, which are poor conductors, score low on the number scale and produce grunt-like bleeps, while gold, silver or copper, which are highly conductive, score top marks, with a higher-pitched, excitable sound.

This is the general idea, but the story is more complicated than this. Iron, for instance, may be a poor conductor *per se*, but a big chunk like a bit of old plough will return a high-ID reading due to its sheer size. And precious metals will respond differently when alloyed with other metals. A gold coin, for instance, may give a similar signal to the ring pull of a drinks can. But I wasn't ready, at this stage, for such fine-tuning.

I switched on the machine for the first time and watched the digital calligraphy chase itself around the display screen. When the detector bleeped I gave it a nod, anticipating the odd kind of almost-bond that can develop between humans (well, *men*) and mechanical objects. Then I fed it with tidbits, wafting the different items across its coil and duly noting, on the opening page of a new notebook, the ID number and beep tone of each.

The iron ring registered 18 and sounded pissed off, as I would if shaken from a drunken sleep. The gold coin and the brass legs scored high marks and sounded crisp and upbeat – the 'happy bleeps' that were Kris Rodgers's watchword.

While I was doing this, my partner came out to spy on me and spotted the gold coin, which was a family heirloom she had inherited from her aunt in Spain. I had taken it from her jewellery box without her permission, but she didn't seem to mind. 'As long as you don't actually *bury* it,' she joked.

When the coast was clear I proceeded to the next stage, which was to create a 'test garden' – to dig holes in the ground, bury my test objects in the holes and find them again using the detector, noting its reaction and readings. The bit of garden I chose for this experiment was called, somewhat optimistically, 'the orchard'.

Though it did contain some apple trees, calling it an orchard was really an excuse not to mow the grass there very often, or do any weeding at all. The orchard was also where I intended to make my first attempts at metal detecting for real. This was partly so that I didn't leave the lawn surrounding the cottage pockmarked with holes, as Pete Welch had warned me would happen. But it was also because I reckoned the orchard was a really promising search site.

Earlier in the year, while digging a hole for an apple tree sapling, I had found a fragment of Victorian glazed pottery and an oyster shell. The shell probably dates from the nineteenth century when oysters were a poor man's fast food, though it could be many centuries older. A few years earlier, while clearing nettles in the orchard, I had also stumbled on the spelter figurine I used in the bench test.

This object was the forerunner of finds I would make with the detector and gave me a preliminary taste of the thrill of the process. When I'd cleaned the soil off it, I found myself looking at the face of a bewhiskered military gent wearing a fez. The top of the fez was hollow and plugged with earth. Letters on the base of the bust spelt out the name GORDON. The fez, the Victorian facial hair, the name – I had dug up one of English history's more bizarre minor characters, Major-General Charles George Gordon, known as Gordon of Khartoum.

After his martyr's death at the Siege of Khartoum in 1885, Gordon had posthumously enjoyed an outpouring of patriotic adulation. Statues were erected in his honour, a hospital in Westminster changed its name to Gordon Hospital (though the suspicion has to be that the Western Hospital for Fistula, Piles and other Diseases of the Rectum was just waiting for a pretext) and a manufacturer of Victorian mantelpiece knick-knacks spotted an opening for a new product line.

The hole in General Gordon's fez was a puzzle. But an internet search revealed an identical object – a match holder and striker. The matches were kept in the fez and you struck them on the textured surface of the striker plate behind his epaulettes. For many years, no doubt, General Gordon was a fixture in the inglenook fireplace that still lay at the heart of the cottage. But at some point his function became redundant, the man himself a forgotten figure, and the bust was taken out and lobbed into the undergrowth.

I began to look on the orchard as a holder of secrets, a sense only reinforced when I did some research on the local area in preparation for the arrival of the metal detector. On a tithe map of 1839, I found that in the middle of the nineteenth century the strip of land we called the orchard had been a plot of arable land (which explained its long, thin shape, suitable for ploughing) belonging to 'D. Stevens' and rented by 'Sarah Prior'.

Sarah was listed as living next to the plot of land, in a house and barn she also owned – the cottage and (converted) barn that was now our house. I pictured Sarah Prior and generations of rural folk before and after her subsisting on the crops and vegetables they grew in this narrow strip. As they worked, oyster shells were thrown from their hands, coins dropped through holes in their pockets, oxen harnesses snapped and fell to earth and the piece of land now called the orchard filled steadily with memoranda and signatures.

I dug the holes for the test garden with another new piece of equipment, a high-strength 'digging tool' designed specially for metal detecting that lies somewhere between a garden spade and a trowel and extrudes pleasingly well-formed plugs of earth. The holes were scattered across a flat section of the orchard and I marked each location carefully with one of those wooden 'lolly sticks' used by gardeners. Once I had noted the ID number and tone of a find, I dug it back up and tamped the earth back into place.

That was the idea. It went off without hitch with the first couple of objects. But the gold coin didn't seem to be in the hole where I had put it. It wasn't just me that couldn't find it. Neither could my 'carrot'. This is a crucial bit of specialist kit, otherwise known as the pinpointer, that in colour, size and shape looks like, well, a carrot. Designed to detect metallic objects at close range, it has a durable plastic snout with which to rootle in the bottom of muddy holes. When it gets within a few inches of a target, it bleeps. When it's almost touching, it chatters excitedly, like the fruit bats I once heard in Fiji when the breadfruit were ready to eat.

But the carrot remained silent. I thought I had dug each hole to a depth of about six inches, but maybe for the gold coin I had gone a little deeper. I carried on digging, tried the pinpointer again. Nothing. Then my partner's rubber gardening clogs appeared in my eye line. 'Everything OK?' she said from far above.

Sitting back and wiping my brow, I reassured her that everything was fine. But I was suddenly feeling the heat. The coin was worth about £3,000 – I'd looked it up the night before – quite apart from the sentimental value of having belonged to a recently deceased and much-loved aunt.

'It's the gold coin, isn't it?' she said.

When I admitted that it was, she uttered two words that always freeze my blood: 'Traveller's cheques'. Over the years these apparently innocuous nouns have become shorthand for, 'Oh no, you've done it *again*, you complete moron.' The specific reference is to a trip to Corsica on which she gave me her envelope of holiday money to look after for five minutes and in that time a thief somehow managed to nick it from under my nose. Having re-fired a bullet she had fired many times before, she went back to the house, leaving me sweating.

I could have returned fire with a recycled bullet of my own and it was also expressible in two words: 'Dress pin'. When I returned from that first metal-detecting outing with Kris in Kent, I had taken my day's find from the top pocket of my shirt and waved it proudly in front of my partner's nose before placing it in a bowl by the kitchen sink.

I was going to rinse the mud off it just as soon as I'd checked out 'Tudor dress pins' online, but in that time she decided to do the washing-up. Small enough to be mistaken for a piece of food detritus, the dress pin was never seen again. But I decided that discretion was the better part of valour, given that her gold coin had possibly hit a sinkhole and slipped down hundreds of feet into Hampshire's chalky substratum.

In the many videos posted online by detectorists, often professionalised with soundtracks and graphics, the bit when they dig for an object is always skated over or speeded up, as if it were no more problematic than tying shoelaces. Having picked up a promising signal, they deftly hold the detector in one hand while levering up an accurate divot with the digging tool held in the other, giving it a helping toe poke with, usually, the left foot (right in my case, as I'm a left-hander).

Dropping to earth, they then truffle out the booty within seconds and, without breaking sweat, brandish the find aloft with a gleeful exclamation. But the earth is an alien, unfathomable place. Even its nearest depths are less familiar than deep space and I found the digging/finding process bothersome. It was as if the soil were playing entry-level magician's tricks that were still diverting enough to baffle me.

One beginner's mistake is to not check the plug of soil you have removed – you're digging deeper and deeper while the target is right there next to your knee all along. With the gold coin, it turned out that I was digging in the wrong place. After I'd widened the hole, the carrot finally led me to it and a domestic crisis was averted. But after that scare I was wary of the tricks that soil could play.

The groundwork had been completed. It was time for me to detect in anger. Pete Welch had had advice for me on this score. He had, for example, recommended not doing it in June – the month I bought the detector and we met – when the soil is likely to be dry and hard to dig. But it had been a damp early summer and then, just when I was ready to start detecting, it rained solidly for three days.

Waiting for the rain to stop, I watched detectorists' videos and read *Treasure Hunting* magazine, to which I had recently subscribed. From this I learned that many of the things that detectorists find in the ground of the British Isles are quite astonishing – beautiful, rare, moving, provocative. Most are unearthed in England: a map of finds reported to the Portable Antiquities Scheme (PAS) in any given year will show the rural acres of the South-east, the Home Counties, the East Midlands and East Anglia peppered with dots, while Devon and Cornwall, Wales, the North-west and the North-east remain largely unblemished.

The reasons for this are varied and overlapping but the main one is that this is where the Romans and Saxons settled, taking advantage of climate and trade links and establishing for ever the south-eastern third of Britain as the richest and most populated part of the country. Geology also plays a part – copper alloy does not survive well in the acidic soils of Cornwall, for example – as does urban development. If it were possible to metal detect beneath the pavements of Winchester or York, or the sprawling conurbations that cover much of the south-east of England, who knows how loud and frequent the 'Wow!'s would be? And some regions have a more active metal-detecting scene than others.

But every day someone somewhere is finding a Celtic gold stater, Britain's earliest coinage, or something Roman. This may sound like a free hit but there are responsibilities involved and detectorists who ignore them, either through ignorance or deliberately, give metal detecting a bad name. The worst offenders are the so-called 'nighthawks' – another word that archaeologists don't like because they feel it confers a spurious glamour on people who are essentially crooks and scumbags.

Nighthawks are detectorists who operate on land without the landowner's permission, or on scheduled ancient monuments (such as Hadrian's Wall) or archaeological sites for the purpose of looting and then selling valuable historical artefacts, thereby depriving wider society of our common heritage and archaeologists of potentially vital information.

That information, incidentally, resides not just in the object itself but in where it was found – the 'find spot', which can be measured down to the square yard. Find spots to archaeologists are as important as *terroir* to wine buffs. They enable stratigraphic excavation of a site – analysing it by layers to provide 'context' in relation to other objects or features. The process builds a picture that might include a date when the site was in use, its purpose, the status of people associated with it, their way of life and so on. Detectorists are not so bothered about this. To push the wine analogy (and to generalise), they don't care where the plonk comes from, they just want to get their hands on it – a fundamental difference.

'Heritage crime' – the illegal trading in artefacts and the looting of historical sites – is hardly new. The venerable museums of the Western world are stuffed with its results. But as metal detecting grew as a hobby through the 1970s, some archaeologists believed it was turning every detectorist into a potential safe-cracker, gleefully spinning the combination lock on the strongbox containing our heritage. They started a campaign called STOP (Stop Taking Our Past), which detectorists countered with a pressure group of their own under an acronym calculated to wind up their opponents: DIG (Detector Information Group). The battle lines were drawn, the argument polarised.

Before I took up the hobby, I was aware of this aggro and had put it down at least partly to good old English snobbery, reflecting binary divisions that have been around for a long time: Saxon and Norman, town and gown, peasant in the field and toff in his castle. The novel and film *The Dig*, based on the discovery of the Anglo-Saxon burial site at Sutton Hoo in 1939, is built on that division, pitting self-taught 'excavator' Basil Brown, who speaks like a yokel, against plummy-voiced Cambridge luminary Charles Phillips OBE FSA.

Matters came to a head in 1983 over the fate of Wanborough Roman temple in Surrey, described by the British Museum as 'one of the saddest stories in British archaeology'. Two detectorists stumbled on the site through the discovery of a number of Iron Age coins that they handed in to Guildford Museum. At the resulting inquest, conducted under the old law of Treasure Trove, the find spot was made public and the site was subsequently looted on an industrial scale by nighthawks, with the loss of thousands of objects.

The outrage that followed triggered reform that led to the replacement of the common law of Treasure Trove in England, Wales and Northern Ireland (that had existed since the time of Edward the Confessor) with the Treasure Act (1996). The definitions of 'treasure' and the obligations of the finder were sharpened up. Treasure is now: any object (other than a coin) that is at least three hundred years old and has a precious metal (i.e. gold or silver) content of at least ten per cent by weight; a prehistoric object containing precious metal; any group of two or more prehistoric metal objects found together (e.g. a hoard of Bronze Age axe heads); two or more coins from the same find (e.g. a hoard that was hidden, a purse-full that may have been dropped or a religious offering) provided they are at least three hundred years old and contain ten per cent gold or silver (if the coins contain less than ten per cent gold or silver, there must be at least ten of them); any man-made object whatsoever that was found with an object or objects defined as treasure (such as the pot the treasure was found in).

Anyone who finds treasure is legally required to report it to the coroner within 14 days of finding it, or within 14 days of when 'the finder first believes or has reason to believe the object is treasure'. This clause covers the possibility that you might, for example, take an object home covered in mud and not realise its true identity or worth until you clean it several days or weeks later; it also bends over backwards to encourage rather than criminalise the finder. The penalty for failing to report treasure you have found is a maximum prison term of three months or a fine of up to £5,000.

Once its treasure status has been declared, the object passes to a body of experts known as the Treasure Valuation Committee, which puts a value on it based on what it might fetch on the open market (a figure that may be challenged up to three times by the finder/ landowner if they think it's too low). A museum may then purchase it for that price, with the proceeds split (usually but not always 50–50) between finder and landowner. If no museum wants it or is able to raise the asking price, the find is 'disclaimed' and returned to the finder and landowner, who can do what they like with it.

When the Treasure Act (1996) came into force, in 1997, it was welcomed by archaeologists but their concern was that it didn't go far enough. What about stuff that was pulled from the ground that wasn't technically treasure but was still of enormous archaeological importance? This loophole was plugged by the PAS, which started up in the early 2000s. Managed by the British Museum and funded both nationally and locally, it is a voluntary scheme that encourages and enables detectorists (and anybody else who discovers an archaeological object by chance) to record potentially significant finds with a locally based archaeologist known as a Finds Liaison Officer (FLO). There are now more than 40 FLOs operating across England and Wales.

Legislation and organisation, together with educating detectorists through local groups, has put the heat on the looters. But the philosophical divide between archaeologists and detectorists will always be there. One archaeologist I spoke to, a bit further along my learning curve, likened it to the difference between sports fishermen and marine biologists: 'Both are interested in fish but they have entirely different perspectives on it.'

Thanks to the PAS, the two sides have learned to share the riverbank without kicking lumps out of each other, even if the resentment still smoulders. Among the detectorists I've met, I've heard plenty of chuntering directed at the world of archaeology, though they tend to get on with their local FLOs. One said: 'Heritage belongs to us *all*, not just them. You don't have to go to university to walk across a field waving a computer on a stick.'

Another complained that detectorists were made to feel like 'working-class layabouts and heathens'. For him, at least, the resentment pre-dated metal detecting and went deeper than archaeology. He told me that at his state comprehensive school, he and fellow pupils were paired with boys from a nearby public school on a fundraising project. The posh boys didn't seem to be taking it seriously, and when my friend had the temerity to point this out, he received a formative lesson in an unwritten rule of English life. His counterpart from the school with ivy on its old walls jabbed his finger at him and said, 'People like *you* don't get to talk like that to people like *us*.'

As well as tension between archaeologists and detectorists, there is internecine strife. The National Council for Metal Detecting (NCMD), which I joined (not least because the annual £8 membership fee includes public liability insurance), is the longstanding 'voice' of the hobby, proclaiming itself 'the only metal detecting council formally recognised by the UK government'. But amid much bad feeling, some erstwhile members have peeled off to form the Association for Metal

Detecting Sport (AMDS), with the aim of 'fill[ing] the vacuum that exists between ordinary detectorists and the decision makers that have influence over the hobby'.

Meanwhile, there is a Federation of Independent Detectorists (FID) for lone operators, and an Institute of Detectorists (IOD) is in the pipeline, its lofty-sounding mission being 'to research, create and provide an educational programme to suit many stakeholders'. When I assured one detectorist that I was a fully paid-up member of the NCMD, he replied, 'Just as well – if you'd been a member of the breakaway group I wouldn't have given you the time of day.' Without delving any deeper on this, Freud's 'narcissism of minor differences' comes to mind – as do the People's Front of Judea and their bitterest enemies, the Judean People's Front, in the Monty Python film *Life of Brian*.

What's for sure is that if it wasn't for detectorists, modern historians would have a more partial view of history, archaeologists would have a lot less to do and FLOs would be out of a job. In the last 20 years the PAS has recorded more than 1.5 million objects (the overwhelming majority found by detectorists) and added their details to its database, a brilliant, endlessly expanding resource available free online at finds.org.uk.

Given this volume of material, you'd think England would be fished out by now, and some of it is. Pete Welch may have claimed that England was 'largely unexplored' but he also likened the land that farmers have made available to detectorists to 'an incredibly small pond' that is getting ever smaller as the hobby grows in popularity (metal detecting lends itself to fishy metaphors, as well as attracting lots of people who actually fish; there is also a crossover activity known as 'magnet fishing', which involves chucking high-strength magnets into rivers and seeing what they drag up – supermarket trolleys usually).

Pete, who was described to me variously by archaeologists as 'totally honest' and 'one of the good guys', has turned metal detecting into a full-time commercial operation, running a club that charges detectorists (£20 a day for members, £23 for non-members) to take them out on one of his many long-term permissions and sharing the fees with the landowners. This means of monetising the hobby is welcomed by detectorists who don't have their own permissions or live in towns and cities with no obvious access to their own fields. But archaeologists aren't keen – as one said to me, 'The motivation has become monetary gain from the maximum number of people attending, rather than increasing our knowledge of the past.'

Meanwhile, the suspicion among detectorists on some rallies is that they're being fleeced, especially when they find nothing all day. 'It's like selling someone a fishing rod for a lake that's got no fish in it,' Pete told me. 'Do I keep on taking the money?' He said that when a field of his is fished out, he chats up another farmer and gains a fresh permission. Others are not so scrupulous.

That's only part of the story. Almost all of England is spoken for in one way or another – one eye-catching statistic is that half of the country is owned by less than one per cent of the population, namely the aristocracy and the super-rich. Most of the rest belongs to the Forestry Commission, the National Trust, the Ministry of Defence, utility companies and local and county councils, while the Crown owns almost all of the shoreline. Thus much of Surrey is off-limits to detectorists, while neighbouring Hampshire, being a largely rural county with huge amounts of potentially accessible agricultural land, is still fertile ground provided you can secure the necessary permissions.

This was my neck of the woods but even here the sense of shadowy entities encroaching on your surroundings can feel personal. According to the deeds of our cottage, the 'Ecclesiastical Commissioners for England' (i.e. the Church) own the rights to 'all mines, minerals and mineral substrata lying at a greater depth than 200 feet' on part of the land, while an old sign hanging in a nearby wood declares it to be the property of Magdalen College, Oxford.

As everywhere else, detectorists in Hampshire operate more or less on sufferance on a limited number of sites while there are vast numbers of acres that will never be disturbed by their digging tools. For good or bad, whatever miraculous objects from our shared history lie beneath the surface of these forbidden places, we shall never see them.

This was why I was excited by the prospect of detecting in the orchard. It was an ancient pond that had never been fished. And it was mine. Pete Welch cautioned a methodical approach. 'The technical side of it, as a novice, is to dig everything, dig all the iron and that way you'll learn to gradually increase your machine's capability to match your own,' he said. 'In other words, you're not digging up rubbish any more, or at least you're minimising it.'

He also gave me headspace to dream, mentioning two recent finds his group had made on a permission he had out towards Basingstoke: a lead seal matrix with Lombardic writing (common in the medieval period) on it that proved to be the personal seal of a descendant of a Bishop of Winchester, and, just one field away, a papal bulla from the same era. Here was the connective tissue of place and history, as revealed in the discovery of apparently random objects.

When I told Pete about the age and location of my house, he said, 'You'll definitely find something. Civil War? You could find musket balls. It's not that long ago.' I thought back to the detectorist I had met in the fields above the cottage and the Cavalier who scurried across my imagination. The Battle of Cheriton had taken place three miles from the cottage and a story linked the cottage to the battle.

In the aftermath of the day's fighting, that routed Royalist officer, Sir Benjamin Tichborne, had fled the field and hidden in a hollow oak tree close by. Backing up this story, the Ordnance Survey map of 1871 shows 'Sir Benjamin's Oak'. It is no longer marked on the modern OS Explorer map but there is evidence on the ground – in the exact spot a new oak tree has been planted, fenced off from browsing cattle, as if the local landowner had wanted to honour the tale and give it a new lease of life.

As Sir Benjamin hid in the tree, so the story goes, a monk and a Cavalier brought him food and drink they obtained from our cottage, which was then an alehouse. And since then these figures have acquired the status of ghosts that are said to haunt the locality. Not that I'd seen them. I was hardly a ghost person.

On a bright summer morning, with beads of rainwater still sparkling across the orchard grass, I metal detected for the first time. Within 20 seconds I'd found something. A good clean beep, a high ID number, a delve with the digging tool and a rootle with the carrot and there it lay, glinting silver in a shallow hole. A coin? I lifted it. A button, circular and flat, with a central loop on the back.

Assuming from its good condition and general shininess that it was 'modern' (by this I meant twentieth century), I nevertheless bestowed on it the honour of being the first object I zipped into the secure pocket of my brand-new finds pouch. I imagined a video camera catching the moment. It had been so smooth, practised, no hacking around haplessly. My mother used to tell me I was a natural cyclist who had just jumped on a bike and shot off in a wobble-free line, with no need of stabilisers. Perhaps I was a natural detectorist.

For the next hour I shuffled around the orchard making unsightly holes in the ground, stumbling over my unfamiliar equipment and finding nothing. I had stuck by Pete Welch's advice to 'dig everything' by responding to even the lowest ID readings and grunts. But the soil was playing those tricks on me. Some of the targets I just gave up on, having dug for several minutes, ever deeper and wider and more frantically, and still not hit metal.

On a couple of occasions my carrot jittered crazily, only for me to realise that I'd laid it down next to the metal digging tool. I gave up wearing the headphones (designed to keep the bleeps private, essential for metal detecting with other people) because they were making my ears sweat and I kept getting tangled in the cord. And at one point a tall nettle swung down and stung me deftly on the small patch of bare back exposed between jeans and T-shirt.

Laying down the kit, I took a break and gave myself a talking to. A decade earlier, I had made a trip to Ladakh in the Indian Himalayas to spot snow leopards in the wild. Every night in the tent (before my eyelids froze together) I read a few pages of Peter Matthiessen's *The Snow Leopard*, which relates his attempt to do the same thing in the 1970s.

Being a practising Zen Buddhist, Matthiessen was philosophical about the probability of failure. 'If the snow leopard should manifest itself, then I am ready to see the snow leopard,' he wrote. 'If not, then somehow (and I don't understand this instinct, even now) I am not ready to perceive it . . . and in the not-seeing, I am content.'

As it happened, he did not see a snow leopard and neither did I, but I was not content in the not-seeing. I felt seriously pissed off and short-changed in the not-seeing. I liked to think I had learned from that experience. But far from approaching metal detecting with the Zen-ness of Peter Matthiessen, I was craving instant gratification and getting ratty when it didn't happen.

I now reminded myself that these objects I expected to find in the ground did not exist – if they existed in the first place – solely in order to satisfy some primitive acquisitiveness in me; a person of yesteryear had not lost or discarded them for the benefit of an unspecified person at a notional moment in the future! Deep breath . . . I needed to be content in the not-finding.

The next find was technically junk, but junk is a relative term in metal detecting. One detectorist showed me a day's finds that included at least ten objects of antiquity I would have been thrilled and proud to have found. Then he dismissed them all bar one – the end piece of a Roman fantail brooch – as 'hedge fodder'.

Buttons in fields are as common as pigeons on municipal statues, though I learned to like them for being both personal and classless. Then there is real junk, typically 'shotties' (old shotgun cartridges), ring pulls, nails, featureless coins (Kris Rodgers's 'coins of nothingness'), bullets, 'canslaw' (shredded drinks cans) and bits of iron known as 'boats' – Bits Of A Tractor. Yet even these, depending on context, can have something interesting to say. This new orchard find was textbook boat, yet I found meaning in it.

It was three links of a big iron chain, so heavily rusted together they had taken on the form of a single organism, like a fossilised mollusc. Being of uncertain date, this fragment of heavy-duty chain linked me to wherever and whoever I wanted to be linked to. Plausibly it was a relic of the Sarah Prior era when the orchard was ploughed. The Prior family had bought the cottage in 1830 after the previous owners, the Budds, suffered a pile-up of ill luck.

According to an unpublished local history, Thomas Budd's wife had died in 1828 and two years later Thomas and his seventeen-year-old son William were convicted of sheep stealing from a farm at nearby Chawton, the village where Jane Austen had lived until her death in 1817. Thomas and William Budd were transported to the penal colonies of Australia and the remaining Budd children were sent to a workhouse. This was the kind of rural reality that reached to Jane Austen's front door but she never mentioned in her novels – no room for it on the 'little bit (not two inches wide) of ivory' on which she painted her words.

The Prior paterfamilias, William, was in his seventies, nearly forty years older than his wife Sarah, when they moved into the cottage. He died within two years and Sarah became head of the household, raising a stepson, Henry, eleven years her junior, and two daughters of her own. In the 1851 Census, Sarah and Henry are listed as sole occupants. Were they still maintaining their stepmother–stepson relationship, or were they, as my mother used to say out of the corner of her mouth, *more than that*?

Sarah was a hard worker. She cites her occupation as 'farmer' and the tithe map of 1839 shows her as owning – in addition to the cottage, barn and land immediately surrounding them – one plot of arable land (now the orchard) while renting another. She is buried in the local churchyard and when I walk across the fields to the village I sometimes drop in on her, this tough old bird who once lived in my shoe.

Within a few minutes of digging up the chain links, I got a button, small and convex with some sort of design on it that I hoped was military, and five minutes later and close by, what I decided was a small bullet casing. Into the pouch they went and while I continued to sweep I created the backstory around button and bullet, which can be summed up in the image of a slumped Roundhead, knackered after a day's footslogging, not caring much about anything any more as he huddled against the late winter cold and tried not to think about what might be expected of him on the field of battle the next day.

The session's final signal came as I swept my way past the recently planted apple tree sapling. The target was deep and I almost gave up on it. I wished I had when I lifted it to the daylight. It was a small piece of indeterminate shape, smeared with mud. I was about to toss it in the nettles, then remembered that the cardinal rule for beginners is not just to dig everything but to keep everything and then make sure you check it all out. In any case, as I walked back to the cottage – detector propped as nonchalantly as I could manage on one shoulder – I lifted the fragment back to the light and spotted a possible symmetry to it.

Having parked the detector in the porch, I transferred button, chain links, second button, possible bullet and mysterious fragment from the keep net of the finds pouch to their new permanent home, a large clear plastic tub that had originally contained fat balls for the birdfeeder. Then I cracked open a beer and carried the tub up to my desk.

The second button was an early lesson in the danger of confirmation bias. The button did not relate to the army nor to the Civil War era as I had assumed. Under my little magnifying glass – actually a plastic gift from a Marks & Spencer Christmas cracker but it did a job – I could see that the raised motif was a 'fouled' anchor (i.e. with rope twisted around it) surmounted by a crown, while the edge of the button was 'braided' in a rope pattern. I had found a button from the jacket of an officer in the Royal Navy.

Pinning down the era was not so easy and I spent an hour tumbling through endlessly subdividing internet wormholes in search of an answer. The key seemed to be the shape of the crown on the button – did it show the Tudor Crown (as worn by English monarchs pre-Civil War before it was apparently melted down on the orders of Oliver Cromwell) or the St Edward's Crown (made especially for Charles II on the Restoration of the monarchy and worn by kings and queens ever since)? The former had a smooth, round arch, the latter a looped double arch.

Since the early nineteenth century, the designs of the royal crowns on military buttons and other insignia had alternated between these two, depending on who was on the throne. *Why?* As I dug further into the arcanery of royal headgear and symbolism, I was gripped with a feeling that would become familiar over the coming months – a sort of compulsive, propulsive boredom that I revved up with slurps of beer or wine as I hunched over my laptop trying to match the muddy objects on my mouse mat with images on the screen.

One of the wormholes led me to a field near the abandoned medieval village of Little Oxendon in Northamptonshire. In 2017 a detectorist called Kevin Duckett, a restorer of classic cars, was detecting there when he found a one-and-a-half-inch figurine made of solid gold with traces of enamel on it that turned out to be a likeness of Henry VI. It caused a stir not just for its intrinsic treasure value or the quality of its craftsmanship but due to the provenance that Kevin and others claimed for it: they believed it was the statuette of Henry VI that once adorned the Tudor Crown, the crown that hitherto was presumed to have been destroyed on the abolition of the monarchy; all its gold turned into coins, its jewels and precious stones sold off.

As the crown itself no longer exists, the main point of comparison was a portrait in the National Portrait Gallery of Charles I painted in 1631 by Daniel Mytens in which the crown sits on a red-velvet-covered table next to the standing monarch. This image, along with contemporary inventories of the components of the crown, formed the model for a replica Tudor Crown made in 2012 and put on display at Hampton Court Palace. When Kevin Duckett went down to Hampton Court and set eyes on the figurine of Henry VI in the replica crown, he was, he said, 'absolutely overwhelmed . . . it was exactly the same. It was mind-blowing.'

Historical and geographical context backs up the theory that Kevin's golden find could well have been part of the Tudor Crown. The place where it lay buried for so long, Little Oxendon, is very near the site of the Battle of Naseby, the decisive battle of the English Civil War in 1645 in which Charles I's forces were routed by Oliver Cromwell's New Model Army. As well as losing most of his fighting men, the king also lost his personal baggage. Was the figurine tucked among it, having already been removed from the Crown and taken along as a precious keepsake? Conceivably. People – Kevin Duckett especially – wanted to believe it.

Others held the line of academic rigour. The British Museum said that more evidence was required to deliver a firm verdict and on the PAS database Kevin's find is listed as a 'pilgrim badge', sumptuously described: 'Henry is shown crowned and carries an orb in his left hand

and a sceptre in his right hand. His robes are partially enamelled with traces of flecked white enamel on his cloak representing ermine fur . . .'

Lucy Worsley, the historian, TV presenter and Chief Curator for Historic Royal Palaces (including Hampton Court), steered a middle path: 'It's tantalising to imagine its true history. Is this part of a long-lost crown? I'm not sure we'll ever know . . .' Beered up over my laptop, I was rooting for Kevin.

Then I remembered that I had completely lost my own plot. Establishing a date for the Royal Navy button I had just found in the orchard had been the objective when I launched myself down those chutes of possibility. Clambering back up while checking the side tunnels, I reached an answer to the button question: it probably dated from between 1901 and 1952.

The bullet, by the way, was a modern .22, used for shooting rabbits (the land around the cottage is honeycombed with their burrows). The small and unremarkable piece I had found at the end of the day's detecting was an afterthought at this stage. I held it under the desk light and trained the little plastic magnifying glass on it. It had a greenish patina that had me nodding sagely and mouthing 'copper alloy'. Not that I really knew what I was talking about. I was just aware that copper turned green as it aged, and I had already noticed that many detectorists' finds are described as 'copper alloy', so it seemed a safe bet.

It was about the size of a thumbnail and had one broken-looking edge that suggested it had sheered off from a larger piece, which would make it, I had read somewhere, a 'partefact'. The possible symmetry of it lay in the three identically sized shapes above the broken edge, as if they might have been a decorative addition to something much larger.

That was as far as I got that day. I made a mental note to show it to fellow detectorists, when I finally started meeting some, and put it in the plastic tub with the rest. My collection of memos from underground was up and running.

2

READING THE RUNES

There are various candidates for the title of 'inventor of the metal detector'. My favourite is a French *ingénieur* with the appropriate name of Gustave Trouvé, who plied his whimsical trade in Paris in the second half of the nineteenth century. Mr Found was so forward-thinking that his mind vaulted the dirty era of fossil fuels and contemplated only things electric.

He produced early versions of the head torch, the endoscope and the electric vehicle (a tricycle) as well as *bijoux électro-mobiles* such as a battery-powered drumming rabbit. His prototypic metal detector was designed to locate bullets in bodies, a basic idea that twentieth-century manufacturers adapted into the function of land-mine detection.

It was brooches – Roman, Saxon, early medieval – not bombs that detectorists were after when the first metal detectors went on sale to the general public in the late 1960s. In the spirit if not the intention of Gustave Trouvé, these funny stick-and-disc devices became go-betweens, shuttling between the present and the past; lending their ear to the whispers below, and passing them on above ground.

You can explain how they work in terms of physics and the interplay of electromagnetic fields. Or you could say that a random and plaintive calling into that other country is going on. And every so often you get a response: a call-and-response across history. And when that happens and you finally lay hands on the target, well – something remarkable happens. So I was told and so I was to learn, for the handling of historical artefacts – the touching through the grain of one's fingertips objects that were last held by distant ancestors – has a transformative power to it, as if the object were momentarily imbued with the spirit of the long-dead person it once belonged to. This is the dopamine rush we all quickly learn to crave.

My first public outing as a detectorist was in a field in the north of Hampshire with an 'old feel' to it. So said Andy, and I knew what he meant without quite understanding why. It covered less than five acres and had a trapezoidal shape, sloping down to a stream on one side. Big trees cast inky shadows along the edges. Looking afterwards on a map from 1871, I noticed that a building called Burnt Cottage had once stood near the corner where we parked our cars, though there was no trace of it on the ground. This was the beginning of me getting the feel of land, sensing a voltage coming up through the feet.

It was Andy's permission. He had come out with my new detectorist friends, Sally and Rob, and his son Patrick, known as Paddy – 11 years old and a metal-detecting prodigy – to cosset and coach me on this public debut. The drive there had taken me into a corner of Hampshire I had never been in before, of tight lanes hemmed in by swaying cow parsley and burdock, and the grainy fragrance of freshly cut fields.

On a couple of occasions, the dashboard dominatrix who usually ordered me from A to B was reduced to suggesting that I 'refer to the map'. I was barely 20 miles from where I lived and 40 miles from London, yet felt, as they say in Newfoundland, 'far away from far away'.

When I reached our agreed meeting point in front of a pub, Sally and Rob were already there, waiting by their hatchback in boots and caps. Rob wore a red Liverpool FC windcheater, Sally was the talker. I had emailed her through a mutual contact after hearing that they were novices too, having taken up the hobby 'for something to do' during lockdown. From the pub, I followed their car to the field where they'd arranged to meet Andy and Paddy. Then we stood by our open car boots and made tentative detector talk – none us being quite fluent in it – as we waited for the others.

Sally and Rob might have been beginners, but I was secretly dismayed to discover that they had already made two finds – on the Hampshire–Berkshire borders – important enough to register with the local Finds Liaison Officer (FLO). The first was a sword belt hanger, once the possession of a man of high social class, that had been dated to 1550–1650. Sally swiped up an image of it on her phone. Three plates were suspended on loops from a mount that would have been fixed to a belt. From those dangling plates our man of means would have attached the scabbard of his sword, the movable quality of the attachment making it easy to tilt the scabbard and draw the sword.

The rapiers worn in the sixteenth and seventeenth centuries were fashion accessories and status symbols. They were also as sharp as sashimi blades. Living in paranoid and violent times (that time span started with the death of the Tudor boy king, Edward VI, and ended with the Civil War and the execution of Charles I), a smart man tools himself up.

Sally and Rob had also found a coin from the same period, the reign of Mary I. It was a silver groat and it represented a landmark in the career of any detectorist – their first 'hammered' coin. If metal detecting had a Big Five like game viewing in Africa (you supposedly haven't done it properly unless you've seen, and photographed, a lion, elephant, leopard, buffalo and rhino), a 'hammered' would be one of the objects you'd need to find to prove your credentials. The word describes how the coins were made – a piece of blank metal, usually silver, know as a 'planchet' was placed between two dies or moulds bearing the designs of the two sides of the coin. The top die was then struck with a hammer and the blank planchet was transformed into a unit of currency with the reigning emperor or monarch on the obverse ('heads' side) and a symbolic image on the reverse ('tails'). Apparently a moneyer who was really on his game could produce up to 2,500 coins a day.

This laborious means of manual coin production was in use from the Iron Age to the mid-seventeenth century, creating the monies of the Celts, Romans, Anglo-Saxons, Normans, Tudors and Stuarts. It ended in the early 1660s when the milled machine method was introduced. Hammereds ceased being valid currency and over the centuries have become charismatic curios. Their charm lies in the fact that due to being handmade no two are quite the same.

Many were struck slightly off-centre or double-struck to create a shadow effect in the design. For this reason it was often difficult to identify the precise centre of the coin and the proper diameter was therefore also unclear. People took advantage of this by 'clipping' pieces off the edge and collecting them till they had enough to melt down and sell. Milled coins put an end to this counterfeiting practice by incorporating lettering and marking on the edge itself. Hammered coins were also, legitimately, cut into halves or quarters to produce smaller denominations and detectorists occasionally find these tiny half-moons and pie-slice shapes, though the most commonly found hammereds are complete medieval pennies.

Hammered coins are not exactly rare but they are special. Finding one is a rite of passage for new detectorists, like losing your virginity or passing your driving test. Until you have overcome those hurdles it is hard to imagine life on the other side, yet once you do, you pretty soon forget the hurdle ever existed – though I remember driving everywhere at 100mph for a while. Sally and Rob, I noted, had wasted no time reaching the other side. I wondered how long it would take me.

After they had told me about the sword belt hanger and the hammered coin, I thought briefly of trading them my mysterious orchard find. But the truth was that after looking promising it had died in my hand. A few days after finding it, I had been browsing through finds.org.uk, the database of the Portable Antiquities Scheme (PAS), when a shape caught my eye. A shape in triplicate, just like the fragment from the orchard. It was described in the accompanying text as a 'trefoil' – the symbol of a three-leaved plant – and was one of six attached to a much bigger object identified as a 'harness pendant', an item that was hung from the harnesses of horses from Roman to medieval times.

Before finishing for the night, and admittedly after more than a few beers, I found the email address for one of my local FLOs (there are two) on the PAS website and sent her a breathless email with a picture of the 'trefoil' attached. I went to bed feeling as whizzy as Howard

Carter after he had peered through that crack into the disarranged jewel box of the boy pharaoh's tomb and declared he saw 'wonderful things'. I woke with a hangover and the sad clarity that this affliction can bring: in this case that I had been following my own detector up the garden path.

Calling up the image of the harness pendant, I realised it had a centimetre scale alongside it. My 'trefoil' was about three times bigger than the ones on the pendant. And it was not, as the text described, 'moulded in imitation of a leaf'. There was no moulding or decorative quality to it at all. Was it even a trefoil shape? Mmm . . . nah. The shape was probably random. I regretted the email to the FLO (and never did get a reply) and decided it was best to leave the 'trefoil' in the tub, a small defeat known only to me.

Andy and his son Paddy arrived in a dark SUV and tumbled out in dark garb, looking ready for a yomp across the Brecon Beacons.

'Let's face it,' Andy said, casting his eyes down his front, then perusing my own clobber, 'it's a hobby for middle-aged men in khakis and combats.'

When I asked Sally about being a rare woman in a male-dominated world, she said, "Well, I'm not a girly girl. I like football and motorbikes.'

'I'm a fisherman too,' Andy went on, 'and I used to be a trainspotter when I was a kid. I'm that kind of person!' The field we were about to detect on, he said, was one of his best and he regarded the permission he'd extracted from the landowner as a testament to his powers of persuasion. 'Mind you, it helps, being in sales for 25 years. And he's my wild card.' He pointed proudly at Paddy, a scale model of his dad.

Paddy has his own YouTube channel, Paddy Detects, on which he posts 20-minute videos filmed by Andy. Paddy's commentary oozes a casual authority that is comical in one so young. On some of his films, detectorists four and five times his age defer respectfully to Paddy's knowledge.

His greatest find so far has been a four-inch piece of Bronze Age 'ribbon' gold, a thin strip decorated with several ribs on one side. The FLO who recorded the find described it as 'enigmatic' because its precise use, besides adornment, was unknown. Was it a hair band, or did it perhaps fit around a dagger handle?

When he put it in his finds pouch, Paddy thought he'd picked up scrap and intended to bin it when he got home. Fortunately he showed it to his dad before he did so. The story was pure gold, earning this headline in the *Daily Mail*: 'Boy, 10, discovers Bronze Age gold in Andover using metal detector – but almost threw it away because he thought it was a bit of FOIL'. Not quite on a par with 'Toddler finds cure for Alzheimer's' but on the stopping train there.

Having seen a couple of episodes of Paddy Detects before I came out, I was slightly in awe of The Boy Detectorist. Most detectorists with their own social-media brands or channels – and there are lots of them in the UK – cultivate an upbeat, attention-grabbing on-screen persona. Paddy pitches his appeal higher, addressing the lens with an engaging gravitas, treating the viewer as equally knowledgeable.

In person, I was relieved to discover, he was not quite the bonsai boffin of Paddy Detects but a modest kid who just wanted me to do well on my first-ever public outing. Previously, he said, he'd found a 'Roman', i.e. a Roman coin, on this field. 'You never know, you might too,' he said sweetly. A Roman was another find I coveted. As Romans were also by definition hammereds, it would be a case of killing two birds with one stone.

During all this chat we had been standing by our respective car boots, tailgates aloft, gear inside waiting to be grabbed. Now it was time. I lifted machine and digging tool from the boot. Detectorists have a neat way of balancing their machines on their digging tools so that they tilt together in mutual support to form a shape like the Greek letter lambda, thus: λ. It's a useful way to park them out on the fields while you're scrabbling in a hole with your carrot. I tried it now, while the others were distracted with their own preparations – propped them into one another and took my hands away. The lambda immediately collapsed into an X and then a couple of underscores like this: _ _. I looked around. No one seemed to have noticed. I made a mental note to perfect my propping technique in the privacy of the garden.

At this moment, poised on the very lip of becoming a fully fledged detectorist, I felt ridiculously self-conscious. How to even carry the detector across the short track to the detecting field without looking like an impostor? Could I pull off the over-the-shoulder look? I stole glances back at Andy and Paddy, nonchalantly handling their equipment as if they were extensions of their own limbs, then ahead to Sally and Rob, who already seemed to have the air of a well-oiled team. I had no muscle memory for this.

The two bags I had slung around my neck – one for finds, the other containing a water bottle and sunblock – felt bulky and disobliging. The cord for the headphones had already wrapped itself like bindweed round one leg.

This was technically a public place, but the track was a dead end and no traffic nor people had passed since we arrived. At least, I told myself, these awkwardnesses were being played out with no audience bar my new friends, who had all gone through the same reinvention. Then, just as we were about to cross the track, a group of runners appeared and we had to hold back to let them pass. This was an ordeal I had wondered about – being rumbled up close as a detectorist by a group of non-initiates, or 'civilians' as I was starting to regard them.

There were six or seven of them, men and women, a couple with fitness trackers strapped to their upper arms. They were sweating and heavy-breathing and moved in a jostling pack, like grazing animals lumbering towards fodder. As they drew alongside us, two runners in the middle of the pack looked across, exchanged glances with each other and smirked. In return I raised my eyebrows and cocked my head on one side, in a way that I hoped looked sardonic and defiant, with a touch of 'You don't look so cool either' about it.

The field had just been cut for hay and was nicely damp after overnight rain, which meant that signals were improved and the soil was easy to dig. This was when Andy described it as having an 'old feel' and pointed out the salient points of stream, slope and spreading trees. Shyly, I started detecting along the edge of the stream, with my back to the others – as if, because I couldn't see them, they couldn't see me.

Then Andy walked over and suggested gently that this was not the best place to do it because a lot of modern junk got dropped along the edges of streams. Before leaving me to it, he swiped up an image of a gold coin on his phone and held it out to me: 'That's a gold Celtic quarter stater. If you find one of these you're allowed to dance around, Nigel.' Thinking about this afterwards, I realised he was referring to the fabled 'gold dance' that detectorists supposedly do when they find an object made of the ultimate precious metal.

I pushed up the slope and into the middle of the field, where I could discreetly study the others – how they swept the coil, how they carried the digging tool, how frequently they hit a promising target and decided to dig for it. In fact, Sally and Rob were atypical because they detected together, taking it in turns to sweep and carry the digger. This got around the need to do both at the same time, which struck me as a bit of a cheat.

My digging tool caused me an immediate problem, though I didn't realise it for several minutes. Sweeping the detector from left to right to left – the coil will only work when in constant motion, for a reason I don't quite get, but never mind, it's not important for me to understand – I was picking up a crisp signal on each rightward sweep, but no corresponding signal as I swept left. Normally a target will identify itself through a synthesis of the two signals, so I was puzzled. I felt like a dog chasing its tail.

Then I realised: each time I swept to the right, the coil was reacting to the stainless-steel digging tool that I was dangling carelessly near to the ground with my right hand. I hoisted the spade on to my right shoulder and the problem was solved. But I had wasted 15 minutes. I then wasted ten more digging a hole that got wider and deeper while yielding nothing.

Andy, who was keeping a paternal eye on me, came over. He confirmed with his machine that I was digging in the wrong place. 'And your digging tool is too small – if you don't mind me saying so,' he added. I took this on the chin and set to afresh, eventually hitting a slice of iron junk.

Meanwhile, Sally and Rob had got their eye in. I had already watched with envy as, twice, they paused, stooped and dug. Each time the dig had been brief and I assumed the target was worthless. On the third occasion their body language assumed increasing self-importance as they lingered over the find, turning and turning it in their gloved hands. Finally, Rob raised his arm and shouted, 'Got something!'

Andy and Paddy propped their machines on their spades and walked over. I reprised my propping attempt and failed again. Leaving the machine on the ground, I hurried over in time to hear Paddy pronounce, 'Coin.'

Rob held it out on the tip of his gloved finger: a small, dark, soil-smeared, unevenly edged disc with what appeared to be writing on it – possibly a P and an R. Paddy had a closer look and said, 'Could be a Roman.'

Andy thought it could be even better than that.

'Could be a skeet,' he said. At least 'skeet' was the way I pictured the spelling of the word he used, which was then unfamiliar to me. Later I found that the word is spelt 'sceat' and denotes an Anglo-Saxon silver coin – a beautiful rarity.

As Rob and Sally stared at him, Andy grinned and held up his hands.

'I'm just putting it out there,' he said.

We all agreed – me through gritted teeth – that Sally and Rob deserved congratulations.

As I trudged back to my recumbent detector, it occurred to me that though the coin was yet to be firmly identified they had almost certainly just found another hammered.

Now I concentrated hard, focusing on my sweeping technique – keeping the coil parallel to the scuffed, muddy grass stubble – but also willing the ground to answer me back. I thought about the 'old feel' of the field, absorbed the soft slope, the lip of tufted grass above the invisible stream, those shadows under the tree skirts that looked dense and mysterious in the watery sunlight and the flutter of black wings in the branches.

There was suddenly no filter between now and a faraway then. No scale by which to measure time. I liked very much this feeling and attributed to it what happened next. A good signal, a swift dig, a target found: a button, smallish, grey, scuff marks on the front, an incomplete shank on the back. I knew it was hedge fodder to the rest of them and wasn't going to announce it, but Andy spotted me turning it in my hand.

'What you got?' he called.

'Just a button.'

He and Paddy came over.

'Cool,' said Paddy. 'A tombac.'

Tombacs are generally flat buttons made of pewter or copper alloy that were worn on jackets in the eighteenth and nineteenth centuries. They litter the landscapes of Europe. (Researching them afterwards, I realised that the button I had found in the orchard – my first-ever find by detector – was also a tombac.)

Pretty soon I got another one. It had an older patina, a jagged edge. It was decoration-free, functional, like the farmhand who had probably last touched it.

My best find came as summer mist shaded into fine rain and we had started to walk towards the cars. It was about the size of my little fingernail and had a bell-like shape that curled over into some sort of fastening at the thicker end. Paddy was polite about it, spotting on it a decorative motif and pronouncing it 'interesting', though nobody knew what it was. It was often the pieces you couldn't identify, said Andy, that proved the most significant.

The previous week, he and Paddy had been to see the local FLO with their latest finds. Andy swiped up another image on his phone. It showed buttons, coins, a Roman brooch and an unwieldy piece that didn't look like much and he hadn't thought to get excited about. It was this mysterious object that the FLO made a beeline for, as he recognised it immediately as an Anglo-Scandinavian horse stirrup strap mount from the eleventh century, i.e. the period between the Viking and Norman invasions of England. 'Proper cool,' said Andy.

Today, his and Paddy's return was meagre: a medieval lead weight, a post-medieval silver thimble, a modern coin, some buttons. Still, it amazed me that five acres of land, on such a cursory search, had surrendered such finds to us. Sally and Rob's coin was certainly the best of them. They said they would let us know what it was. Then we melted away from the field with the old feel, leaving it to the rain and the cawing of rooks.

On my drive home through those mazy lanes the sun came out again and mist rose from the wet and warming tarmac like feathery wisps of smoke. Through it old cars started materialising – lovely open-top machines built in pre-war English factories, with dinner-plate headlights and, apparently, no reverse gears. They were driven by middle-aged men dressed up as the middle-aged men of their grandfathers' generation, in tweed caps, Rupert Bear scarves and Biggles goggles. I was caught up in a vintage car rally and I was driving against the flow of them.

As the lanes were single-track and there were few passing places I found myself, in my jelly-mould hybrid (with its origins, like my detector, in several faraway countries), feeling obliged to defer to age by reversing or pulling over into hedges and field openings to let them pass. As they did so, the driver (often accompanied by a wife in a straw bonnet) would give me the kind of entitled wave that made me want to reply with a raised middle finger.

As I backed off for yet another Austin 7, I asked myself if my new-found interest in the secrets of the soil was just a reversing away from reality. More like a reordering, I decided. The reason I had not been to this part of Hampshire before was that I had chosen instead to be in places like Albania or Madagascar. As you get older, time ceases being precisely linear. It loops back on itself, throws up clues, invites you to examine evidence that was there all along but you were too busy to notice. What I'd been doing that morning felt like breaking new ground, not going over old.

Pete Welch is a looper-back, an examiner of small things that others miss. On our first meeting, when I told him where I lived, he had talked about a field near the cottage he called Roman Ridge on account of all the Roman stuff he has found there over the years. On his first dig on the field, he had been looking for evidence of the course of a Roman road that a local archaeologist had narrowed down to three fields.

'There were Roman coins scattered all over it,' Pete told me. Then he discovered hobnails from Roman boots: 'Only along the ridge of the field, nowhere else, not down the sides, just along the ridge, which makes sense – why would you walk along on the slope?' This was the derivation of his name for the field – and the beginning of his obsession with solving its secrets.

Up to this point, the field Pete knew as Roman Ridge had been to me a spine of arable land that rose to the south as I drove to the nearest

Tesco Express after running out of milk or beer. I would half-notice its changes of colour according to the time of year and the crop it bore and as such it was part of the wallpaper of my immediate world. But I had never given it actual thought, and harboured no curiosity about it. Until now. Now it seemed to me as exciting as an Angkor temple site.

'Are you going to be detecting on it this year?' I asked Pete anxiously.

The answer was yes. He would invite me along when it was ready. We were in the becalmed yet nervy period when the farmers are about to start harvesting the fields, and detectorists with permissions on them wait for information on which will become available and when. Often there is only a narrow window between cutting the crops and sowing the winter cereals for next year's harvest. So Pete was keeping his phone close and planning his rallies, which could be anywhere from Winchester to Buckingham.

In this limbo we met for another drink, in a pub owned by one of his farming landowner friends. The first thing I did was pull out my find from the old field and wave it under Pete's nose. I had hopes for this piece. At one point I had even convinced myself it could be a Roman brooch. There were Roman brooches on the PAS website that fell into the category of 'not dissimilar' if I'd had a bit to drink and squinted hard enough, and the motif on it – which looked like a sunflower growing from a wicker basket – could have represented a vine, which implied to me a Roman connection. But I had learned from the 'trefoil' not to see what I wanted to see.

'Clog clasp,' said Pete, barely glancing at it. 'He probably lost his clog as well – fell off in the mud.'

Later I found an almost identical piece on the PAS database: 'A Post Medieval copper shoe or clog clasp dating to circa AD 1700–1900.

The object has been machine stamped [in my case with the basket-and-flower design] and would have been used with a similar hasp to secure a wooden shoe to the foot.'

I felt moved, holding it in the palm of my hand, by the thoughtfulness required to decorate something as small and functional and barely seen as this – in the words of one archaeologist I was to meet later, 'the investment of ideas and iconography in the design and manufacture' of even so humble an object as a clog clasp.

But my clog clasp was trumped by Sally and Rob's coin. She had emailed me to say it wasn't Roman, or indeed a sceat, but was still 'pretty cool': a Charles I 'rose farthing' dated 1636–44. 'Our second-ever hammered!' she wrote blithely.

Pete had brought along his laptop to show me the background he had done on Roman Ridge. I supplied the relevant OS (Ordnance Survey) Explorer map, which is where we started, pushing back our coffee cups, unfolding and flattening it across the wooden table, then getting our bearings above it.

'The thought is that the Roman road from Alton to Winchester goes through here,' he said, turning the map, hovering his finger, then landing it on a precise spot, 'but the archaeologists just aren't sure of the exact course. It's not a military road, it could have been an agricultural road. There's not a rigid rule that it has to be dead straight.'

Lying less than half a mile to the south-east across the wavy red line of the modern road was a fragment of ancient woodland that is one of the remaining pockets of the vast forest known as Andredes Weald, which in early medieval times covered roughly the area of the modern-day South Downs National Park and, over in East Sussex, the High Weald Area of Outstanding Natural Beauty. I used to walk

Bertie the dog in the old wood and one day some ten years previously I had come across a group of archaeologists staking out a trench for excavation. One told me they were investigating a Roman road. 'More a farm track probably,' he said. 'See the camber?' He pointed out a wide seam of raised ground running through the undergrowth.

Romans plonked their size XIIs all over this area, on a network of roads that often followed prehistoric tracks. To the west lay Venta Belgarum, Roman Winchester, to the east a settlement called Vindomis that was almost certainly on the site of a place called Neatham, north-east of Alton. Vindomis, mentioned on a fourth-century Roman route map, was a *mansio* or stopping place at the point where two important highways crossed: the east–west route from London to Winchester and the north–south route from the major town of Calleva Atrebatum – near the village of Silchester, north of Basingstoke – to Noviomagus Reginorum, Roman Chichester. The copy-editor of this book, Sarah Hulbert, told me that she grew up in an old cottage and forge on the line of the Silchester–Chichester road and her father once found a Roman coin in the garden.

The original line of this north–south road is marked on OS maps as a dotted line. The site of the Roman settlement of Neatham lies near it, just to the north of the Holybourne recreation ground, where an English Heritage sign warns against illegal metal detecting. The field is a scheduled monument and has been left to grow wild. I pushed through a gap in a hedge to find it, having been directed there by a dog walker who told me, 'Legend has it there's a house in the village with a Roman tomb in it.' He added that he thought this story was rubbish.

'Well, you never know,' I almost replied, for it reminded me of an ancient settlement called Qurna in Egypt. Visible to the tourists being bussed to the Valley of the Kings, its mudbrick houses still dot a hillside near the Ramesseum, the mortuary temple of Ramses II, though it is now purely an archaeological site. A community of Bedouin had lived here for hundreds of years, until turfed out by the authorities in 2007, building their dwellings on top of pharaonic tombs and latterly using the tombs as storage for bicycles and fridges – and, in one case, for keeping their ducks safe at night.

By the time I met the dog walker, I had been walking the tracks and fields around Vindomis for an hour or so. Wild bees hummed in the trees. There was a sense of displaced energy that drew my eye to dark openings in thickets and hedgerows. The field itself, under its mat of undergrowth, seemed to roll slightly like the deck of a ship as I brushed through the tangled grasses.

Vindomis was a pit stop where two major roads crossed that grew into a settlement of 30 acres. In the post-Roman period, the Saxons lived and traded here (Neatham being a Saxon word for 'cattle market'), judging from coins found on the site. And there is evidence that they adopted local traditions – at least one house had a wall painted with a faux marbled effect, a sophisticated Roman fashion and technique.

I found all this out almost by chance, on a visit to Alton to buy a sealable sandwich box and some foam rubber for the safekeeping of any delicate finds I might make (having decided that they'd get shaken around too much in the bird ball tub). Just at the top of Alton's sloping high street stands a U-shaped cluster of public buildings, created in a spirit of Victorian philanthropy, that includes the Curtis Museum of local history. It was founded by and named after the son of Jane Austen's apothecary, who had rooms on the other side of the street. Just as I had been to Peru's northern highlands but never to northern Hampshire, so I was familiar with the sardine-canning museum in Stavanger but had walked past the Curtis Museum a hundred times without giving it any thought.

This time I swerved inside, where I found galleries that were the equivalent of lined sandwich boxes, protecting modestly exquisite things. Chief among them was the Alton Buckle, found in the grave of an Anglo-Saxon warrior during excavations in the town in 1959–61. There, in its cabinet, it reposed, glowing not just in its spotlight but with the luminescence of beautiful age. The size and shape of a bottle opener, it is made of silver with 'cloisonné garnets' (i.e. red gemstones divided by enamel bands) and gold filigree. The museum claims that the level of craftsmanship and aesthetic sophistication rivals the best of the finds at the Sutton Hoo Anglo-Saxon ship burial, arguably Britain's greatest-ever archaeological find.

The Curtis Museum also features objects found near our cottage by metal detectorists – notably a seventeenth-century silver swivelling seal matrix (showing Cupid firing his bow and arrow on one side and two hearts pierced by an arrow on the other) and a Bronze Age gold ring. And there is plenty of material – artefacts, maps, scholarly research – on the Roman occupation of the area. Aside from Vindomis there were, according to the display, 'twenty-six known or probable [Roman] villas' dotted around Alton, some built to a high spec with hypocaust heating systems, mosaic floors and bathhouses.

When, on leaving the museum, I mentioned the figure of 26 to the small, masked person peeping from behind the collecting boxes and leaflets on the front desk, she said it had been revised upward. 'We now think there were as many Roman villas as there are big farms today,' she said. This person was Jane Hurst, a local historian who has the kind of love and knowledge of her home patch that is an infectiously beautiful trait in a person.

A Roman pulse beats strongly through this region and I was more impatient than ever to find it on Roman Ridge. While Pete Welch waited to get the nod from the farmer, he arranged digs on other permissions. One sounded like a dress rehearsal for Roman Ridge although it was 80 miles away in Oxfordshire. According to Pete in his weekly newsletter, the field in question was bisected by 'Margary's Roman road no.161' – a reference to Ivan Margary's definitive text *Roman Roads in Britain* first published in 1955.

The newsletter included a link to an aerial photograph of the field on which 'you can clearly see the double ditch and *agger*' – an *agger* being the embankment on which a Roman road was built. On the aerial photograph this showed up as a varicose bump crossing on the diagonal. On the ground it was more difficult to make out.

'So where's the Roman road exactly?' I said to Pete when I got there on a sticky, overcast morning.

He looked smug. 'You're standing on it,' he said, pointing at a plucky red poppy growing from the stubble at our feet. 'It goes right through here where the cars are parked and across the field. See where the ground rises as it hits that far hedgerow? That's the *agger*.'

Beyond the hedgerow, cutting the Roman road in two and flowing below the level of the field, was the M40 that I had just driven up. High-sided trucks slid ceaselessly in either direction, creating a compressed roar in the cutting. At my feet and in no less of a hurry, blue-back beetles shouldered their way through the grains of cut wheat. Forty or so other detectorists had turned up, which made this my first proper public outing, the Sally-and-Rob field having turned out to be a gentle and semi-private introduction.

When Pete's watch hit 9.30am and he declared the field open, I stood back and watched the others pour in. When detectorists are unleashed, they each start following their own head plan. However gregarious the preamble and aftermath of a day's detecting, the meat of it is solitary and cagey, each detectorist a wily sole operator. Now bulky men began to move with startling swiftness and purpose on imagined tracks of advantage that mostly seemed to relate to the course of the *agger*.

I decided to be counter-intuitive and start in a corner that no one else found interesting. After an hour of no signals, I moved towards the *agger*, which was clearly traceable if you stepped off it a bit, but found nothing there either bar junk. Back in the car, I ate the cheese-and-pickle sandwiches I had made for lunch six hours earlier and drank stewed tea from the Thermos. When I looked across at the row of parked cars, I saw, framed in each side window, the head of a middle-aged man masticating a sandwich.

For the afternoon session I picked another part of the field but had no more luck. My left arm was beginning to ache. My mind kept wandering – to the high-pressure jet cleaner, for example, and the paving stones I was looking forward to relieving of their lethal slipperiness – and though it made no sense, I believed I stood less of a chance of finding anything interesting if I was no longer able to focus on the ground and the possibility of what it might be about to reveal. Then, contemplating the longish drive home, I got a scratchy signal. It was probably iron, but I'd had so few signals that I decided to dig it anyway.

As I knelt spooning the earth out, a pair of old-fashioned slip-ons appeared by the hole, and above them, dusty slacks.

'What you got there then?' said a voice. I looked up. It belonged to an unruly-haired man whom I surmised, correctly, to be the farmer who owned the field. 'Neat little tool that,' he added, admiring my digging tool.

'It's too small,' I replied.

'So what you got?' he said again and l realised he assumed I knew what I was doing.

Deflecting him away from my target, which I was having the usual trouble finding, I took a break to say casually, 'There's a Roman road through here, you know.'

'Is that definite?'

'Yes. It goes right through where the cars are parked and across the field. See where the ground rises as it hits that far hedgerow? That's the *agger*, the Roman embankment.' He looked impressed and I pictured him repeating this information in the pub later, with the same spurious authority as me. Slowly, though, he grew bored as I continued to dig fruitlessly and eventually he went back to his combine harvester.

As I was returning to the car, having found nothing at all, the farmer finished baling a third field and opened it up for detecting. I decided to give it half an hour. An elderly man, wearing a face mask low on his throat and, it seemed to me, bundled into far too many clothes for the humid conditions, was detecting near to me. Suddenly he exclaimed, 'Hammered!' and held one arm aloft as if he'd had a number nine on his back and he'd just hit a bullet of a shot into the top corner in front of adoring fans. As I turned towards him, he pulled the face mask up over his nose and said, 'Don't come too close. I've got cancer.'

I apologised and backed off.

'No, it's OK,' he said, wanting me to see the coin. 'It's just I've got no immunity [sic] system, see?' He leaned towards me and dropped the cut coin into my hand. 'It's the first time I've been out this year!' I pictured him in a hospital gown undergoing gruelling treatments and yearning for open fields. Hammereds are not necessarily impressive-looking specimens – this one was cut into a quarter and could have been a scrap of foil – but he was buzzing and I felt pleased for him, the poor bastard. I also felt envious. I was envious of an old man who was probably gravely ill.

On the drive home, I reviewed the day's encounter with the cancer patient. He'd made me realise that detecting was turning into a far more all-encompassing pastime than I had bargained for and giving me life lessons at an age when I thought I was beyond classrooms. Reliving the man's goal-scoring moment, I decided that my failure to find a hammered was becoming analogous to a striker who can't score for toffee.

The terraces – in the form of my own id – had been giving me the benefit of the doubt, but I was feeling them turning. I was becoming a laughing stock to myself, the striker who falls over his own feet with the goal at his mercy. I was also becoming mean-spirited, begrudging a sick man a moment of small joy.

With the crops coming off the fields, Pete Welch's digging days were now happening at the rate of three a week. Though Roman Ridge was still out of bounds, he had, he told me, so many acres of permissions that he had lost count. In the pub he had opened his laptop to reveal an extraordinary paradigm of three-dimensional reality rendered in documents of detail and complexity. The starting point was GPS navigation software called Memory-Map that enabled him to access all OS maps on screen and operate them on the ground by means of the GPS facility on his smartphone.

To this he had added data from the Historic Environment Records (HERs), an exhaustive online resource that maps and details the recorded archaeological finds, sites and structures across every square inch of the county (these are available for other counties in varying degrees of accessibility and thoroughness). A rectilinear enclosure, for example, might be evidence of Roman activity, whereas traces of 'curvilinear' structures were more likely to be Anglo-Saxon. 'What you do,' he said, demonstrating, 'you get the grid ref and hit the button and bang – the info will appear on the screen at that spot.'

He then customised the maps to reflect his own knowledge and experience, by means of a series of icons and annotations. A green tractor on a field meant the permission was his. If it faced in the same direction as green tractors on other fields nearby, it meant all the fields belonged to the same farmer. A yellow tractor denoted an old field that he was unlikely to go back to; a red tractor equalled no permission. I also spotted a skull and crossbones – a farmer who, metaphorically at least, had chased Pete off his land with a shotgun and was unlikely ever to play ball.

He had also noted where and when significant objects had been found on his digs, e.g. 'full stater, 2012' (a reference to a rare Celtic gold coin). The mapping software had a proximity feature that he connected to his phone so that when he was in a field he had put in the system, the phone would tell him when he was standing on a spot of archaeological significance.

All this homework fed into the seductive newsletters Pete posted to advertise his upcoming digs. The next one was on a field of 84 acres near Winchester from which the crop of oats had just been removed. 'Our past digs on this field have been rewarding with many hammered coins from Stephen [the twelfth-century king] to James [I],' said the newsletter. 'Plenty of cut 1/4s and 1/2s randomly spread, a beautiful gold poesy ring, a silver gilt ecclesiastical ring plus odd Roman coins have also been good finds. There is an Anglo-Saxon spot where sceats have been detected.'

This field also abutted a motorway, in this case the M3. As we dug and hoped for hammereds and sceats, the modern world rushed past heedless of their proximity. There were about a hundred of us and we detected to the Doppler effect of sirens, further distorted by the angle of the motorway cutting. The stubble was dense and tall but I stuck at it and eventually found a squashed lead bullet that looked like a wad of old chewing gum. Soon after that I found a musket ball, smooth, roughly spherical with a white patina, little bigger than a blueberry yet as heavy as my shoe; and finally, a rusted belt buckle.

Walking back to the car, I created a story around these objects that gave me the wished-for Civil War connection my orchard finds had failed to do. Royalist forces had been based at Winchester before the Battle of Cheriton. The field lay on the Cheriton side of the city and soldiers had conceivably ridden or marched over it or camped on it in those days of late March 1644.

The belt buckle, which had a flamboyant largeness to it, could have belonged to a swashbuckling Cavalier. But it looked suspiciously modern when I got it home and I had to concede that it was more likely from the same era as bell-bottoms and stacked shoes. As for the squashed bullet – probably nineteenth century. Only the musket ball had been equal to my fanciful interpretation. It was a lead shot from a seventeenth-century musket.

Later, Pete told me that 53 hammered coins had been found on the field that day. 'Not bad for just over a hundred people,' he said.

'Wish I'd been one of them,' I replied gloomily.

'Well, half of you weren't,' he said, trying to buck me up.

The following week, on another of Pete's permissions, I found my first 'moo tube' – a landmark of sorts. A moo tube is an aluminium tube that once contained an ointment that farmers rub into cows' udders for the treatment of mastitis. On any field that has had cattle on it, moo tubes will be lying there like cruel tricks, giving off superb signals.

It was a frustrating morning, my only other finds being big, rusted iron – horseshoes, chain links, an iron ring and general plough or tractor bits that I chucked in the hedgerow – and the afternoon session was equally frustrating. 'Any luck?' asked a passing detectorist with a white beard as I was about to clock off.

'No. Lots of iron. You?

'Three farthings. One George VI.' He shrugged.

'Plenty of moo tubes,' I exaggerated, enjoying the jargon.

'Two Red Bull cans,' he countered.

The following day, I had to go to Andover to see a man about a horse. Traipsing around the town centre, I came across the Museum of the Iron Age, which is essentially a repository of finds from Danebury Hill Fort south of Andover. These include iron rings labelled 'chariot fittings' that looked very like the iron ring I had chucked in the hedge the day before. I tried not to dwell on this.

*

Each new field is hope, each old one reality. On a field of freshly cut peas, a small woman with grey hair escaping her straw hat was covering the ground methodically, up and down, up and down, like an ant on an errand. As her path intersected with mine, she paused and looked up. 'Anything?' I shook my head. 'I got a Roman but it's small.' She produced an old film canister and tipped out a tiny dark coin. 'See? Grot.'

'Grot' is detectorist slang for a coin, especially a Roman coin, with few or no markings left on it (archaeologists get all maiden-auntish over the disrespect implied by such a word). But still, it's *Roman*. I wanted to magic up a megaphone, place it to the woman's ear and shout at the top of my voice, 'Lady, to me that is not grot!' Instead I said airily, 'Way it goes.'

Finally, finally, I received an excellent signal, easily the best of a poor day. So I dug. And dug. Deeper and deeper. This scenario was becoming familiar. A positive signal followed by a deep target usually meant big iron and I was about give up when I noticed that my frantic digging had attracted the attention of a willowy man in a floppy England cricket hat. 'That's deep,' he said, strolling over. 'Better be good!'

'Probably big iron.'

'You're below ploughing depth there.' He checked the signal on his detector. 'You're right, good signal. Could be a hoard.'

Hoards are the holy grail of detectorists (although, to borrow a funny line from *Detectorists*, you could say that their *ultimate* holy grail is in fact the Holy Grail). A hoard is a stash of miscellaneous items buried in the ground – usually for temporary safekeeping but sometimes as a ritual offering. Famously, the seventeenth-century diarist Samuel Pepys buried bottles of wine and a 'Parmazan cheese' in his garden during the Great Fire of London. The following year, during the Anglo-Dutch War, he sent his father and wife off to the country with family savings of £1,300 (over £100K in today's money) in a 'night-bag' and instructions to 'hide', i.e. bury, it.

Detectorists have found hoards of Bronze Age axe heads, Iron Age gold staters, Roman coins and much more. But the most famous hoard found by a detectorist (in 2009) was the Viking swag bag of Anglo-Saxon treasure known as the Staffordshire Hoard, a breathtaking cache of mangled-up weaponry in finely worked gold and silver, some pieces being adorned with red garnets 'backlit' with gold foil. The level of craftsmanship and artistic vision is so exquisite that modern-day commentators ask, in all seriousness, 'How did they do that?'

The finder of the Staffordshire Hoard, Terry Herbert, was using a detector he picked up for peanuts in a car boot sale. He and the landowner shared a windfall of nearly £3.3 million (and fell out spectacularly over the money, with Terry later reportedly claiming, 'Sometimes I wish I'd never found that hoard'). Now here was someone suggesting I might be about to find my own hoard. I thought he was joking but then he said, 'Mind if I have a go? I mean, it's your hole . . .'

I thought, *Of course, there is* hole *etiquette*. I said, grateful for the rest, 'No, go ahead.'

We took it in turns to dig and scrape – he had a nifty archaeologist's trowel – till we were nearly two feet down. The carrot was chattering more and more excitedly, telling us we were getting close, but there was still no sign of the target. 'Trouble is,' said my new friend, 'when do you decide to call it a day? You don't want some bloke coming along in ten years' time and finding the axe heads you missed. It's known to be an Iron Age area round here.'

This was news to me. Then I thought back to the museum in Andover, and the ring I had chucked away. That was just two fields away from where we were today. For the next few minutes, I dug like a maniac, picturing the story in the papers. The two of us would be generous in our moment of triumph, each acknowledging the effort of the other, like marathon runners crossing the finishing line hand in hand.

Finally we hit the target. A patch of rust-red iron. Big. Bigger the more we scraped. Not so much 'boat' as 'moat' – Most Of A Tractor.

3

CHASING BOUDICCA'S HARES

'You wanna go to Norfolk,' said Kris when I told him I was struggling to find anything interesting or even to feel that I was making any meaningful progress.

Norfolk is a detectorists' El Dorado. Between 2012 and 2019, more treasure finds – 917 – were made in Norfolk than in any other county or region. In 2019, Norfolk cleaned up (as it does every year) on the number of objects reported to the local Finds Liaison Officer (FLO) under the Portable Antiquities Scheme (PAS), with nearly 11,000, and Suffolk was second with 6,000 (Hampshire was third with 5,000; Northumberland registered just 82).

East Anglia has always been in a league of its own. The Sutton Hoo Treasure, found near Woodbridge in Suffolk in 1939, is one of the greatest finds in world archaeology. Three years later, also in Suffolk, the Mildenhall Treasure of Roman silverware was unearthed by a ploughman. It is regarded by the British Museum as one of its most precious treasure collections.

In 1979 and 1992, detectorists found late Roman hoards of extraordinary quality and significance in Thetford, Norfolk and Hoxne, Suffolk; in 2008, a detectorist locked on to a hoard of more than 800 Iron Age gold staters near Wickham Market, Suffolk. There are various explanations for this apparent abundance, one being that there are more detectorists operating in East Anglia than anywhere else. Then again, they exist here for a reason.

People have been leaving traces in these fertile flatlands since barefoot mollusc hunters left footprints on the beach at Happisburgh up to 950,000 years ago, making them the earliest evidence yet of humans in Britain as well as the oldest human footprints found outside Africa. By the Middle Ages, a thriving wool trade had turned East Anglia into the most densely populated and affluent farming area in England.

But the Industrial Revolution left it behind and its heritage consequently remained largely undisturbed by extensive urban development or road building. The land is flat and easily detected; the many thousands of arable acres, refreshed by the plough, are the gift that keeps on giving. And Norfolk has been a pioneering county in terms of its attitude to amateur archaeologists and detectorists.

When the anti-detectorist STOP campaign was at its height, an inspirational Norfolk archaeologist called Tony Gregory had the counter-intuitive idea of narrowing the divide between the two camps, visiting detectorist clubs and using amateur detectorists on archaeological excavations. Norfolk became the model on which the Portable Antiquities Scheme was based and both Norfolk and Suffolk have continued that good work.

Surely even I, a beginner who had so far shown little aptitude for acquiring the skill and related good fortune of successful metal detecting, could not fail to score well in Norfolk. Doing so should be, to borrow the phrase, Normal for Norfolk!

When I asked Kris if he had any contacts in the county, he put me on to a social worker from Norwich called Christopher Holmes who posts smartly made videos on YouTube under the name The Discriminator. 'An open and friendly guy. He's made some great finds.' These include a 'purse spill' of 24 Henry III coins.

I spoke to Chris on the phone, an immediately easy conversation that involved advice to do with big iron and knowing when to stop digging, and finished with an invitation to join him on a weekend rally high up near the north coast of Norfolk.

The county's narrow and meandering roads were a relief after the roaring straitjacket of the M25, at least up to the point when I got stuck for the second time behind a giant metal grasshopper with spiked accessories as lethal as the hubcaps on Boudicca's chariot. Anticipating such agrarian-related hold-ups, and given the distance involved, I had decided to break the journey overnight in Thetford, leaving me a final push of 50 miles to the rally site the following morning.

My hotel in Thetford was just a few doors up from the Ancient House Museum, a repository of local history housed in a half-timbered Tudor merchant's house. It was closed when I was there, which meant I was unable to see a temporary exhibition of items from the Thetford Treasure, a late Roman hoard of gold jewellery and silver spoons found in the town by a detectorist in 1979 and usually on display in the British

Museum. The finder of the hoard, a salesman named Arthur Brooks, was a chancer who ended up getting it all wrong.

Brooks, who was being treated for cancer, and his wife Greta stumbled on the hoard one late November day as the light was fading. They had been out for a drive (with his detector conveniently in the boot) and were passing a place called Gallows Hill on the outskirts of Thetford when Arthur remembered that he had heard stories of Roman coins being found there.

'He said, I just want to have a, whatever you called it, a swish around,' recalled Greta in a radio interview. The finds came up straightaway – gold rings, gold bracelets, a gold belt buckle, the silver spoons. They carried them off in a rolled anorak and Greta washed them with baby shampoo when they got home.

Arthur did not report the hoard, apparently because he did not have permission from the landowner, Breckland Council, and feared he might be deprived of the reward. The site was about to be developed as a light industrial estate and, to the subsequent dismay of archaeologists, a large metal warehouse was soon built on top of the find spot, obliterating whatever else may lie in the ground as well as vital contextual features. Meanwhile, Arthur placed the items in a bank vault in Doncaster.

Dealers were approached and in early May of 1980 one was taken to a secret location – by a stranger who was not Arthur Brooks – and shown the treasure by torchlight. He reported this to the British Museum and the cat was out of the bag. Two months later, Arthur Brooks died of cancer. The hoard was valued at £261,540, which would have been divided equally between Arthur and Greta Brooks and the council had they declared the treasure in the proper manner.

Ignoring calls from some archaeologists that nothing should be paid out because the finder had tried to cheat the system, the coroner directed that Greta should receive a third of this amount, around £87,000, to be shared with the landowner. Sounding like a broken woman in her radio interview, she described the whole episode of the Thetford Hoard as 'awful'.

The following morning, I discovered that a flock of pigeons with dysentery had roosted overnight directly above my car. An unsuccessful attempt to clean the car roof delayed my departure from Thetford and when I finally reached the weekend dig site I was one of the last arrivals. I drove gingerly across the stubble, past a food truck, a horsebox and a portable flagpole flying the St George's flag, through an avenue of campervans and enclosures made of windbreaks and found a tight pitch between a substantial red tent and the high white side of a mobile home.

There were about 60 vehicles here, which worked out at about a hundred people. No time now to put up my tent. I staked my claim by dumping down tent bag, sleeping bag and folding Quick-Seat and headed out in search of The Discriminator. At the entrance to the site, by the flagpole, a group of people were milling behind and around a table, trading jokes and looking generally proprietorial. I decided that these people must be the organisers of the weekend's gathering.

'Hello, mate, do you know Chris from Norwich?' I said to the nearest of them, a man with his head in a cloud of vape smoke. He half-turned and looked sharply at me in a way that I interpreted as a non-verbal version of 'Who wants to know?' Then he said, 'No, mate.'

I slunk away, feeling defeated, an outsider. I knew I stood out. I had not had time to cultivate the disguises of clothing, jargon and banter. 'Combats and khakis,' Andy had said. Plenty of that here, plus camos, tats, buzz cuts and tool belts. It struck me that a lot of these blokes were probably ex-army.

This rebuff triggered an association with an event in 2001. On the eve of 9/11 (not strictly relevant but it added retrospectively to the weirdness of what happened), I had been accused of being a spy for the British Army. The setting was a traditional music pub in the centre of Belfast and my accusers were two Republicans from the Falls Road with whom, up to that point, I had been chatting good-temperedly. I got out by legging it, not looking back till I'd run about half a mile into a crowded area of the city. This moment of jeopardy proved that not-belonging can be dangerous and it has stayed with me.

No one here was accusing me of anything, but I had a kind of flashback, a controlled panic attack, and wanted to leg it again. Shouldering my detector, I headed for the permissible fields behind the camping area, vast acreages domed with a fierce blue midsummer sky and dotted with hunched figures whose appearance and movement gave them an extra-human air as they operated in careful isolation from each other, their headphones looking like compound eyes on the sides of their heads.

This was the moment I first experienced the relief of detecting in a large field, and how anxieties can be dissolved away. It was about 60 acres and the wheat had just been cut. The stubble that remained retained its tarnished-gold colour, and a couple of times I mistook a stalk lying on its side for a band of gold, so brightly did it reflect the sunlight. The field also seemed to cup the warmth of the sun and slow-release it back at ankle height. I was paddling in an invisible warm sea while less than a mile to the north lay the real thing in a band of deep blue dotted with the white of yachts and wavelets.

The stubble was about four inches tall, which meant that effectively the machine was forfeiting the first four inches of soil penetration, rendering it far less efficient. Over 20 minutes I found no decent targets and dug nothing but didn't mind. Then, just as I was getting frustrated, a klaxon sounded. I looked around. A man in a high-vis waistcoat was standing in the far corner of the field holding up the orange noise-generator like a trophy. The other detectorists in the field looked up, shielding their eyes from the sunlight, then started making their way towards the man in the high-vis jacket with the klaxon.

The scene was like some sort of zombie ritual. I assumed the explanation was that something extraordinary had been found – a hoard of Roman gold, Saxon jewellery – and the klaxon was the signal to gather round and admire. The detectorists detected as they went, rather than shouldering their machines and hotfooting it. Like birdwatchers with binoculars at the ready on their chests, they are always 'on' – legion, and not always apocryphal, are tales of amazing finds on the edges of car parks and the fag ends of days. I followed suit, then noticed that the man in the high-vis jacket – who I assumed to be the keeper of the special find – had disappeared. Still the detectorists streamed, beyond the corner of the field and over the horizon. Into a spaceship maybe.

A man motored past me, sweeping as he went.

'What's happening?' I said.

'Next field is open now,' he replied. 'The ploughed and rolled one.'

It doesn't get any better – a field newly ploughed, so any objects buried deep are churned nearer the surface, then flattened with a roller to make for perfect detecting conditions. Hence the swift exodus from the wheatfield. This was pretty much the definition of shooting fish in a barrel.

As I walked into the field, a Tiger Moth looped the loop two thousand feet above, its engine screaming, then fainting before it flattened out and burbled away. How many hours did the pilot take to learn to do that? Fewer, I reckoned glumly, than I would need to become a competent detectorist. In the new field the signals were better, the soil easier to dig. But I seemed to be regressing with my pinpointing. Targets became will o' the wisps. I started sweating in the sunshine and glugged down some water. After peering for so long into the world of worms, I shifted my gaze to the horizon. A wind farm appeared like a *fata morgana* on the sea.

After three hours I headed back to camp for lunch. On my way I passed a female detectorist – in a small minority on the rally – dressed in black, and deployed the phrase, 'Found much?'

'Not really. Coupla pieces of shrapnel.' She was Australian. 'They pinged off nicely. You?'

I shook my head, wondering what she meant by 'pinged off nicely'.

Back on the campsite, I bought an egg bap and a cup of tea from the food truck and had my lunch sitting in my folding Quick-Seat, making use of the beverage holder in the armrest and reflecting ruefully on a feeble morning's work. My only consolation was that the Aussie woman had fared no better. For the afternoon session I returned to the freshly ploughed field and found a lead bullet. I also peed in the adjacent field of tall maize. At one point a ginger-haired man in a red singlet veered towards my swing path. 'Any luck?' he said companionably.

I grimaced. 'Bullet. You?'

'Coupla hammereds,' he replied. 'Just on that first hill where you come in.' He said this as if it were an admission of failure. 'Still,' he went on, 'it's a nice little field to dig on.'

In the middle of the afternoon, and having had no success, I suddenly remembered Chris from Norwich. The person I had arranged to meet. The main point of being here at all. The onus had been on me to find *him* and after my initial unsuccessful attempt I had just given up. I had assumed I didn't have his mobile number but now remembered that Kris in Kent had given it to me and I had called him. Chris's number was in my phone somewhere. I reached into my old canvas bag – where I kept sundry items for a day out in a field – for the phone but couldn't find it. I had lost my phone.

As I panicked all the way back to the campsite, it started to spit with rain. I found the phone wedged in the beverage holder in the armrest of my folding seat, pocketing it before it received a terminal soaking. Then I hurried to pitch the tent. It was a pup tent made for two slim, short people, and now that I looked it was by far the smallest tent on site.

Most exceeded the square footage of flats in London. People could stand up in them, had created front gardens with barbecues and bar areas. One was festooned with twinkling fairy lights. Another had its own WC tent out the back. Then there were the vehicles, which unfolded like Swiss Army knives into mini gin palaces. There was a one-upmanship going on here that I hadn't bargained for.

Tucked in my tent, with rain pattering on the flysheet, I found Chris's number. My idea was that the day could be salvaged if I could hook up with him by the bar – which was concealed in the horsebox – and buy him a drink or two. But when I called him, apologising for the mix-up, he'd already left the site.

'Mate, I thought you hadn't bothered,' he said.

I felt my eyes pricking with tears of mortification.

Then he said that he was staying locally and coming back in the morning at 7am sharp. He described his car. Bullet dodged, just about.

Feeling relieved, I contemplated the evening ahead. My plan now was to ease myself into the atmosphere and camaraderie of the rally by hanging out by the bar truck and buying people drinks.

But there was to be no drinking scene that night. The rain fell harder. People hunkered in their canvas castles. I lay listening to the man in the tent to my left farting exuberantly while talking on the phone to (judging from the occasional perfunctory endearment) his wife.

'Plenty of stuff's been found (*parp!*),' I heard him say. 'One bloke found a Roman ring. I think some Roman gold (*parp! parp!*).'

Was it true, this information? Such rumours must fly in camps like these. In any case it increased the foulness of my mood and general sense of failure.

When the rain eased to a light drizzle, I put on a rain hat and scored a hamburger and chips from the food truck (noting there was zero action around the horsebox bar). Then I unscrewed the bottle of red wine I had brought, filled my plastic wine glass and had dinner sitting in the drizzle in the folding chair in front of the tent. The relative decorum of the ritual cheered me up a bit. As I was finishing off the chips and contemplating a return to my nylon pupa, there was a rustling and unzipping in the red tent to my left and the portly figure of my flatulent neighbour fell out.

His crumpled features looked like a semi-deflated air mattress. He wore a T-shirt that said 'Just another ring pull'. Looking over at me, he broke the ice by remarking on the pigeon shit on the roof of my car. His name was Glen and he had cramp in his legs.

'How d'you get on in a tent that small?' he said. 'Mine's bad enough.'

His was in fact big enough to stoop in and had separate 'living' and 'sleeping' areas.

'Found much today, Glen?' I asked.

'A terret ring.'

A terret ring, it turned out, was a loop from a horse's harness, from the late Iron Age or early Roman period. Beckoning me over, Glen opened the boot of his car and unclipped a plastic sandwich box. Inside, nestling in protective foam rubber, was a curved piece of copper alloy with a raised, decorated section in the middle.

'Two thousand years old,' said Glen. 'Sort of thing Boudicca would have had on her chariot.'

His pronunciation of her name was old-school, Bodi-*see*-er, rather than the revisionist *Boo*-dicker.

I coveted the terret ring. It seemed to me an astonishing find. But Glen seemed more proud of his homemade charging box, which used three household burglar-alarm batteries housed in a wooden Fortnum and Mason presentation box he had found in a skip in Ipswich.

'Does everything,' he said. 'Detector, headphones, smartphone. The lot.'

This self-sufficiency was evident in a general vibe across the camp. There was an off-grid feel to many of the people there –

a bit Swampy the eco-warrior, a bit nutzo survivalist, but probably tending to the latter.

Glen said he worked for a big supermarket chain and was due to retire the following summer.

'See that tent?' he said, pointing to the inflatable one on the other side of his that was big enough to fly model planes in. 'I fancy one of those. A blow-up. Stick that in the back of the car and head off to a dig. That'll do me. I'm never going to be a millionaire now, am I?'

As dusk dwindled to near-dark, two men walked past with shouldered detectors, returning from a late-evening session in the fields.

'Found anything?' someone called from the doorway of his campervan.

'Nah,' said one. 'Think I'll take up nighthawking.' The camp echoed with a sinister laughter that unsettled me.

Glen went to bed and was soon snoring. I stayed out in my chair, drinking wine and enjoying the atavistic feel of camping: barbecues and fire pits glowing through the dark, muffled laughter, the plosive sound of beer cans being opened. Until a few years ago there had been a re-creation of an Iceni village in Norfolk (the old signposts were still up), the Iceni being Boudicca's tribe. At night it may have looked and felt similar to this. As I lay down to sleep, I felt a closeness to the land that was certainly literal – the tent was pitched on stubble and the spikiness pushed up through the groundsheet and thin airbed – but also figurative. What objects lay just below me? This was my final thought before I feel asleep.

I woke to the rapid squeaking of an oystercatcher and the tolling of the bell in the squat church tower a mile to the south. Chris turned up on the dot of 7am. He was a slim, energetic, warm man with a ready smile, the kind of rare person you feel you have known for five years after just five minutes.

He waved away my apologies for the previous day's cock-up.

'More important, how did you do?' he said.

'Oh, terrible. Yourself?'

He took me round to the boot of his car. While I had been labouring and cursing to find a solitary bullet, Chris was bagging beauty and rarity. A Henry III hammered cut quarter, a George III coin and then . . . 'I have to admit, my heart skipped a beat.' He produced from its protective box a sizeable, elaborately decorated buckle that he believed to be Viking.

'It's a bit of a thing,' he said, his eyes sparkling. 'The zoomorphic style. I can almost convince myself I can see a Viking helmet in the design of it. See the eyes there? It's intricate, it belonged to someone of note. It's tantalising!'

He'd found it in a place that suggested the opening scene of a film: on a shoulder of land set back from the shoreline.

'You'd come ashore, find high ground to get your bearings,' he said. 'Perhaps a raiding party came ashore and set up camp on the hill.'

Chris had brought along previous, equally astonishing finds for me to see. That 'purse spill' of 24 Henry III coins. 'A hoard is kind of the Holy Grail,' he said – at which I resisted the temptation to answer with the *Detectorists* comeback. He added thoughtfully that each hoard is – or was – also 'a tragedy'. A Celtic coin from the Iceni tribe dated to 60 BC. 'My most precious find. Because it's local. So individual and unique.' Seeing all this gorgeous material, I felt like a parks footballer in the forcefield of Lionel Messi.

For the new morning's detecting, we drove a mile to another field, L-shaped and sprawling over many acres, just harvested of potatoes. It was next to the church whose bell I'd heard tolling in the night.

While we were setting up our gear, Chris introduced me to the concept of 'recovery speed' – how quickly you can investigate a target and move on to the next.

'It's the crucial element,' he said.

I felt relieved he hadn't seen me yesterday, digging and digging for ages on one hole like a mole with OCD.

As we started on our sweeping trajectories, Chris promised: 'We'll get you a hammered today.'

The soil was damp and soft, and within five minutes a mate of Chris's had come over with encouraging early finds.

'Tealby penny,' said Ray, his chest puffed with modest pride as he held out an irregular smudge of a thing.

Chris explained that Tealbies were coins issued in the second half of the twelfth century, in the reign of Henry II, and named after a hoard of more than five thousand of them found near the village of Tealby in Lincolnshire in 1807.

Ray had also found a medieval lead ampulla, which looked like a wad of pre-masticated chewing gum.

'Makes sense,' said Chris, pointing to the church – ampullae being tiny flasks that, once filled with holy water from a religious site, took on the miraculous power of a relic. They were cast into fields to bless the land and bring forth a rich crop. Amen to that, I thought.

A short while later, I had a promising signal. Mindful of Chris's words about recovery time, I dug decisively and had the target in my hand within a minute: small but heavy, the shape of a squat cone. At first I thought it was a pebble and couldn't understand why the detector was reacting to it.

'Lead weight,' said Chris. 'Probably medieval.'

I was reasonably happy with this possibility. At least it was *something*, and had some age to it.

The question of age had been puzzling me. Why did I venerate it in objects as a quality – perhaps the most important quality – in its own right? Why did a scruffy old clog clasp that might have been worn by a Hampshire farm labourer three hundred years ago mean more to me than the button from the uniform of an officer who served in the Royal Navy in the mid-twentieth century?

Human existence, compared to that of the universe, spans, it's true, the mere proverbial blink of an eye. But within that blink there are infinities. I was beginning to understand that holding something humanly old was a way of combing out those knots of time; each piece a brush with a specific mystery. And the older it is, the more cobwebbed, the more *mysterious*, the mystery.

'Or could be a gaming piece,' said Chris. 'Could be Viking.'

'*Viking*?'

'Sure.'

'Like the Top Hat in Monopoly?'

A couple of years earlier, an ex-miner detecting alongside the River Trent near Torksey in North Lincolnshire found 37 pieces similar to the one I found in Norfolk. Torksey had been the location of a camp established in the winter of AD 872–3 by what the *Anglo-Saxon Chronicle* called the Viking 'great heathen army', the force that through the 860s had swept into Northumbria, Wessex and Mercia.

The use of these lead objects as pieces in a board game was confirmed after they had been compared to stone counters in Oslo Museum. The game was a chess-like contest of battlefield strategy called *hnefatafl*, and as the Vikings used only stones when they played in their homelands, it has been suggested that the lead pieces found in England were made here – probably at Torksey, where there was a source of lead – rather than brought over.

Each player of *hnefatafl* started with 37 pieces, so the detectorist had bagged a complete set, making it a unique find. In September 2020 the set was sold, along with a specially made reproduction wooden board, for £3,224 by a Mayfair auction house.

At the time, in the field, I had not brushed off the mystery to this satisfying degree. All I knew was that I had found something older than anything else I had yet found, possibly/probably Viking. Half an hour later, I got the anchor-shaped 'chape' (pin) of a buckle. Chris thought it was Roman at first but corrected himself to Georgian. Later still, on the PAS database, I spotted a near-identical piece found in Oxfordshire, 'dating to *c*.AD 1660–1720'.

These finds inoculated me against envy when Chris proceeded to pull out his plums for the day: firstly, a narrow copper strip bearing the classic Saxon 'diagnostic' of a ring-and-dot pattern, probably part of a bracelet; then a greenish patterned disc, slightly bigger than a 2p piece, that prompted him to call over, 'Mate, sorry to do this to you . . .'

He whizzed off a picture to a friend for confirmation, and received it straight back.

'Yep. Saxon disc brooch. More ring-and-dot. Classic catch plate, like a safety pin. Never thought I'd find one of these.'

What he couldn't make out then, but confirmed later, was the detail of the design. It showed a serpent eating its own tail.

It was a rich weekend for finds. That ecstatic soil gave up, besides Chris's notable objects, more than two hundred hammereds, a chunky Roman bronze ring, a Saxon 'porcupine' sceat (the pattern looking like the raised quills of a porcupine), a half noble gold hammered 'Eddie' (from the reign of Edward III), a silver *denarius* from the rule of Septimius Severus, the Roman emperor who invaded Caledonia and died in York in AD 211, and an Edward the Confessor penny. And, skittering across its surface, a hare.

Hither and thither ran the hare, into invisible dead ends and back out in reverse gear, finally hitting a groove that flew it over the horizon. The hare was revered by the Ancient Britons as a 'shapeshifter'. I saw more hares in that first summer of metal detecting than I had previously seen in my life. On one of my Hampshire days out, I was admiring a dashing leveret when a fellow detectorist clocked it too and – like Glen – started talking about 'Bodi-*see*-er'. That was when I discovered that the statuesque, tawny-tressed scourge of the Romans kept hares up her dress.

This sounds like one of those burned-cakes takes on history, but it has a respectable source in the form of the Roman historian Dio Cassius's account of Boudicca's revolt in his 80-volume history of Ancient Rome. After pumping up her 120,000-strong army with a spear-rattling speech, 'she employed a species of divination, letting a hare escape from the fold of her dress; and since it ran on what they considered the auspicious side, the whole multitude shouted with pleasure, and Boudicca, raising her hand toward heaven, said: "I thank thee, Andraste . . ." ' – Andraste being the Icenic goddess of war.

*

Divination was what I needed. A few weeks later, Chris invited me back up to Norfolk to detect on one of his personal permissions. I'd had no luck in the meantime but had been encouraged by my second day's efforts on the Norfolk weekender. Maybe this famously giving soil would crumble even more obligingly. I took the train, having arranged to borrow Chris's spare gear at the other end. It was mid-morning when he picked me up, from a dusty rural halt like Edward Thomas's Adlestrop, where 'no one left and no one came'.

Next to the railway line lay one of his best areas, where he'd found his hoard of Henry IIIs – and 20 hammereds in a single field. But those fields were currently out of commission, having just been re-sown. We had to make do with a recently dug potato field and 40 or so acres of wheat stubble. He'd been out for an hour or so before I arrived and had already found a D-shaped Georgian buckle and a musket ball.

The machine he loaned me was a good one, better than mine on paper, and I appreciated the wireless headphones, as the lead of my basic plug-in variety was the worst-performing feature of my kit. It was constantly wrapping itself around one or other of my legs, or skewing the cans off one or other ear. But the borrowed pinpointer was a problem. It chattered crazily – like an a capella choir of fruit bats – in proximity to just about anything.

We started on the potato field, and while I was still grappling with the delinquent carrot, he had turned up a clod with a disc-shaped object embedded in it – a tantalising sight for detectorists.

'A round in the ground!' he exclaimed.

The next few seconds, when you extricate the target, clean it off with gloved thumb and a squirt of water and make a stab at what it could be that you are holding – a sceat, a Roman, a Tealby penny? – are delicious. You give yourself permission to dream. These dreams are often short-lived.

'A farthing of nothingness. Wank!' said Chris cheerfully.

There is a choreography to detecting with a buddy. You don't do it on top of each other, you respect people's solitude and their right to be alone with their thoughts and, sometimes, their demons. Kris, in Kent, had hinted to me of the therapeutic qualities of detecting. In one of his videos he gestures at the Kentish countryside around him and declares that 'This is my church. Metal detecting is my prayer.' In another video, devoted to 'Mental Health and Metal Detecting', he acknowledges how the hobby has helped him 'through dark times, depression and anxiety'.

These 20 minutes of thoughtfulness, delivered as Kris sits in a field on an overcast day, attracted responses from 164 detectorists who said they also suffered from depression and that metal detecting was a life-saver. One wrote: 'It's how I reset my mind. The rhythm of the sweep, the dopamine hit of the target, the focus required for concentrating on the target tones, it is all a way of recentring my soul.'

In Hampshire I had met a policeman who was a response officer in a rural town I didn't know well but had always thought of as well-heeled and law-abiding – it had an Aga shop, for God's sake! He said that the reality of life in that town – in *any* town, come to that – was far grimmer than people realised. 'Last week,' he said, 'I had to tell this lady her husband had died at work. Young kids upstairs. I could hear the words coming out of me and her world just collapsed in front of me . . .'

When I commiserated, he hesitated, then launched into a story of the time he was called to a flat with a long-dead person in it. The carpets were littered with dead bluebottles and empty cider bottles. The body was bent over the bath and the bath taps were still running. Dressed in a full forensic suit, he was instructed to carry the body into the lounge and lay it on its back on the floor for the CSI team to investigate.

'My initial contact with the body was the right shoulder and as I applied pressure my fingers broke through the skin, which was all gelatinous, and went under the collar bone. I hyperventilated several times, I felt completely rancid,' he said. 'Time alone out metal detecting, concentrating on those beeps, it seems to push all this shit into another place in my subconscious where it can't harm me.' He apologised for giving me 'too much information' and I thought, no, the sorrow is mine for not knowing that people go through such things so I don't have to.

Chris had his bugbears too. Being a social worker was, he told me, 'non-stop, completely non-stop and you can't escape it. You're run ragged and you're fed up with people. Then you go shopping and you see the same people. You go to the cinema – same thing. The only way to escape is to get away from people. People are what cause a lot of the problems in my life. Being out here is about getting away from them.'

I was beginning to realise that we are all of us, as we poke around 'out there', hiding from something or seeking something else. In my case I had thought metal detecting was a way of elevating an interest in tokens of the past but something else was coming through. Something like seeking where I belonged. During the Brexit debate, the then Prime Minister, Theresa May, had referred in a snide way to people she called 'citizens of nowhere' and I had been cut by the remark.

Did she mean me? I had a disrupted childhood that left me not knowing whether I was an English southerner or an English northerner (quite different things) and I had since lived most of my life in either London or Hampshire (with frequent trips abroad) without feeling a particular connection to either. If you were to have asked me where I wanted to be buried, or have my ashes scattered, I wouldn't have known what to tell you.

Detectorists give each other room to work on such questions. On some of those vast prairie-type expanses, a person seeking thinking space can disappear from view, over the brow of a rise that you hadn't previously realised existed. But you always, eventually, loop back towards one another and re-establish contact by comparing your finds.

The next time I crossed paths with Chris, he was on his knees poring over a hole. By this time I had partially tamed the carrot. There *was* a knack, as Chris had suggested – you 'earthed' it by laying its snout in the soil before switching it on but I was still not convinced it was giving me reliable signals. So far I had found just two shotties.

'Silver in the hole!' announced Chris. It was a Victorian threepenny bit from 1860. Though he could make out the date, the design was worn, Vicky's features almost blank. 'Not the best of conditions, bless her. She's seen better days,' said Chris. The image, could we have seen it, shows the Queen at the age of 18, though she was in her early 40s by 1860 and already taking on her formidable matriarch look. (The famous likeness of her in old age, wearing a widow's veil, didn't come in until 1893.)

Five minutes later, as Chris and I were drifting again into our separate and diverging patterns across the field, he yelled out 'Hammered!'

I walked back with mixed feelings – pleased for him, eager to know what it might be, yet piqued by a childish sense of unfairness. *He's already got hundreds of the things – 20 from one field, for God's sake*, I was thinking to myself as I smiled my way over.

'Let's have a rare one, Saxon or something,' he said as he carefully lifted the dulled disc from its long slumber. 'It's really soft. You can bend it.' He peered. 'Ah. It's a "short cross". Richard, John or Henry III.'

Coins, he had told me, were his gateway drug.

'Just up here I found my first-ever hammered coin and I had no idea who King Edward I was. No context. Was that three hundred years old or a thousand years old? So I looked him up and that was the first time I put historical context to what I was finding in the ground.'

Since then, the small change of small change had become his area of expertise.

He explained that 'short cross' coins replaced the Tealby pennies and covered the reigns of Henry II, Richard the Lionheart, John and Henry III. The 'short' crosses (they did not extend to the edge of the coin) on the reverse acted like a dotted perforation line, indicating where to cut the coin to reduce it to smaller denominations of halfpenny or farthing. But the design was open to exploitation.

As the cross did not reach the coin's edge, it was impossible to say where the edge was and people took advantage of this by shaving or 'clipping' slivers of silver from the edges. The problem was rectified with the introduction, in 1247, of 'long cross' coinage. 'They learned their lesson, you could say,' he said.

Chris sprayed the coin, gently rubbing away the soil disguise until the portrait of the curly headed monarch began to emerge.

'See the face coming through? The eyes in the middle?'

This likeness of a medieval monarch was oddly 1970s, like a singer who was on *Top of the Pops* just before the punk explosion. The hair looked permed, the eyes were flash-bulb wide under the big Norfolk sky. After eight hundred subterranean years, he looked as startled to see me as I was to see him. Chris, being a regular visitor to the courts of the short-cross kings, was pleased but not fazed. I felt awed and unworthy, a new courtier crouching behind a pillar.

For our afternoon in the stubble field, we switched to 'sniper' coils – with a reduced diameter, they were supposed to be good for poking around in small spaces and bristly undergrowth. But after an hour or so I knew in my bones the day would not be the one lodged in my memory as the moment my luck turned. And that at least unhitched me from the desperate hope that usually plodded dutifully in my bootprints.

It was a dramatic flatland day, seven-eighths of the landscape being flint-blue sky. The perimeter of the field was spaced with oaks, their trunks woolly with ivy. A horsewoman in a hi-vis waistcoat trotted placidly between them. The only sound, apart from the ever-present crackle in my headphones, was the distant roar of jet fighters from RAF Lakenheath.

Then even that subsided and the headphones fell silent. 'God it's *quiet*,' I muttered to myself. Five minutes later, Chris was by my side.

'Mate, you've got your headphones switched off.'

The usual white noise from the detector was now leaking externally but I hadn't heard it. He sounded embarrassed on my behalf.

My return for the four-hour afternoon session was more shotties, a bullet, a button and the minor consolation of a coin so worn it was unidentifiable. Chris pronounced it a 'halfpenny of nothingness', though he reckoned it could be Georgian. He, meanwhile, had pulled more decent coins and buckles, Victorian, Georgian and medieval, as well as medieval potsherds and pieces of clay pipe. All in all, he said, with the Vicky threepence and the short-cross hammered, a good day.

'I think there's something about your home turf, for some reason,' he mused as we waited for me to catch my train back to Norwich and beyond. 'I always do well here and today's a good example coz we've both had exactly the same opportunities, haven't we? And I've got an absolute stack there, and I feel like, how have you not found more?'

There it was, the question I had sensed hanging in the air all day, except this was the polite version. What must he have thought when he noticed I had inadvertently switched off the headphones? I worried that I was being a burden to him, a loser tainted with ill luck.

'Either I'm attuning my hearing better or I'm used to the ground and what it sounds like, I don't know,' he went on. 'Because I'll go to someone else's permission and I'll do really poorly.'

'Really? *Seriously?*'

I suspected he was just saying this to make me feel better. But we were getting into other realms.

'Yeah. I went up to North Lincolnshire, right next to Ermine Street, the Roman road. This guy John said, "You've got to come up here, it's filled with Roman", and he found Roman all day long and I didn't get a sniff of it. It was getting to the point of embarrassment. I hadn't changed anything. I had all the kit.' He sighed and glanced at the darkening sky. 'I can't put my finger on it.'

4

BADGERS WITH SPADES

In those early metal-detecting days, I saw it as essentially a self-centred activity. I just wanted to find really old stuff, to feel that buzz that archaeologists as well as detectorists agree they get when handling an object of age and knowing they are the first person to touch it since Boudicca was giving the Romans a run for their money or Charles II hid in a tree.

My familiarity with the purpose and techniques of archaeology was negligible, my knowledge of British history full of holes – though I claimed for myself a kind of half-intuitive understanding born of a random accumulation of ill-sorted facts and an affinity with landscape. I gave little thought to the wider responsibilities we all have to a sense of common heritage.

But as I started making historic finds, it dawned on me that this was a serious business I was getting into. Before I went much further, I needed some basic puppy training, as I could barely cock my leg without falling over. This was what drove me over the county border from Hampshire into Sussex.

Through social media I had discovered an initiative to educate detectorists in best practice for recording, handling and conserving their finds, and generally to bring hobbyists and archaeologists closer together. Sussex Heritage Community is the brainchild of one of life's selfless optimists, Daryl Holter, who for seven years was the heritage crime officer for Sussex Police.

The crimes he dealt with in that role covered everything from driving a quad bike over an Iron Age hill fort to stealing church stained glass to order, with nighthawking featuring prominently. When the Sussex force merged heritage crime into 'rural crime' (where it has had to take its chances alongside tractor theft, poaching, fly-tipping, hare coursing, dognapping and morris dancing), Daryl decided to continue his good work out of police hours, as a civilian.

I first met Daryl at the pub on Beachy Head, the infamous suicide spot where the South Downs plunge abruptly to the sea and England ends in a toothpaste smile of despair. If anyone could talk you back from the brink it would be Daryl, who has a Dixon of Dock Green air about him – both kindly and a little bit sorrowful at the scrapes people get themselves into. For him, human folly and negligence manifest themselves most regrettably in our attitude to found historical objects.

He himself has an emotional rather than a transactional relationship with them.

'I'm not so bothered about the precious metals,' he said as we sat down beneath a print of storm waves crashing on to Eastbourne seafront. 'What I want to do is understand how people *lived*. When you find a Neolithic axe head or scraper, you realise that that object took a very long time to make, to find the flint material, to shape it.

'That was your knife, it killed an animal, it enabled you to butcher an animal, it allowed you to live. Without that, you're up against it. When you hold something like that, you just understand something of what living was like back then and how very different we have it now. That connection is important.'

Important but lost, in too many cases.

'There can be something happening at, let's say, Pevensey Castle,' he said, 'and people will drive past and go, "It's not mine, it doesn't bother me", but if it was their car in the driveway being smashed up, they would do something. The connection isn't really there. It's stealing our history, but I don't think everybody gets that.'

Daryl flipped open his laptop to run me through images of recent heritage crime in the locality: 52 brass memorial plaques prised from a graveyard; historic structures on Brighton's seafront stripped of ten tons of copper and lead; stolen Georgian mileposts and Victorian postboxes.

The final image showed the handiwork of nighthawks on a scheduled monument. 'There's a hardcore of detectorists who will say that was done by animals, not humans, and because no one has witnessed it you can't prove it,' he said. 'But when you're looking at square-cut holes, it's quite obvious it's not a badger with a spade.'

Daryl then mentioned the Sussex connection to the case of the Herefordshire Hoard, the most notorious example of looting by metal detectorists in British legal history. Later, I sat at my laptop and filled in the gaps, starting in Eastbourne, the seaside resort once dubbed 'God's waiting room' for its high proportion of elderly residents. The fuddy-duddy factor of such towns can be measured in the incidence of antiques shops. In March 2011, the *Eastbourne*

Herald featured an item about an unusual variety of the genre in the town's back streets:

> *A treasure hunter opened his Aladdin's cave of historical*
> *finds in Eastbourne last week. Simon Wicks has been legally*
> *plundering historical sites for the past 40 years unearthing*
> *everything from trivial Victorian coins to a golden garnet cross*
> *belonging to Anne Boleyn. His shop, Britanicus in Terminus*
> *Road, holds everything from £5 medieval buckles to £15,000*
> *gold snuff boxes . . .*

The shop also sold metal detectors, for Simon Wicks was a particular kind of 'treasure hunter': a detectorist. An unintended clue to the kind of detectorist he was is contained in the newspaper report. You can no more 'legally plunder' than you can 'tidily bomb'. In 2014, Wicks received a criminal conviction for nighthawking but, seemingly undaunted, continued to operate at the shady end of the antiques and antiquities world. And there – in the dusty corners of pubs and eBay – he would have stayed but for a phone call he received on 10 June 2015.

The man who dialled his number was George Powell, then 34, a fellow detectorist from Newport in South Wales. Powell, who had multiple convictions for offences including burglary and deception, told Wicks that a bit of business had come up that he might be interested in. They met the next day at a motorway service station on the M4.

A week later, Wicks walked into the offices of Dix Noonan Webb, an auction house in Bolton Street, Mayfair that specialises in coins. There, he produced seven coins and showed them to an expert called Jim Brown. Had he been sitting on a chair, Jim would have fallen off it, for he identified the coins immediately as Saxon and of the highest value. Two of them, known as 'Two Emperors', were of particular rarity and historical significance, as they bore images that suggested an alliance between the kingdoms of Wessex and Mercia in the ninth century that historical records did not reflect.

Wicks had little to say about the provenance of the coins beyond the fact that he believed they had been found by detectorists in Herefordshire. On a quick mental calculation, Jim Brown reckoned they could be worth several hundred thousand pounds. He explained that it would take some time to assess and value them accurately and locked them in the company safe. Wicks went home to East Sussex, but he wasn't done.

On 28 July, reversing the principle that when you're in a hole you should stop digging, he returned to Dix Noonan Webb with a further nine coins. This time, he had bothered to concoct a story, albeit a feeble one: the coins had belonged to a man who had died in the 1970s and bequeathed them to his wife, who had in turn left them to their son, from whom Wicks had just bought them.

The auctioneers took them into safekeeping with the others and on 31 July – as rumours circulated in the intersecting worlds of coin collecting and archaeology of a huge scam in the making – passed the 16 coins on to the police. Wicks was subsequently arrested and four years later appeared in the dock of Worcester Crown Court alongside Paul Wells, a fellow coin dealer, and two metal detectorists named George Powell and Layton Davies.

The case of what came to be known as the Herefordshire Hoard is well known in metal-detecting circles – the ultimate example of nefarious practice that casts the hobby in the worst possible light and makes it that bit more difficult for all of us to gain trust and permissions from landowners. I remembered reading about the trial in the papers in 2019, but that had been in my pre-detecting days and I hadn't paid that much attention. Now the case intrigued me, and the more I read, the more it dragged me into its forcefield of mystery and greed.

The Hoard was unearthed on 2 June 2015, when Powell and Davies decided to search with their detectors in a part of Herefordshire – in the ancient kingdom of Mercia – that they reckoned held particular promise of plentiful historical finds. The fields they plumped for were in a remote spot near the town of Leominster where an Anglo-Saxon monastery had once stood.

The first mistake they made – or perhaps it wasn't a mistake – was to be cavalier in obtaining the necessary permissions. A woman called Yvonne Conod had agreed to them detecting on a field she owned. Her son Mark, a tenant farmer who ran the 200-acre Eye Court Farm nearby, had also given them his blessing even though he was in no position to do so, as he was not the landowner. It was on land belonging to Eye Court Farm – owned in fact by the Old Etonian 4th Baron Cawley – that Powell and Davies made their history-redefining discovery.

As they dug down, they probably first hit a lead box or covering (a piece of lead sheet having been discovered at the home of one of them) from which they extricated more and more coins and objects. Powell and Davies were experienced detectorists, Davies having previously behaved by the book in reporting more than a hundred finds to his local Finds Liaison Officer. It must have been immediately obvious to both that they had stumbled on a treasure hoard.

From what is now known (based on deleted photographs on their smartphones as well as on what they declared), they found: a ninth-century gold finger ring, octagonal on the outside, each facet decorated with a pattern highlighted in a black compound known as niello; a ninth-century oval gold bracelet in the form of a serpent eating its own tail; a spherical crystal pendant held in a harness of gold, each strip incised with a herringbone pattern, dated to the fifth to the seventh centuries; one silver ingot from the late ninth or early tenth century, with the likelihood that there were more; and maybe as many as 300 coins, though only 31 have been retrieved.

These 31 include 5 'Two Emperors', each with the image of twin rulers on one side and a Roman imperial bust on the other, together with the name of either Alfred the Great of Wessex or Ceolwulf II of Mercia. The significance of the coins lies in this symbolism, which suggests both an alliance and a balance of power between the two Anglo-Saxon kings that is at odds with the generally understood events of the period based on the *Anglo-Saxon Chronicle*, which was written after the Mercian king's death in the court of King Alfred. This dismisses Ceolwulf II as a foolish thane and a puppet of the Vikings, no more than a footnote in early British history – but these coins suggest a rethink on Ceolwulf's status could be due.

The hoard had been stolen and hidden by Vikings. In the ninth century, the Vikings' 'great heathen army' was marauding its way through the Saxon kingdoms, plundering monasteries of their gold and silver and hiding the booty for temporary safekeeping. But in this case something went wrong and the treasure was never retrieved – or not, at least, for more than a thousand years, when a couple of chancers from South Wales hit the detectorists' jackpot.

Powell and Davies stood to make a lot of money under the Treasure Act, but they had a problem – the 'permission' they had obtained for detecting on Eye Court Farm was not sound because it was the tenant, not the landowner, who had given them the nod. Even then, had they come clean straightaway, they might have blagged their way through, which would have been the best way to guarantee the highest reward, as the Treasure Act itself emphasises: 'It is important to bear in mind that a finder who fails to report a find of treasure . . . and sells it to a dealer has not only committed an offence but is likely to obtain a much lower price for it than if he had reported it in the proper way.'

Thinking they knew better, Powell and Davies were acting like characters in a bungled heist movie. On the permission question, they tried to cover themselves by making a misleading disclosure to Yvonne Conod and her son Mark. Powell visited both, telling them he had found valuable items on Mrs Conod's land and giving coins (worthless, not from the hoard) to both. Mark Conod said Powell also sent him pictures of a bracelet and a ring, saying they were Anglo-Saxon and claiming he had handed them in to a museum.

But Powell had trouble containing his excitement. How else to explain why he posted an image of coins from the hoard on the website of a local detecting group? The world of metal detecting is small but highly connected and incorrigibly nosy. Posts of finds on social-media platforms spread rapidly, especially when rare and possibly highly valuable objects are involved. As one archaeologist said to me, 'The looters can't help but boast on Facebook and if you don't alert them by asking questions they'll keep on doing it till they give everything away.'

The day after their discovery, the coin dealer Paul Wells received a phone call from a 'very excited' Powell. On 4 June they met in a cafe near Wells's market stall in Cardiff. Powell had brought Davies along and Wells invited an antiques dealer called Jason Sallam. From their pockets Powell and Davies spilled out about a dozen hammered coins. They then produced three bundles of kitchen towel from which they unwrapped the gold ring, the gold bracelet and the crystal pendant. 'I knew straightaway they were something special,' said Wells in a statement.

According to Wells, a heated conversation then followed in which he told Powell and Davies that they must declare the finds immediately; Powell argued that they could be worth as much as £40,000, here and now, to the right people; Davies backed Wells up and Powell doubled down on the instant profit they stood to make if they went their own way. They finally agreed that Jason Sallam should take the objects away and examine them properly to establish exactly what they were dealing with.

Sallam had little doubt of the extreme rarity and value of the finds, but he sought a second opinion of a colleague; and when he had had his suspicions confirmed, he returned everything to Wells with the injunction to tell Powell and Davies to declare the items. Wells in turn handed the loot back to Powell and repeated the message to do the right thing. According to Wells, Powell promptly handed back five of the coins to Wells 'for safekeeping' and said that the hoard had already been reported.

It was at this point that Powell called Simon Wicks, the Sussex 'treasure hunter', and arranged the meeting in the motorway service station. He and Davies then fixed a meeting at the National Museum Wales with the Finds Liaison Officer (FLO) for Wales, Mark Lodwick. They were probably spooked into doing this by an email they had received from Pete Reavill, the Finds Liaison Officer (FLO) for Herefordshire and Shropshire where the hoard was found. Reacting to rumours, Reavill had warned them that if they had indeed found treasure they were legally obliged to report it.

At the meeting with Lodwick, they surrendered the ring, bracelet and pendant, and two Saxon coins, claiming the coins had been found at different spots (which according to the Treasure Act meant they were not 'treasure'). But this partial declaration, far from dampening the rumours, only fanned them. In August, Powell and Davies were arrested by West Mercia Police on suspicion of theft. In September, a detective constable from WMP, Gareth Thomas, interviewed Paul Wells at his home in Cardiff about his meetings with Powell and Davies.

During this interview, Wells enacted an odd *mea culpa*. Producing the magnifying glass with which he scrutinised precious objects, he fiddled with the lining of its leather case and extracted five coins that he had hidden there, saying that three months earlier Powell had given them to him to look after and he had intended to give them back. DC Thomas arrested him. Two months later, Simon Wicks was picked up in Sussex. The looters of the Leominster Hoard had been rounded up.

On 3 October 2019, following a lengthy investigation that went around the houses of Anglo-Saxon history and smartphone technology, the four of them went on trial at Worcester Crown Court. 'This case, in two words, is about Buried Treasure,' said Kevin Hegarty QC, opening the case for the prosecution.

There was a time when I might have had a sneaking admiration for the defendants. Simon Wicks could have been one of the 'knocker boys' – dodgy antiques dealers – I drank with in pubs off the Western Road in Brighton in the 1990s. I was also reminded of the Bedouin of Qurna village in Egypt, the ones who lived in pharaonic tomb-houses and whom I wrote about in a magazine article in 2007.

The people of Qurna traded craftily in the funerary goods – and, occasionally, mummies – they grew up among. They also became experts in the manufacture of fake artefacts, some of them so brilliant they were works of art in their own right. I was shown, by a man who used to work as a conservator in the Valley of the Kings, how to make a plausible fake – he dipped a newly carved wooden priest figure in a chemical solution that included tea, then rolled it in mummy shrouds (astoundingly, as he worked he recited 'Ozymandias', Shelley's poem of Ancient Egypt).

People had always been on the steal and on the make in the valleys of the pharaohs – this was the means by which museums and private collections across the world acquired their mummies and amulets. Even Howard Carter, the discoverer of the Tomb of Tutankhamun, and his patron Lord Carnarvon were at it. Throughout the Victorian and Edwardian eras, the looting of cultural artefacts was considered a perk by Britain's imperial class. Sometimes it was facilitated by murderous violence.

The British Museum acknowledges that the controversial Benin Bronzes – controversial because many believe they should be returned whence they came – were lifted by British forces in 1897 in the course of the 'widespread destruction and pillage' of Benin City in modern-day Nigeria, and that 'thousands of objects of ceremonial and ritual value were taken to the UK as official "spoils of war" or distributed among members of the expedition according to their rank'.

As part of a 'de-colonisation' process, the Museum has devised a self-guided 'Collecting and empire' trail that 'shows the different, complex and sometimes controversial journeys of objects to the Museum' – all, needless to say, removed from their find spots in an era when context was not a consideration. Room 33 contains pieces acquired on Britain's 1903 invasion of Tibet and, as Sathnam Sanghera points out in *Empireland*, the explanatory text doesn't pull any punches, admitting that 'although some objects were paid for, many were forcibly taken by military officers from monasteries and the homes of Tibetans . . . British machine guns killed over 600 Tibetans, armed only with bayonets and wearing *gau*, during a battle in Guru in March 1904'. A *gau* is a lucky prayer box – in this case not so lucky.

The poor villagers of Qurna in Egypt, who lived without running water, turned looting into a way of life but at least they didn't commit wholesale murder to make it happen. Theirs was an innocent cottage industry compared to the ruthless acquisitiveness of Europe's imperial powers. Weren't people like Davies, Powell, Wicks and Wells from a parallel English tradition to the crafty Bedouin? Not so different, you might say, from that affable spiv Del Boy in the TV sitcom *Only Fools and Horses,* one of British popular culture's most loveable characters. But now that I was coming to understand the concept and importance of common heritage, the charms of the Del Boys of this world were wearing thin with me.

The next time I met Daryl Holter, the indefatigable upholder of correct heritage practice, was on a hidden slope of fields and paddocks in Ashdown Forest in the High Weald of East Sussex. Daryl had put out a request on social media for someone to lend us their land for the day and a stranger called Julia, with no connection to metal detecting, had made the acres surrounding her Arts and Crafts farmhouse available. There were molehills in the pasture and mist lying across the surrounding folds of copse and heath; and though a good two hours' drive east from my cottage, it still felt like home, as if I'd found a secret place at the end of my own garden, for both my land and Julia's were once within the thick canopy of Andredes Weald.

With a hovering smile, Julia set up a table of tea and lemon drizzle cake in the stable block as we gathered on the wet grass with our machines – newbies like me, some experienced local detectorists, the custodian of a scheduled monument (mid-nineteenth-century Shoreham Fort), a military historian. We talked through permissions, sweeping technique, hole-digging protocol, the reporting of finds, with accurate find spots ideally, and the dangers of unexploded ordnance.

'If you think you've found a bomb,' said Ray, who runs a group called Detecting the Weald, 'step away. Call the police. Walking into a police station and putting it on the counter is not a good idea.'

The subject seemed to animate the group.

'And don't take a grenade to a charity shop – that really happened,' someone added, while the man from the fort pointed out, with some relish, that 'just the fuse from a Mills bomb – not even the explosive, just the fuse – can take your arm off up to the elbow.'

As the introductory spiel progressed, I felt cautiously smug. I'd obviously already picked up more than I realised, for I was not hearing anything I didn't know already. And some of the new detectorists here were even more wet behind the ears than I was. One person, equipped with a box-fresh detector with not the faintest mud smear on it, did not even have a pinpointer.

'Carrot?' he said, looking nonplussed, when I asked where his was.

I liberated my orange vegetable facsimile from its holster on the shaft of the detector, turned it on and pointed it at the zip on my fleece until it gibbered obligingly.

'Good for close hole work,' I said with lofty authority.

A group of three caught my eye: a slim young man in a hoodie; a big lad in black; and a slight, older woman with white hair and delicate features. They had two detectors between the three of them and I was curious as to how that would work, who would pair off with whom, when we were finally let loose on the fields.

Then I forgot about them. I was drawn by those fields. The deep greenness of them, the dampness, the crinkles. Detectorists will tell you that a freshly ploughed and rolled piece of arable is the real caviar but tufted grass and pincushions of clover, loomed over by veteran trees, cast a deeper spell for me. Only later did I discover that the PAS discourages detecting on 'undisturbed pasture' (as opposed to arable land, where the soil has already, repeatedly, been disturbed by the plough) in case you damage fragile archaeology. But by then I was hooked on the green.

Today I felt convinced of the presence out there of intricate ancient objects and their desire to be found. When the talking finished and we fanned out across the paddock, the zone between my headphones filled with intensity and I paid no heed to the others.

Those early minutes are always energy-filled. I was picking up good signals straightaway, and even though they yielded only tin foil, a horseshoe and a strange piece of bendy lead tubing, I remained optimistic. Then I found two more pieces of bendy lead tubing. One of the old hands veered towards me and showed me his growing collection of the same. We had no idea what they were but there were lots of them and little of anything else.

Slowly my attention wandered as hope of the special find ebbed. Detecting encourages idle thoughts. I'd frequently fantasise about running into Andy and Lance from *Detectorists* – just as Lance, in one of the episodes, imagines detecting with the former 'glamour model' Linda Lusardi.

I read a ridiculously pleasing article in *Treasure Hunting* magazine written by a detectorist called Matthew Payne. He described how he was detecting on a field in Hampshire when he spotted a man and woman watching him from the garden of a house next to the field. 'As I got close enough to talk the penny dropped,' he wrote. 'In front of me was the actor Toby Jones and his wife. Not knowing what to say I just blurted out, "I know you don't I?" To which he replied, "Yes, I play Lance in *Detectorists*." ' Authenticating this inherently unlikely encounter, there was a photograph of Matthew and Toby Jones together on the day in question.

Now I lifted my gaze to the ridges of Ashdown Forest, receding like stage flats into a gauzy distance, and became nosy about my fellow detectorists. On the far side of the paddock the man in the hoodie and the woman with white hair were detecting together, him sweeping the detector, his left arm linked through her right.

When they found a target, she was the one who did the digging. I assumed this was a Sally-and-Rob-type arrangement but their obvious age difference didn't add up. And where did his mate fit in? The lad in black detected on his own but always fairly near to them and I could see they were in constant communication.

After a couple of hours there was a drift back towards the stable block. Time for my cheese-and-pickle sandwiches and some of Julia's lemon drizzle cake. While I was waiting in line with Daryl for a slice of cake, the white-haired woman approached Daryl with an object she had evidently mentioned to him earlier.

This was not a find she had made today, but one that represented the highlight thus far of her short detecting career. She didn't know what it was but knew it to be special. In her hand was an almond-shaped piece of lead with a pattern of grooves in it.

'It's not a coin but it's got some funny writing on it,' she said.

We pretended to study it, then handed it back, neither of us having a clue what it was but agreeing that it had an air of age and importance. She said they had sent pictures of it to the local FLO and were awaiting a reply. When she had gone back outside, I asked Daryl about her and the set-up with the other two and he explained that she was the mother of the man in the hoodie – Dean – and that Dean was blind. The penny dropped. *Of course Dean was blind! Of course she was his mum!*

Her name was Lucy and the mate, always keeping an eye on them both, was called Alex. I wandered out to Dean with my slice of cake and introduced myself as a fellow beginner.

'So you're sight-impaired,' I said, thinking I was being sensitive to use such language.

Dean smiled and replied, 'I'm blind.'

His mum said they had permissions on Romney Marsh, the watery wildness straddling Kent and East Sussex. I had not been there but had a sense of it – the smuggling, the sheep, the mists. Water snakes too for some reason. Mention of the Marsh always made me think of water snakes. On the arable lands of the Marsh was where they had found the strange object.

'We go out Sundays,' she said. 'You can come out on the Marsh with us if you like.'

It was an invitation I planned to take up, but I still had plenty to learn; I didn't want to disgrace myself again as I felt I had with Chris in Norfolk. The next morning, I abandoned plans to do a little light strimming in the garden and went out in the orchard to hone my sweeping technique and pinpointing skills. I was detecting in a far corner bordered by woodland when I got a superb but possibly misleading signal.

It could have been something small and wonderful but equally something big and worthless. I dug, deployed the carrot, dug some more. It was big, whatever it was, very big. I should have admitted defeat and abandoned the search but a compunction to discover the worst took over.

By the time my partner came out to see what I was doing, the hole was two feet deep and a foot wide and looked hideously disfiguring. I had, however, preserved the initial cap of turf, and when she remonstrated at the apparent vandalism, I assured her that I would make it good. Then curiosity got the better of her. She peered over my shoulder into the depths. 'What do you think it is?' she said.

'Junk. I don't know why I'm bothering.' But I kept digging. Finally I struck metal. It was flat. And big. I cleared away more soil and rapped it with my knuckle. And hollow.

'Could be a coffin,' she said cheerfully.

'Don't be ridiculous,' I said, then decided to be equally flippant. 'Could be a bomb, though.'

I blurted this out before remembering the warnings about unexploded bombs delivered the day before. Could the cottage have been under the flight path of the Luftwaffe bombers that inflicted such heavy damage on the port cities of Portsmouth and Southampton in World War II? Was this a bomb designed to sink a battleship? Hurriedly I dragged the soil back in the hole, tamped the turf plug back into place and tried to put from my mind the big metal thing under the orchard.

The next meeting of our group of learner detectorists was at Worthing Museum and this time we were supposed to be looking at things from the archaeologists' viewpoint. The starting time was 7.30 in the evening, when the museum was closed. Walking in dimmed lighting past cabinets of curiosities – Georgian costumes, a prehistoric logboat levered up from a bog – I felt a prickle on my neck, as if the tables were momentarily turned and the exhibits were giving *me* the once-over.

At the back of the assigned meeting room, the museum's curator of archaeology, James Sainsbury, had put out some trestle tables and arranged across them objects from three hoards (late Bronze Age, Roman, late Roman) from the museum's collection as a well as a gold Bronze Age 'torc' (neck band) and an object labelled 'enigmatic', known as a 'Sussex loop'. These, it turned out, were for later, a tactile coda to the evening's business.

That business concerned the unique role of metal detecting in delivering to museums both local and national many of their most popular and valuable exhibits. For Worthing, explained the bearded, enthusiastic James, that means above all the Patching Hoard, 'probably the most important late Roman hoard in the whole country'. It was found by two detectorists in 1997 near the Downland village of that name.

The 23 gold coins and 27 silver coins, along with 2 gold rings and 54 pieces of 'hacksilver' (i.e. silver bullion), were buried around AD 465 when Britannia was on the skids, the Roman army having left us to our own devices, and monetary exchange had been replaced by a barter economy. The coins are in exceptional condition because they were barely in circulation. The hoard's value lay solely in its metal content, but that would have been extremely high because of the purity of the gold and silver.

Who buried the Patching Hoard and why is a mystery of the Dark Ages that engulfed Britain at this time. Did they do it against the hoped-for return of the Romans and the reimposition of order in turbulent and terrifying times? Or to hide their wealth from the home-grown brigands (Picts, Irish) and foreign invaders (Anglo-Saxons) who were piling into the power and security vacuum?

It's hard to imagine Worthing or Eastbourne being on the front line of conflict, but in post-Roman Britain, Sussex was a lawless and violent place. In AD 477, according to the *Anglo-Saxon Chronicle*, a Saxon invader called Aelle came ashore, at a spot that may have been near the Cuckmere Valley in East Sussex, and killed *monige Wealas*, 'many Welsh' – i.e. 'foreigners', by which was meant the local Romano-British people. Those who escaped fled inland to the cover of *Andredesleag*, Andredes Weald, and Aelle then installed himself as the first King of the South Saxons.

As the *Chronicle* is notoriously unreliable on the origins of Anglo-Saxon England (as on loads of other things, as far as I could make out), this story is probably more legend than truth. But an Anglo-Saxon cemetery was established on Highdown Hill, in the Downs behind Worthing (and just a mile and a half from Patching), as early as the middle of the fifth century.

One theory is that the hill was occupied by a contingent of Roman *foederati* (mercenary) troops, originally from northern Europe, and that the Patching Hoard was an extra inducement for them to 'stay on side' and fight the invading force of their fellow Anglo-Saxons who'd landed in the east of the county. In the summer months, James Sainsbury leads archaeology walks on Highdown Hill on which he brings along grave goods retrieved from the cemetery and reunites them for brief minutes with their find spots – an act that struck me as curiously tender.

From the Patching Hoard, James Sainsbury moved on to a bishop's 'stirrup' ring (i.e. in the shape of a stirrup) also found near Patching, by the Church of St John the Divine.

'As the church was owned by the Archbishop of Canterbury, we *might* be able to display this and suggest the archbishop was visiting and his ring fell off – well, that's my prerogative,' he joked (a nice little comment, as it meant that the professionals are as susceptible as us to wanting to dovetail their finds with their pet narratives).

James also runs a local archaeology project that makes use of two detectorists, and each year, through field walking and detecting, they map the fields in a particular area.

'All of the sites we have looked at have been looted since we were there and we think this is people watching us from afar,' he said.

Making archaeology accessible has its consequences.

West Sussex – especially around Chichester, which has its origins in the significant Roman city of Noviomagus Reginorum – has many traces of Roman occupation that are investigated by archaeologists. One evening, James caught two men with 'top-notch detectors' in a ditch where Roman coins had been found.

'They feigned ignorance, they fobbed me off,' he said.

The police got involved but couldn't pin anything on them. James reckons it was a well-rehearsed operation and it has compromised the archaeological investigation into that site because it's impossible to know how much and what kind of material has been removed by the looters.

Artefacts probably looted from Sussex sites commonly appear on eBay. And there is no shortage of antiques dealers in the prosperous seaside and market towns of the county, not all of whom ask the right questions or, if they do, are fazed by any of the answers – Simon Wicks being a prime example.

'You go to Arundel,' said James, 'and there are Roman silver *denarii* for sale. "Where've you got them from?" They won't answer.'

The coins – including gold *solidi* from the Patching Hoard – and artefacts laid out on tables behind us were rescued from our past for us to learn from and cherish in our present. But they are also examples of what may have been lost. At the end of the evening, James invited us to put on a pair of white cotton conservator's gloves and handle them.

'Hold it with two hands, that's because it's rather delicate,' he said when he saw me looking anxiously at the Cissbury Torc, humming with precious beauty beneath the strip lighting. Designed as a neck ring and now straightened into an uneven line, it is made from a single bar of gold, tightly twisted to give a cable effect, and is dated to 1350–1000 BC. Just four similar torcs have been found, in Cambridgeshire and Staffordshire, and the theory is they were all made by the same travelling goldsmith. I held it gingerly at either end, feeling a certain cryptic buoyancy in it.

'It was found not by a detectorist but by a farm worker who was digging a hole for a fence post,' said James. 'He yanked it out and threw it on a scrap pile. Luckily the farmer knew a metal detectorist, who came by a month or two later and said, "What the hell is that Bronze Age torc doing on a scrap pile?"'

Will the rest of the Herefordshire Hoard also enjoy a reprieve? The trial of the four men who looted it – at least two of whom know the fate of the missing coins – lasted seven weeks through the autumn of 2019. The case turned partly on deleted photos retrieved from George Powell's phone that contradicted their claim that they had found only a few coins and that the jewellery had been taken from two separate holes and was therefore not a hoard.

The four were all found guilty on all counts. Powell and Davies received prison terms of ten years and eight-and-a-half years respectively; Wicks got five years; Wells, sentenced at a later date due to ill health, was given twelve months suspended. The below-the-line comments in the local paper about these sentences (which were reduced on appeal) summed up an attitude I might once have shared: 'Drug dealers and knife-wielding thugs get less time than this. What a travesty of justice'; 'Shame the courts don't hand out long sentences like this to Pedophiles & Rapists'; 'Another failure of the "justice" system. Another judge out of touch with reality.'

An unusual aspect of the case was that a 'victim impact statement' was prepared by local archaeologists including the FLO Pete Reavill and read out in court – the 'victim' being all of *us*. The statement pointed out that 'As a direct result of these actions we may never be able to ascertain the precise sequence of events which relates to the burial or the relationship between the individual artefacts and the hoard.' An opportunity had been lost to display and build a story around the Hoard that apart from anything would have brought pride, identity and the boon of tourism to this remote part of the country.

Powell and Davies maintained their fictions to the end of the trial and beyond. Their failure to cooperate meant that a team from Herefordshire Council's Archaeology Service had to carry out its own investigation into the find spot and its 'context': the possible proximity of archaeological features that might explain why the Hoard was left there.

They started with a number of fields, covering approximately 50 acres, where the looters were known to have detected. These are within sight of Leominster Priory where the monastery once stood, and using existing records the archaeologists identified at the corner of one field an ancient crossroads next to a natural spring.

They then cross-referenced this data with images retrieved from Powell's phone of the objects in the earth and Herefordshire landscapes that proved to show the corner of precisely this field. Cultivation and replanting had destroyed evidence on the ground, so the exact find spot will never be known.

This deprived archaeologists of the opportunity to discover the real story of the Hoard. For example, analysis of pollen traces at the site would have told them what time of year it was hidden and this might have been matched to recorded events. Through stratigraphy they could have found out if it was buried all at once or the site was revisited and the hoard added to or subtracted from. But they did manage to work out the probable year in which the Hoard was deposited, at this auspicious and (you'd have thought) easily memorised location: AD 879.

This was the year in which Ceolwulf II, the king of Mercia, probably died. Alfred then took over much of his kingdom and issued new coinage. A single example of this was among the two dozen coins retrieved during the investigation, and it's this that provides the date for the likely burial of the Hoard. Ninety per cent of it is still missing – many priceless coins and, probably, several silver ingots, just dispersed to the four winds through many sets of light fingers. Or – think about it – reburied.

Experts valued the objects that have been retrieved at about £3 million, while the complete Hoard, should it ever be reassembled, could be worth as much as £12 million. Sentencing Powell and Davies, Judge Nicholas Cartwright highlighted the self-defeating nature of their greed: 'The irony in this case is that if you, George Powell, and you, Layton Davies, had obtained the permissions and agreements which responsible metal detectorists are advised to obtain, if you had gone on to act within the law after you found this treasure, you could have expected to have either a half share, or at very worst a third share, of over £3 million. You could not have done worse than £500,000 each. But you wanted more.'

General Gordon of Khartoum (manufactured *c*1885) performs his official duty once more.

A Monopoly top hat with its Viking ancestor I found in Norfolk.

My buckles – among detectorists' commonest finds. There are nearly 60,000 recorded on the PAS database.

Items from the Staffordshire Hoard of Anglo-Saxon treasure, regarded as metal detecting's greatest find.

Part of my collection of bullets, shotgun cartridges, musketballs etc. Shotties are everywhere.

The dress fastener that lay in a Gloucestershire field, dated 1600–1750.

One of the most exquisite objects rescued from the looted Herefordshire Hoard: the crystal pendant, from the 5th to 7th century.

My 'coins of nothingness' – and a few of significance.
The cartwheel penny is the bruiser in the middle.

Tub of junk – the price you pay for the good stuff.
There are plenty of moo tubes at the bottom of the bucket.

The buckle I found in the paddock near
the orchard, dated 1500–1650.

The rare George IV copper penny
(1827) that may or may not have gone
all the way to Australia and back.

My dandy button, dated 1600–1700 on the PAS database and described as 'decorated with an incised depiction of a stalked flower or possibly an acorn'.

The coin weight, dated 1760–1773, representing 6s 9d, or a quarter-moidore.

I stumbled on all these surface finds in the garden. The Neolithic scraper is in the middle.

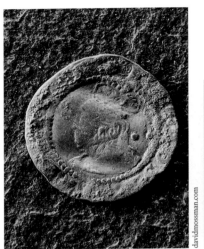

The find that meant so much to me: the silver half groat of Elizabeth I, from the Tower of London mint.

The furniture fitting found in the orchard, 1600s, decorated 'with a hexafoil flower at the centre'.

Buttons, buttons, buttons ... so common they are regarded as 'hedge fodder' by many detectorists.

Part of the Frome Hoard found in 2010. The coin glinting among the grots is one of the hoard's five silver denarii.

The Shippam's Paste bottle I rescued from the mud of Portsmouth Harbour and re-purposed.

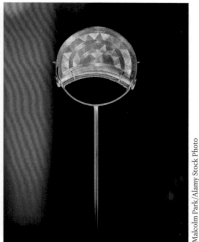

The Shropshire sun pendant, c1000–750BC – a strong candidate for the most beautiful object ever found by a detectorist.

Me detecting in the orchard. I found an old buckle
a couple of minutes after this picture was taken.

Speaking for George Powell, his barrister made a poignant observation: 'It is clear, from his point of view, he wishes he had never found the treasure. It became a temptation – and for him a curse.'

The curse of the gold! All these stories I'd come across of hoards and treasure and the devious greed they engendered were object lessons in the need to be careful of what you wish for. My desire for a hammered – just one and I'd be happy, promise – was a modest-enough goal, but I could still feel it taking me over. For my next outing, to the Detectival Festival in the West Country, I tried to dampen my expectations. It should be about the craic, not the Celtic staters.

5

LUCK AND CHEMISTRY

Detectival markets itself with the slogan 'Bringing the world of metal detecting together'. It's the Glastonbury, or even the Glyndebourne, of the metal-detecting world – an excuse at any rate for a poke-around and a piss-up amid England's rolling acres. Campervans and RVs from all over the country, and beyond, converged on it and on a pallid September morning I rose with the owl hoots and drove west on the M4 to join the fibreglass squadrons.

As I bumped on to the site at 7.30am, campervan doors were open and sleepyheads in dressing gowns yawned down little steps to clear last night's beer cans and plastic plates from folding tables. The flags they had thought to hoist on miniature flagpoles bore crosses or dragons and the occasional saltire. Detectorists feel affinity with the land they tread and now, at the discretion and remuneration of the person who owned this parcel of it – the 12th Duke of Beaufort as it happened – they had come to plunge their hands in for a day or two.

This was the first time Detectival had taken place here and the organisers' literature promised that 'the new site is in a very historically rich area with everything from standing stones and burial mounds to Roman villas and settlements, and medieval deer parks.' The location was described as 'near to Chipping Sodbury', which was true but a bit coy.

In fact it was part of the Badminton Estate, home of the Palladian Badminton House, the Horse Trials, the game played with shuttlecocks and the Duke of Beaufort's Hunt. This was a locus of extraordinary feudal power and privilege that had its origins in the Norman Conquest. The Detectival car park, campsite and arena was bordered by the private Badminton grass air strip, where a few times a year hyper-remunerated horsey and hunting types vaulted the tin corridor of the M4 to fly in on their own planes. An orange windsock was aloft that morning but the detectorists came in Hymers not Cessnas. For once, the exclusive turf was being trodden by people who usually stood on the outside gawping in.

In the reception tent I picked up an orange wristband and a goody bag of magazines, branded T-shirt and baseball cap, then followed the smell of frying bacon to the main arena, an ellipse of trade stands, marquees, food trucks and a Finds Recording Tent manned by professional archaeologists.

As the sun rose, the area filled with tooled-up detectorists, eager for the off. I was standing in front of Mr Tasty's, fishing out the teabag from a Styrofoam beaker of tea, when a group of Poles rocked up looking like a special forces unit in their Polish army surplus. I asked one of them if they had come over from Poland. I had already heard French and German voices.

'No,' he said, 'we live all over England.' He himself had come from Lincolnshire.

'So you meet regularly to go metal detecting?'

'No,' growled his mate. 'We read poetry to each other.'

Periodically during the day's detecting I would run into this little mob out in the fields and they would hail me as a new friend. Now they told me about a Pole who had recently found a hoard in Scotland. His name was Mariusz Stepien and during the first Covid lockdown, on a field near Peebles in the Scottish Borders, he had hit on a group of Bronze Age objects that included a sword still in its scabbard and mysterious bronze rings.

The National Museum of Scotland (NMS) had proclaimed the Peebles Hoard, as it was immediately tagged, 'a nationally significant find'. The reason for this was not just the quantity and quality of the bronze artefacts but the highly unusual presence among them of organic material – leather straps, a scabbard of wood and leather, even traces of thread. The fact that these 'organics' had survived in the ground for three thousand years was down to luck and chemistry (as indeed, when you think about it, are many things).

Bronze is an alloy containing copper that as it corrodes throws a poisonous anaerobic cordon around any organic matter in its vicinity, preventing air reaching it and causing decay. The metal that gave its name to an age of human existence does what it can to keep the story alive. Sword apart, the bronze pieces were identified as parts of a horse harness.

One part, a 'rattle pendant', was designed to jangle as the horse trotted along. The rest of the bronze-studded organics were designed to shine and glitter. Dr Matthew Knight, a Bronze Age expert at NMS who examined the Peebles Hoard for the Scottish Treasure Trove Unit, described it as 'Bronze Age bling'.

He also said that the most exciting piece of the Hoard – perhaps the most exciting thing he had ever found as an archaeologist – was a trace of thread through a bronze looped button. Not the moving 'blingy' parts of the harness, nor even the sword, but a 'tiny piece of string'. I knew how your average detectorist would rate such a fragment. And there lay the difference between 'sports fishermen' and 'marine biologists'.

At Badminton that Saturday morning I was dreaming of big fish. As 9am, the starting time, approached, a funnel of people formed at the entry point to the fields we were permitted to detect on. An excitable Geordie arrived behind me, flashing the red band on his wrist and claiming to no one in particular that he'd got it from one of the sales tents and it entitled him to a free pint from the bar truck. The sound system played Bob Marley and Desmond Dekker; the MC reminded us to record all finds of possible significance in the Finds Recording Tent (and if someone finds the Holy Grail, would they please alert a field marshall straightaway). He then counted down from ten. A klaxon sounded. 'Let's go detect,' he said.

There were 19 fields to choose from, with 6 more being made available for Sunday. They covered 800 acres and most were freshly harvested, though a few were pastureland. As it filled with hunched, purposeful figures, the landscape took on the appearance of an Impressionist painting in the gauzy morning light: *Hommes tristes dans les champs d'hiver*.

Most people headed for the newly harvested acres, on the basis that they were regularly ploughed, but a strip of pastureland, emerald green and thickly grassed, lured me left. It had a pleasing tilt to it, and a long thinness that was perhaps a legacy of the medieval open field system.

It had in other words an 'old feel'. And there were only two people on it. I checked clothing and equipment, like a scuba diver on the lip of the boat, and stepped in.

My finds so far had been meagre, the gaming piece in Norfolk being the best. There were reasons – excuses – for that. Until the previous week it had not rained much in the south and east of England for six weeks. The fields were dry, which adversely affects strength and depth of signal. And much of the time I had been detecting on thick stubble, thus forfeiting the height of the stalks.

Still, it was becoming demoralising. I was beginning to fear rather than relish the prospect of each outing, suspecting that I was simply not very good and never would be. Maybe I wasn't enough of a certain kind of bloke. As I could see as I looked around me, it was a pastime mainly followed by men and built around hardware – not just the detector but the accessories that detectorists wear on hip-slung tool belts – and I have never been a boy's toys sort of male.

Although – late in male adult life and driven by the strange imperatives of the Covid lockdown – I had acquired the strimmer and patio cleaner, I had never owned so much as an electric drill, never mind a jigsaw. Nails, seeing me approaching with a hammer, would move a nanosecond before I hit them. All my life I had been useless with tools and machinery – to the irritation of my father, who spent most of his leisure time at the workbench in the garage, making largely pointless objects for domestic use. He always suspected that my brilliant impression of a practical halfwit was an act deliberately designed to wind him up.

The bias towards white men was very evident at Detectival. The lack of black faces was not so surprising – the hobby developed where the fields are and much of rural Britain remains disproportionately white. Equally there are few black archaeologists in Britain – a situation that one leading archaeologist told me he couldn't account for but needed to be fixed. As for the scarcity of women, weren't they expected to be otherwise engaged on a Saturday morning, fishing their husbands' underpants off the bedroom floor for the weekly wash and picking up their kids from last night's sleepover?

Perhaps too women were put off by the hobby's tendency to quasi-military clobber and an increasingly public competitive side, played out on social media. I had been amazed by the number of male detectorists I had noticed making videos of their efforts. They were software as well as hardware men, turning each outing into a mini *Indiana Jones* movie with surprisingly high production values incorporating drone footage and cleverly synced music.

I was neither a hardware nor a software man. More of a noware man. And each day on which I failed to find much was starting to confirm to me that I lacked a certain blokeish touch, that I'd never make the grade. This did not make me want to give up. Never have I wanted so much to be proved wrong. And there is an addictive quality to metal detecting. However poorly things were going, I was only ever a single find away from becoming a detectorist of distinction.

Such thoughts had been swirling round my head as I waited for the off. But the doubts dissolved the moment I stepped into that green sloping field, its lush grass still damp with dew. Never mind that most detectorists had spurned it in favour of the ploughed soil. I felt somehow at home there and within 20 minutes I had a confusing but tantalising signal, a bleep overlaid with a grunt. I was beginning to interpret the machine fairly well and knew that such a response usually meant iron.

However, when I focused in on the target I realised there were actually two objects down there. I isolated the good signal and spooned up a teacup-shaped clod of earth around it. Then I knelt and probed the base of the hole with the carrot. It chattered excitedly. I delved with my fingers and something moved and revealed itself: dark green, patterned, delicate, like a disc of lacework in metal. I lifted it to a sun that had not shone on it for many years – for I felt its age – and gave it a quick clean with my spray bottle.

It was made of copper alloy, about the size of a pre-decimal penny and had three loops spaced around the outside and a hook. It was the most beautiful thing I had found so far. Everything else had been essentially utilitarian – buttons, buckle, clog clasp, bullet. The clog clasp at least had a design on it – someone had thought to prettify and elevate it through that basket-and-flower motif – but this piece, despite the hook, seemed primarily decorative, and definitely feminine. Then, turning it over and tilting it to the sunlight, I noticed something else. In two places there were traces of gilding, slivers of gold that flashed back the light with something I felt as joy.

Whatever the object was, I had fallen in love with it. Holding it and then – having placed it in the finds pouch – just knowing it was now mine and could not be unfound caused me immense pleasure. After bagging it, I detected for the first time with a sense of lazy euphoria, swinging the coil as if caressing air and with the swagger of a veteran. If I found nothing else for the rest of the day, I didn't give a monkey's. The day was already as sweet as it could get.

So I continued along the pasture, receiving no more good signals but chuffed to overhear a passing detectorist say to his mate: 'Tell you what, I'd be amazed if anybody found anything decent here. I'm not finding shit.'

Presently I moved on to one of the big harvested fields. I didn't think anything could disturb my good mood, but I had not counted on the man who, as he beetled within earshot, called out abruptly: 'Someone said there's a lot of Roman down there. See them people?' He pointed at a corner of the field where several detectorists were snouting around in circles. 'Found much yourself?'

'One piece. Not sure what it is.' I pulled it proudly from the finds pouch and held it out.

He looked unimpressed. 'Oh. Victorian skirt lifter.'

'*Skirt lifter?*'

'Yeah. They used 'em to lift the hem of their skirts when they were working in the fields. I got a Roman.' He showed me a small green grot. 'I'm gonna get some more hopefully.' And he beetled off.

I spent the next hour, as I swept and found nothing, feeling embarrassed by my previous feelings of elation. The piece was unremarkable after all, and not even that old. Its simple function, of keeping a skirt out of the mud, was disappointing. To that seasoned beetler it was evidently barely one up from hedge fodder. But then, as I was heading back to the arena, I rallied. He could have been wrong, he could have just been envious and wishing to rain on my (apologetically small) parade. And what about the gilding? Would a woman toiling in the fields wear such a gilded, decorative piece?

Back in the arena, I ducked into the Finds Recording Tent where a small team headed by a man with a trim beard and a lanyard round his neck, whom I later identified online as the Finds Liaison Officer (FLO) for Gloucestershire and Avon, Kurt Adams, were busy fielding finds behind a barricade of trestle tables. A display cabinet was already filling up with pieces found that morning, recorded by them and put in sealed, labelled bags – 'post-medieval knife', 'spectacle buckle AD 1350–1650', 'English jetton AD 1280–1343'. Was my find worthy of their company? The assistant I handed it to frowned and passed it on to Kurt.

'Worth recording?' he said.

'I think it might be a Victorian skirt lifter,' I muttered.

I wasn't sure Kurt had heard me, but in any case he said '*Nice!*' and I wanted to punch the air. 'Definitely record that,' the archaeologist instructed his assistant. 'It's a dress fastener. See the three loops? It would have been sewn on to a dress or jacket through those. The hook has been bent. It would have fixed through an eye on the other side. Could be 1500s. No, probably 1600s.' He recorded it as 'Dress fastener 1600–1750'. The traces of gilding on the back showed it was for 'Sunday best' – a smart ornamental piece for a woman who took care of her appearance, though she was not especially grand. My kind of person.

Although I didn't realise it at the time, I was tiptoeing through a minefield when I set foot in that Finds Recording Tent. Large-scale rallies attract fierce criticism from metal-detecting detractors, and the Portable Antiquities Scheme (PAS) now distances itself from such events. The problem as they see it is that so much material is found that even if the local FLO is on hand to record it, they are unable to do so properly, and will subsequently be overwhelmed by the follow-up attention that is required – one FLO told me that a single weekend rally can generate a backlog of work that takes months to shift.

The official policy of the PAS is that 'Finds Liaison Officers may attend rallies to promote best practice and may take in finds for recording later, but not (normally) to record finds in the field.' One archaeologist told me that there were stories of FLOs attending big rallies on this semi-informal basis and noting anecdotally just how much was being discovered – then being dismayed by the mismatch with the numbers of finds subsequently recorded with the PAS.

This shortfall indicates that many objects end up in the cabinets of man caves or the shop window of the internet without first passing through the filter of archaeological record. Hence the view that heavily attended, badly managed rallies – rallies full stop, according to some – are like factory trawlers, hoovering up great swathes of marine life and leaving the ocean with bare patches.

The archaeological recording team doing the business that day at Detectival were being paid for by the rally organisers, who were keen to do the right thing, rather than the PAS but such distinctions were way above my head at the time. I was too wrapped up in the discovery of my dress fastener.

After the find had been recorded and returned to me, I had a burger from Mr Tasty's, squirting on a celebratory amount of ketchup from the gallon-sized dispenser, and watched a historical re-enactment show – people wearing bits of sacking and homemade helmets pretending to whack each other with homemade swords.

In front of the tent next door, a man in a hessian dress had made a chimney as big as himself out of mud and grass and claimed it was a replica of a Bronze Age furnace.

'Trouble is,' he said, ducking away from the smoke that billowed from the top, 'I've had to use barbecue charcoal.'

I was dying for him to ask me if I had found anything interesting and he duly did.

'Ahhh,' he said, examining the dress fastener, then handing it back with what I fancied was a respectful look. We speculated on its former owner – the owner before me – and the furnace maker said, 'Wonder if she had anything to do with the big house?' – meaning Badminton House. The woman whose dress was fastened and then suddenly not fastened lived in a significant era in the history of the house and the estate.

Badminton was the story of the landed gentry – rolling acres, a medieval manor, Norman barons, the bung of a dukedom from Charles II in 1682 (for supporting the right side in the Civil War) and a series of increasingly vainglorious makeovers involving cupolas, follies and hahas. What was she doing in this field, a mile from the house, when she lost the wherewithal to keep herself buttoned up? Not toiling, as I had thought at first.

From the map it was clear that the field was on a direct cross-country route between the villages of Little Sodbury and Little Badminton. Did she lose the fastener in the dark, as she hurried between village lights? Or in a muscular roll in the hay, hiding from village lights and eyes? 'Best not go there!' said the furnace maker as we both went there.

The arena was filling again with detectorists returning from the fields and grabbing lunchtime burgers and pints. I tried to read the body language – a trudge probably means you've found bugger all and there was a fair amount of trudging, though I reckoned there were plenty of newbies at the rally who were even less competent than me. Then I spotted a face I recognised. It belonged to a middle-aged woman dressed in black who was ferrying a polystyrene tray of food to the privacy of a marquee in the company of a male detectorist with a certain gunslinger cool.

The woman had big blue eyes and tumbles of blonde hair escaped her branded baseball cap. At first I thought she was someone I had met in another context. Then I noticed that other people were clocking her and I realised who she was. Like them, I knew her from screen and page, for this was one of UK metal detecting's most famous celebrities and 'brand ambassadors', Dawn Chipchase, known to the 20,000-plus subscribers to her YouTube channel as 'Digger Dawn'.

She owed her fame to her irrepressible on-screen personality, a mix of engaging northern bluffness and jumping-bean energy. For its special Detectival edition, which came free in the goodie bag, *The Archeology & Metal Detecting Magazine* had honoured her with a full-length cover shot and a profile inside.

Digger Dawn was a living rebuke to the idea that metal detecting was an inveterately male pastime. It wasn't merely a case of her being tolerated in a male world. She was lauded and lionised, a Boudicca among the Iceni.

The marquee where she had come to rest was the sales stand for the brand of detectors she endorsed and it was plastered with her image. Feeling the pull of her celebrity forcefield, I sidled over, intending to slyly observe her for a bit. Would she be stand-offish with her admirers? Had fame gone to her head? I now wondered if the cool-looking detectorist she was with might be acting as a minder. If so, he wasn't doing the job very assiduously, for a space opened up next to her and before I really knew what I was doing I had occupied it.

'Oh, hello,' she said, looking askance but keeping her cool.

I introduced myself as an admirer of hers and a newcomer to detecting and blurted out something about how tough it must be to be a woman in a man's world.

'I've got to say, I'm never made to feel like a woman if you know what I mean,' she replied. 'There's never a man–woman thing going on even though I'm outnumbered massively. On my analytics on YouTube it's about 92 per cent male. I just feel like one of the guys.'

'You *are* one of the guys!' drawled the gunslinger, who had reappeared. He turned out to be Tim Saylor, aka 'Ringmaster Tim', from Iowa in the American Midwest, a former presenter of an American reality TV show about metal detecting called *Diggers* that ran on the National Geographic channel until 2015. Since then, he and his co-presenter, 'KG' Wyant, have made frequent trips to England to make videos for their web series *Diggin' with KG and Ringy*.

Watching Tim and KG on *Diggers*, explained Dawn, was the catalyst for a life change.

'You know they say that life begins at 50? Well, mine really did because that's when I became Digger Dawn,' she told me. 'And now they're my friends. It's amazing!'

She beamed up at Tim, who gave me his card.

Indulging my curiosity, Dawn filled out a backstory that started when she was playing hide-and-seek in her home town of Rochdale at the age of 13 and she scuffed up what she thought was a gold coin. In those pre-internet days, she had to go to an actual library to find out more about it. The 'coin' turned out to be a gaming token, from the reign of George III.

'After that I always fancied doing a bit of metal detecting. But in the 1980s people who went metal detecting were odd, strange blokes, weren't they?'

This was the decade I could trace my own former prejudice back to, in which amateur metal detectorists were just getting started and stereotypes were rife. The occasional sighting of them (it was always blokes), stuttering about haplessly in a field or on a beach, triggered in onlookers feelings of hilarity and pity.

There was a whiff of onanism about their solitary, anorak-cloaked single-mindedness. They were nerds, geeks, sad bastards, social misfits, not even one up from trainspotters; about as terminally uncool as the bumbling Arnold Poindexter character in the 1987 film *Revenge of the Nerds II: Nerds in Paradise* who, while metal detecting on a beach in his nerdy geek specs, finds . . . another metal detector!

Perhaps the legacy of this prejudice could account for some female detectorists wanting to go it alone. In the previous decade – and despite the male-weighted evidence of Detectival – increasing numbers of women had been taking up the hobby. I had recently read an article in *Treasure Hunting* magazine about a new Facebook group, who also meet in person occasionally, called (with a nod to Alexander McCall Smith's *No. 1 Ladies' Detective Agency* books) the Sassy Searchers Ladies Metal Detecting Tribe.

It was, explained the article, 'a place where other women could come to chat about all things detecting, in a safe, friendly and non-judgmental environment'. So perhaps their desire to exclude men was also driven by something more serious than wishing to establish a youthful, feminine dynamic – that the problem was a predatory tendency among some male detectorists towards their outnumbered female counterparts that could turn detecting days out into obstacle courses for women.

In my own limited experience, metal detecting did not have a libidinous vibe to it, but then again as a late middle-aged bloke – one, remember, who had recently taken up strimming – I wasn't likely to be hit on. One detectorist had told me with no hint of self-mockery that, whereas he used to be derided by women as a nerd, now the 'ladies' found it 'quite arousing' when he told them what he did on Saturday mornings (a remark one can only think of as deluded). I'd certainly heard stories of clubs and Facebook groups having to remind their mostly male members that they hadn't signed up to a dating agency.

Dawn said she had not encountered the problem herself and was doubtful it was widespread.

'I've never been made to feel anything other than a detectorist,' she said. 'If you've found a Roman you've found a Roman. It doesn't matter if you're a man, a woman or a toilet brush.'

The reasons behind the setting-up of a female-only group of detectorists were far from clear from the article in *Treasure Hunting* and as I'm not on Facebook I asked Dawn if she would forward an email from me to the founder of the Sassy Searchers so that I could satisfy my curiosity. In the email I asked impertinently if the entire *raison d'être* of the group could be temporarily suspended in order that I might go out detecting with them. Not surprisingly, I received no reply to this email, nor to a subsequent approach.

One question I would have asked is whether women value different finds from men. To generalise: men like military stuff – axes, swords, bullets, badges, the fins off mortar bombs – and anything blingy:

rings and jewellery made of precious metals that can be sold for a few bob. Men target beaches to find rings that have fallen off fingers that obligingly shrivel in cold seawater – often with a view to keeping or selling them rather than trying to reunite them with their owners. Not all men are looters, but all looters are men (probably).

In *Mudlarking: Lost and Found on the River Thames*, Lara Maiklem's excellent account of foraging on the Thames foreshore through London, she divides fellow mudlarks into hunters and gatherers. Mudlarking is analogous to metal detecting and indeed some people use metal detectors to do it. But, crucially, it can be done without using a detector, simply by looking (known in archaeological circles as 'field walking' and among detectorists as 'eyes only').

The tide on the Thames through London acts like the plough on arable land, continually churning and refreshing the foreshore to bring buried objects to the surface. The 'gatherer' type of mudlark, the category to which Lara Maiklem has chosen to belong, searches with her eyes only, confining herself to what's on the surface. 'There is an element of meditation to what we do,' she writes, 'and as far as I'm concerned, the time I spend looking is as important, if not more so, than the objects I take home with me.'

'Hunters' are more aggressive, focused on the find itself, its rarity or monetary value. Most use metal detectors and digging tools, eager to penetrate the muddy crust and get at the goodies: 'In my experience, the hunters are often men, while gatherers tend to be women. It is rare to see a woman on the foreshore with a metal detector.'

On one of my walks along the Thames in London I met a (male) mudlarker/detectorist near Hammersmith Bridge who was familiar with Lara's book and had an opinion on her hunter/gatherer distinction, reckoning it was really to do with a middle-class writer wanting to distance themselves from the 'common man' type of mudlarker. 'What's wrong with being a hunter anyway?' he said. 'Shows you've got fire in your belly.'

Do female detectorists seek different things from men? As Dawn pointed out, it depends partly on what there is to find in the first place. Her home town of Rochdale rose to prominence in the nineteenth century with the cotton mills and became one of the boom towns of the Industrial Revolution. The mills were everywhere and the millworkers walked to and from work, dropping small change as they went.

'The oldest things we find are from 1700 – but I've got the biggest collection of Victorian and George III coins you've ever seen,' she said. Lancashire scores low in the league table of finds. In 2020, more than five thousand objects were found and reported to the PAS in Norfolk; for Lancashire the figure was less than a hundred. Dawn never finds Roman or Saxon but is, she said, 'joyful of the smallest things', especially if it has a unique local connection. She cited the example of a 'Co-op token', the 'Co-operative Wholesale Society' having started in Rochdale in 1844.

Dawn asked me if I had read the article on her in the free Detectival magazine. 'It's all about the best day I ever went out,' she said. She teaches at a further education college, specialising in teenagers with a range of learning difficulties from autism to ADHD. She started metal detecting in part as a means of relieving the stress of the job. 'I come home on a Saturday knowing I can go out and stand in a field and just chill out. Everything just disappears when you're walking across the grass – you'll know that yourself. I can go for two hours and it's like a complete meditative state.'

One day – her 'best ever' – she brought the two worlds together when she took the kids she teaches out metal detecting. To ensure the success of the outing, she had pre-buried about a hundred coins.

'I've never seen such joy in my life!' she said. 'I was nearly crying I was so happy! One of them, she dug this coin up and I said, "You know what that is? That's a cartwheel penny, George III, from 1797." She said, "Is it?!" Now usually she can't remember her own name hardly. The next day she came up to me with the coin still in her hand and she said, "Dawn, I went to my auntie's last night and I told her, I said, 'That's George III, 1797'," and I nearly collapsed – because she's normally got a memory span of about two seconds.'

While we talked, a small queue of shy fans had been forming under the white canopy. A little girl in purple was pushed forward discreetly by her mother.

'Oh, here's my number one fan,' said Dawn as the kid stood there tongue-tied with awe. 'She's really good, isn't she? Every year I have a picture taken with her and she gets a bit bigger – don't you? Do you eat a lot of vegetables? I like your purple top!'

Suitably dazzled, the girl melted back into the crowd and Dawn said to me with the wistfulness of all celluloid heroes, 'You come to these things and a lot of people just want to say hello. So I "social butterfly" around – then I go home and sit on my own again, like Billy No Mates.'

It was soon time for me to go home. After a desultory afternoon session, I decided that big impersonal events like this did not really bleep my machine, despite having given me my best find (the dress fastener) to date and hooked me up to the excellent Dawn Chipchase. The crowds and the merchandising, not to mention the dodgy burgers, had all the charm of stadium rock.

Rather than U2 at the O2, I preferred the idea of Freewheelin' Bob Dylan at a Greenwich Village cafe – intimate detecting gigs on smallish fields with one or two detectorist buddies and my own sarnies. And even if Dylan fails to show and you don't find that hoard of hammereds, having to make do instead with a Donovan tribute act (some moo tubes), you've still got the consolation of surroundings and company.

It was time I started securing my own permissions. No self-respecting detectorist relies solely on group meets, or the generosity of others in inviting you on to their fields. This meant having to approach local farmers and landowners, a prospect that made me feel uneasy. I didn't have a good track record with the farmer who owned the fields on one side of the cottage. Two years before, he had caught me trespassing on one of these fields.

The trespass was inadvertent. I was on the wrong side of the hedge and had not noticed the footpath sign that directed walkers away from the field margin. But the farmer, who was riding a quad bike at the time, was in no mood to forgive me. Instead, he invited me to remove myself from his land at the earliest available opportunity. The following year he proffered a similar invitation to a friend of mine he caught in the same situation.

A third friend then fell foul of the inconspicuous signage and the man atop his small khaki vehicle but had the presence of mind to come up with a riposte. 'Ah,' he said, 'you must be the farmer who's won all those awards.'

'What awards?' said the farmer, looking suddenly rather pleased with himself.

'The Grumpy Farmer awards!' said my friend.

Eccentric farmers are an occupational hazard of metal detecting. According to Pete Welch, an experience of his had even made it into *Detectorists*. It's the scene in which Andy and Lance call on a farmer with relaxed hygiene standards who's suspected of bumping off his wife and burying her in one of his paddocks.

'It's a true story, *my* story,' Pete said. 'I knocked on the door of this farm in the Home Counties. He's answered the door, he's got no toes in his slippers, he's got his elbows sticking through his jumper, he's unshaven. He says, "Oh yeah, you'd better come in, watch out for the 'landmines' . . ." – there's dog shit from his front door all the way up the hallway. We found out afterwards, he'd only just got out of prison for throwing his wife down the stairs and killing her . . .'

Pete had advised against emailing or even phoning to ask for permissions. An email can remain unanswered. A phone conversation allows the farmer to prevaricate.

'A maybe is a no,' he said. 'You need a yes or a no.' His advice: go for the jugular. 'A farmer's just finished baling his hay in the field and I'm driving along and he's just about to leave the field and I park, whoosh, straight in front of the field and he can't get out. "Look, it's about metal detecting. I want to search your field and I'm not letting you out till you say yes." And he just laughs – I've got permission just for cheek.'

And if the farmer was sitting on a quad bike at the time?

While I worked up a sweat just pondering this approach, an email dropped into my inbox: 'I'm detecting this Sunday and next Sunday in Brookland, Kent on a new field. Ring me when you get there and I'll guide you.' It was from Dean, the blind man I'd met at the detectorists' gathering in Ashdown Forest.

OK, I thought, *just one more gig on a stranger's turf, then I'll start sorting my own.* And I can't say I wasn't intrigued by the idea of being guided by a blind man.

Brookland is in the middle of Romney Marsh, a mini-Norfolk that grew rich on the wool trade in medieval times. Its liminal wetlands lie beyond the eastern margin of Andredes Weald and I had planned to drive there on the direct west–east route of the A272, an old-fashioned road with hardly any dual carriageway that still winds methodically through the centre of towns and villages and the folds of the old forest. But the satnav system kept instructing me away from this heart of darkness and I eventually gave in, climbing north into the orbit of the M25 and letting it spin me efficiently through its twenty-first-century interchanges.

The result was that I arrived early in Brookland. Parking by the old pub – now a private house but the ghostly outlines of a village hostelry were unmistakeable – I went for a nose around the church. Its tower stood in the churchyard alongside it, a pointed witch's hat, as if once doffed and never returned to the head. The floor of the nave undulated, like the floor of St Mark's Basilica in Venice, and the pillars leaned outwards.

A woman was bustling about with a smartphone in the back pocket of her jeans – the vicar in civvies, as it turned out. When she saw me looking at the pillars, she said, 'They're not evenly spaced. They just put them where the ground was solid.' Like the churches of Venice, the churches of the Marsh are built on watery reclaimed land.

The charming oddity of the church of St Augustine – dedicated to the Roman monk who landed in Kent at the end of the sixth century to convert the Saxons – reflects the *sui generis* nature of the Marsh. Like other English places on the edge – The Lizard Peninsula, the Forest of Dean – it developed in its own way, in the case of the Marsh twisted into weirdness by a series of cataclysmic storms in the thirteenth century that rearranged the topographical furniture like a poltergeist.

This is what 'Thomas Ingoldsby', aka the Revd Richard Harris Barham, was getting at in *The Ingoldsby Legends* (a compendium of cheerful baloney, first published in 1837) when he wrote that 'The World, according to the best geographers, is divided into Europe, Asia, Africa, America, and Romney Marsh.'

Dean and his mum grew up on the Marsh but now live away, amid the amenities of a small town in the respectable commuter belt of Kent. The plan had been for me to call him when I got to Brookland and, back in my car, I was just scrolling through for his number when a small car shot by, trailing cigarette smoke from a wound-down rear window: Dean's mate Alex, a roll-your-own man. I gave chase and caught up with them on the edge of a recently ploughed and rolled field flanked by drainage ditches known locally as sewers.

As we put our kit on by our open boots, I broke a certain social awkwardness by asking Dean how he'd got his permissions, as he didn't strike me as a man who favoured Pete's confrontational options. He explained that their numerous fields, dotted across the Marsh surrounding Brookland, all came from the same local farmer. 'I used to work for him as a boy, sorting spuds,' he said.

Dean was born with diabetes but in childhood had normal eyesight. When he was three and playing in the village playground, he spotted a gold half-sovereign glinting in the dirt – it was to become a beckoning finger, like Digger Dawn's gaming token. As Dean grew up, his high blood sugar levels damaged the blood vessels supplying the retina of his eyes, and when he was in his mid-twenties and despite mitigating treatments, he fell more or less completely blind. That had been a decade ago.

'He went into a bit of a black period, thought his world had ended,' Lucy said. 'So we made a bucket list, didn't we? He went round Brand's Hatch in a sports car. He did a skydive. That was to raise money for the eye hospital. He loved that, just wanted to go back up there and do it again.'

Spool on, through his deteriorating eyesight, past permanent dusk ('I can see light. Or dark. I can't see anyone,' he told me) to the lockdown of 2020.

'Obviously he couldn't go out anywhere,' said Lucy. 'He couldn't tell the distances between people and because of his other medical issues it was easier to just stay at home.' Where he felt locked inside a box inside a box.

Then his detectorist uncle was selling a detector off cheap and this is when they realised not just that metal detecting was something he could do, in conjunction with a sighted person, but something that he could do *better than other people*.

'Because obviously his hearing is heightened,' said Lucy.

'Basically every time I've been out I've found something,' Dean said.

Mother and son dovetailed their movements, wordlessly sorting and checking equipment. Then they linked arms, his left through her right, and stepped on to the purple-brown expanse of soil that stretched to far hedgerows and ditches. Dean swept the detector with his right hand, Lucy carried the spade with her left.

As Alex and I followed, he whispered to me, 'I knew Dean when he could see.' But they're not just mates who go back a long way. Alex is

Lucy's back-up should Dean fall into a diabetic coma. 'I can medicate him,' she told me, 'but I wouldn't be able to move him.'

Five minutes into the detecting session, Dean got a 'nice signal', quartering the coil over the target to make sure.

'Eighty-eight, ninety-one,' confirmed Lucy, leaning across to read off the ID number from the display panel.

'Let's go for it – could be a cartwheel penny!' said Dean, referring to the big George III coin that Digger Dawn had buried for her autistic student to find. Lucy did the digging, then handed the object straight to Dean as she always does. It was no cartwheel. He read it through his fingertips: 'Good old tin foil!'

I was detecting parallel to them, but hardly paying attention to my own efforts. The oneness between mother and son with the backdrop of smeared sky and rustling bulrushes kept drawing my eye.

'We had part of an axle one day,' said Dean.

'It was *that* big.' Lucy held her arms as far apart as they would go. 'He made me dig it up.' They both beamed.

Since I'd met them in Ashdown Forest, they had heard back from the FLO on the mysterious almond-shaped lead object Lucy showed Daryl and me. It was a medieval vesica seal matrix. 'Vesica' denotes the pointed oval shape. A seal matrix was used for making an impression on a wax seal, to authenticate a document, to keep it closed and to show it hadn't been opened and tampered with. They were used by individuals of wealth and status – literate people who conducted their affairs by parchment and contract.

The marks on it were an engraved inscription. As the matrix was used to make an impression, this was done in mirror image, which made the matrix itself tricky to read. Archaeologists used to make a cast from them to be absolutely sure of what they were seeing. Nowadays you can reverse the image in Photoshop in a second, though many archaeologists – on the belt-and-braces principle or maybe just for the fun of it – continue to make a cast. The inscription on Dean's seal matrix reads 'S'ROGI F IOhIS', which translates as 'The seal of Roger son of John'.

A few weeks after we went out on Romney Marsh, the British Museum published a list of five 'highlights' from the more than 50,000 objects recorded by the PAS in 2020. They included another seal matrix from Kent, found at Hollingbourne near Maidstone. This was singled out because it was made of silver rather than the usual lead or copper alloy, and because it belonged to a woman, Matilda de Cornhill.

In her email to Dean and Lucy, the FLO wrote that 'Personal seals date from the 13th century so a date of 1200–1300 is suggested.' This was a century in which a greater than usual number of personal items must have been mislaid on the Marsh on account of the panic and destruction repeatedly visited on its inhabitants.

Lucy referred to the main culprit, the storm of 1287 'that took out some of the settlements that were here and washed them away'. But there were others: in 1236, 1250, 1252, 1271 and 1288. Like Covid and blindness, the storms changed things for ever. Coastal villages found themselves inland, landlocked hamlets suddenly had a sea view without having to pay extra for one.

Having been thus discombobulated, in the early nineteenth century the Marsh suffered a literal severing from the mainland when the so-called Royal Military Canal was dug along a near-30-mile loop from the Kent to the Sussex coasts, the intention being to stop the advance of Napoleon's army should Boney invade. He didn't, but the cut was irreversible.

Over lunch – me sitting in my Quick-Seat, them in the car with the windows open for easy egress of cigarette smoke – I asked Lucy and Dean if they missed living on the Marsh.

'It's nice in summer, very bleak in winter. Windy. Cold. Foggy,' she replied.

That morning in Brookland church I had paused to read the inscription on the headstone of a 'grazier' who died in 1816. It likened his loss to 'A dark and wintry gloom'. You imagine they are connoisseurs of wintry gloom round here.

But the Marsh is in their blood and when Dean comes back a mental map unfolds. 'I know exactly where I am,' he said. 'I can picture the road we came down today. The pub. I could guide someone around here quite easily.'

Alex hung his smartphone from the car window to show me images of his other hobby. A red Routemaster bus appeared, in various stages of manufacture. A Spitfire, its engine cowling removed. In his flat in Eastbourne, Alex makes large-scale, finely detailed replicas of charismatic planes and vehicles that can take years to complete. 'He locks himself away for hours,' said Lucy wonderingly.

For the afternoon session, we moved on to the next field and I scored a coin. It lay in the earth looking promising, the copper nicely oxidised to green, and I took my time cleaning it off. It was obviously not so old but I had hopes of Victorian or Georgian. Then I spotted a familiar design: three feathers sprouting from a coronet. Though I had to look up later what precisely this signifies (the badge of the Prince of Wales), the coin itself was all too familiar. It was a 2p piece, the numismatic equivalent of Marks & Spencer underpants, first issued in 1971.

Through the 1970s and 1980s I would keep a stash of 2ps in my pockets for use in the slots of public telephone boxes. A moment in time came to me. A Gilbert Scott phone box making an incongruous splash of red in the green of the Lake District. The heavy door that needed all my weight to shift it; the smell of urine and cigarettes; the sudden sealed quiet and then a spectral voice – my mum's – that made me cry. I was on a school trip and, feeling sorry for myself, just had to call her.

While I was hitting on small memories, Dean was finding a nail, 'a bit of rubbish', more tin foil, 'a bit of shrapnel' – and, as we approached the cars having called it a day, some sort of copper token. These were used on the Marsh at the end of the eighteenth century as trading tokens or instead of currency when coins of small denomination were in short supply. He placed this carefully in a little cushioned container. I had such a container myself but had not so far had cause to use it.

We said goodbye and I drove slowly back towards the village on winding roads, with Lucy, Dean and Alex following in the car behind me. The big flatland sky had turned milky. At a T-junction I hesitated, suddenly unsure of where I was, and Lucy pulled her car alongside mine. Dean, in the passenger seat, wound down the window.

'Are you lost?' he said, smiling with his unseeing eyes, and put me back on course for home.

6

ROMAN (AND OTHER) BREADCRUMBS

Home was calling to me. The week following the Romney Marsh visit, a token of deep time turned up in the lane directly in front of the cottage. It was lying on the tarmac like an envelope on a doormat, having dropped, in a roundabout way, from the sky. The lane winds down from a plateau and when it rains is overlaid by a twisting, plaiting torrent, fed by side streams, that carries with it a silt of stones and twigs. When the rain stops, this detritus is usually left high and dry on the crown of the roadway, but on this occasion a solitary object had been stranded immediately outside the entrance to the cottage. There was an apparent deliberation to its placing, as if someone wanted to make sure it wasn't missed.

'Literally on your doorstep,' said Manni Kirchner, owner of the sharp eyes that spotted it. He bent down to claim it, then handed it gravely to me – a faceted disc of flint, the size of a powder compact, scallop-edged, mottled blue-grey, fashioned to be gripped by human fingers; specifically, the fingers of Neolithic Man, for this was a prehistoric scraper, the talismanic object Daryl Holter had talked about in the pub on Beachy Head. And Manni was my new detectorist buddy.

Rather like the scraper, he had turned up on the doorstep a few days before, declaring his interest in local history and wondering if he might be allowed a closer peak at the cottage, seeing as it was one of the oldest houses in the neighbourhood, with a signature involvement in the local side hustle of smuggling back in the jolly old day. He had a winning line: 'I've never had the privilege of living in a house I'm younger than.' Manni was 18 years old.

The cottage did occasionally summon people. A couple of years after we bought it, a car halted hesitatingly in the lane outside, right where the scraper would turn up. Inside were two Australian women, one elderly, one (the driver) middle-aged. They had come from Northampton – more than a hundred miles away – on the off-chance that someone would be at home. The elder, the mother-in-law of the other, produced an old photograph of the cottage just after World War I (she had also brought a copy for me to keep; it now hangs in a frame on the stairs). The photograph was taken from the bank that climbs above the lane to the north-east and this perspective gives it the feel of an overview, as if it were summing up an entire era.

In this old print the lawn is given over to vegetable beds. A man in a flat cap stands directly in front of the cottage leaning over a bicycle. Behind him, two women and a man stand in a huddle, apparently chatting. Next to them, unheeded, is a little girl in a long dark dress and boots. She is looking towards the camera, as if perhaps she has spotted the man on the distant bank stooping over to take the photograph. As if perhaps she is seeing her own future.

'That's me,' said the old lady, pointing at the little girl. 'I was born in the cottage.'

As I made tea in the kitchen, the woman explained that shortly after the photograph was taken she had emigrated to Australia with her family. After 70 years, this was her first visit back to England and she had had a yearning to see the cottage again.

The experience evidently wasn't as overwhelming as she had expected. She glanced around the kitchen, at the fitted cupboards and microwave oven, and said, with a note of disappointment, that it didn't ring any bells. The women thanked us and said they had to be getting back to Northampton.

'Before you go, have a quick look through here,' I said, leading the way from the kitchen into the living room.

The former little girl in the photograph followed me through – and started sobbing. Her daughter-in-law put an arm around her.

'What's the matter? What is it?'

The old lady pointed at the beehive inglenook.

'The fireplace!' she said. 'I'd forgotten it existed.'

Now, through its gaping and sooty mouth, an entire biography was pouring. Thinking back, I realised that the dynamic of this moment was similar to the story rush that transmits itself from found objects to a detectorist's fingers in the first seconds of discovery.

Manni's route to get here was through Hampshire's Historic Environment Record (HER). This tells you that in 1956 two pieces of old pottery were found – you could say hardly surprisingly – in the garden of the old house that lies a couple of hundred yards up the lane from us. These sherds, while evidently old, were 'too small to identify' with any certainty and were therefore classified as 'Roman/Medieval', with a terminal question mark to emphasise their unknowability: 'Roman/Medieval?'

The pieces themselves have long since disappeared into some storage vault, but the idea of them stirred in Manni an excitement sufficiently percussive to propel him on to his bike and up the hill from the other side of the village where he lived to our remote little lane. Having informed the startled owners of the adjacent house that two small pieces of old pottery had been found in their garden 60 years ago, Manni then knocked on our door.

In the kitchen, after he'd accepted my invitation to have a snoop round, he rummaged in his backpack and, looking pleased with himself, hoiked on to the table a lump of old brick and plaster.

'What's that?' I said.

'*Opus signinum* – Roman concrete?'

'Oh. Where'd you find it?'

'Village.'

Manni was a field walker. He walked the fields around his home patch with his head and eyes down, scouring the earth for signs and objects. His eyes were attuned to ground clues, which is why he spotted the scraper so readily. I asked him if he metal detected too. His answer was interesting: 'I have a metal detector but I'm not really a detectorist.' Here was the same philosophical faultline that Lara Maiklem identified, between the mudlarks who hunt and those who gather. In Manni's case it was because his main interest was pottery and other surface-level finds, which in turn was underpinned by his politics.

'It goes back to the idea that for me history is a proletarian thing,' he said. 'With field walking you're finding a real person's real waste.' He meant the clay pipe, the oyster shell (the organic equivalent of the polystyrene burger box), the piece of basic cooking pot. 'With metal detecting, you're finding a rich person's belt buckle.'

You could argue this point. Detectorists turned up plenty of proletarian, utilitarian objects – coins of small denomination, my clog clasp, Digger Dawn's Co-op token, poor people's clothing buckles. But Manni was a smart kid whose views I respected. Despite the fact that I was old enough to be his granddad, we became detecting buddies and I frequently deferred to his greater knowledge on potsherds, Roman history, the Inclosure Acts, Neolithic tools, the Labour Party and personal identity.

His arrival in my metal-detecting world coincided with my early attempts to acquire local permissions. I had already discounted the farmer on the quad bike. The farm estate that owned most of the fields on the other side of the cottage was the one on which I had encountered the detectorist whose sandwich was stolen by Bertie the dog. Though I had not run into the detectorist again, a neighbour assured me she had see him very recently. He was still active.

That being the case, I couldn't expect a second permission to be granted on the same land. And even if it was – the farmer figuring there was plenty of land to go round – that way trouble lay, as Pete Welch had warned me. He had a friend who became his 'arch enemy' by setting up a rival club and obtaining permissions on land that Pete regarded as his.

So I suspended the idea of approaching the local farmers and explored the landed-gentry route instead. There were two rich landowners in the neighbourhood – both baronets – who owned fields with great promise for detectorists. One lived in a vast Grade I-listed country mansion that has featured in several TV murder mysteries, surrounded by hundreds of acres landscaped on Picturesque principles. The other had a Tudor farmhouse up on the Downs, with land that included the site of an abandoned village.

There were three abandoned villages within a seven- or eight-mile radius of the cottage marked thus on the OS Explorer map: 'Medieval Village (site of)'. I had studied them on Google Earth and the one up on the Downs seemed to have left the most ghostly traces. One weekday I drove up there, parked the car on the road and walked along a public footpath, past the Tudor farmhouse where the landowner lived, to the village (site of). Pete Welch's advice was going round in my head: don't phone, don't email, knock on the door – chat 'em up. I'd decided to sneak a look at the field first while I girded my loins for that knock on the door.

For the chat-up line I had done some homework by Googling the baronet in question and discovering one of his interests, which could (on a good day, with a fair wind) be said to have a connection to metal detecting. I planned to steer the conversation in this direction if I wasn't flattened by a metaphorical quad bike first.

Another detectorist had suggested an even less scrupulous tactic: buy some hammered coins online (he knew I hadn't found any of my own) and, to stimulate the farmer's interest and impress him with my professionalism, pass them off as ones I'd found in the previous few weeks in fields similar to his – the implication being that I would find such wonderful things on his land too. This idea also had wider merit.

The longer I went without finding a hammered, the more desperate I was growing. Friends and fellow detectorists alike were becoming embarrassed to ask. A modest little specimen would shut them all up. With two clicks I found an 'Unresearched medieval hammered silver long cross' for 99p on eBay. My finger hovered, then snapped shut the lid of the laptop. My pride had been shredded, but not that far.

The visible remains of the medieval village occupied just one field, of about eight acres. Black cows with white faces were in it and they bumped towards me in a show of a curiosity as I paused to take pictures over the barbed-wire fence. Ridges and saucer-like depressions were visible beneath the knotty and nettled pastureland. It had been a tiny, humble hamlet.

The houses, made of timber and wattle, would simply have rotted. There had been a church apparently but its stones had been carried off to make other walls. Over in the south-west, the old rooflines of Winchester and its squat cathedral tower lay in a misty hollow. That view would not have been so different when people lived here in the fifteenth century, gazing out in the pauses of their days.

My walk back towards the farmhouse was slow as I gathered my courage and rehearsed my patter. The path turned a right angle and there, where there hadn't been when I walked out to the field, was a man mending a section of fence. We nodded at each other and I told him I had just been looking at 'the' field, the one where the abandoned village had been. I was hoping this might elicit a promising reaction or useful information but the man just said, 'Yeah?'

'Yeah. There must be loads of interesting stuff in the ground there. I was wondering, has anybody ever metal detected on that field?'

The man held his big yellow staple gun aloft as he considered the question. Finally he said, 'The boss don't like metal detectors.'

'Detector-*ists*,' I said. This correction was a running joke in *Detectorists*. As soon as I had said it, I regretted it. It came out wrong, made me sound like a smart arse. Maybe I *was* a smart arse. Ignoring me, the man went back to his barbed wire. I continued walking, past the farmhouse, straight to the car and drove home, reasoning to myself that it wasn't cowardice but a sense of realism that had caused me to change my mind and not walk up the garden path and knock on the door.

Thanks to the fence-mender, I knew in advance the answer I would have got – no point in wasting time and losing face. But deep down I knew Pete Welch wouldn't have given up so easily. Somehow, deploying sly humour, he would have turned the encounter with the fence-mender to his advantage.

This failure left me with one more landowner, the one in the house that appears in TV murder mysteries, to approach. But cowardice once more won the day. In order to save a journey of several miles on public roads, a friend's son had requested of this man permission to cycle across a portion of his many hundreds of acres, on existing paths, to his place of work, a small cottage industry located on farmland beyond the big estate. The man had turned down his request, and done so with uncalled-for brusqueness apparently. What chance would I have (I said to myself), with my intention not merely to glide over his demesne on inflated rubber that leaves no trace but to *dig holes* in it? Once again, I chickened out.

While I was absorbing these setbacks, Manni invited me out on a field-walking morning. You could say that field walking is the foreplay of metal detecting – the foothills of the real excitement, the getting-in-the-mood for the buried pleasure of breaking the ground and digging for targets; or, to give it a snobby slant, metal detecting for the middle classes, without the geeky gear and overlaid with a patina of archaeological respectability.

There is even a scientific-sounding phrase for it: 'surface artefact collection', which describes it accurately if a bit pompously (like 'ambient replenishment control' – supermarket shelf stacking). The idea behind it is the same as for metal detecting. When fields are ploughed, artefacts buried in the lower layers are churned up to the surface. These include not just metal objects (by definition, the only targets recognised and identified by metal detectors) but 'ceramics' (bricks, tiles, tesserae, i.e. pieces of mosaic, pottery, clay pipes), 'lithics' (worked flint such as the Neolithic scraper, stone from buildings) and glass, from bottles/vessels and windows.

For archaeologists, field walking is an important tool that has the simplicity of requiring no equipment, unlike geophysical or aerial survey. But it needs to be done systematically, on a grid basis, to ensure the field is properly covered. Manni and I were content to just amble, chatting as we went. He had chosen a field on the edge of a market town very much in our Roman zone that included the village and environs. It had made itself known to him a few months before when he was walking the footpath that runs along one edge and spotted a Roman roof tile lying in a furrow.

We did not have permission to field walk on this field, which was wrong and meant we were trespassing, so don't try this at home, folks. But in mitigation we felt the question of ownership was largely beside the point, as the land and what it contained had been sold to a property developer and would soon be bulldozed to oblivion prior to more than three hundred 'traditionally styled' houses being built on it.

Manni had gone along to a council meeting where the principal objections to the new housing estate concerned the fate of owl boxes, not the loss of archaeology. And whatever we found we had agreed to leave in place even if it meant it being sealed for ever under foundations and patios. This was just an exercise in observation.

In the car before we started, Manni gave me a quick lesson in basic identification of pottery: 'Iron Age is very shelly, like dog biscuit. Your Roman stuff is much finer. Medieval feels like sandpaper. On this field you can pick up pretty much any potsherd and know it's pretty old. My best find here is a Roman beaker base with maker's mark, almost like a trident.'

Fields, I was discovering, have a mood music to them. It might be a literal sound, of rooks, the hum of powerlines or the roar of jet fighters; or a fragrance, of wild garlic from adjacent woods; or a lush symphonic greenness. Today's soundtrack was the high-pitched excitement of a primary-school playground, all innocent faces and sly kicks.

The soil had been sown with a cover crop before building work started. Within a few seconds, Manni stooped among the low green shoots. 'Pig's tooth,' he reckoned. I picked up an oyster shell. Then a piece of red clay.

'Might be Roman,' said Manni, turning it in his hand. 'No, it *is*. It's been overfired. The thickness, the shape. A basic tile.'

It triggered a memory that I related as we walked the furrows. In the 1970s, in the Spanish Basque Country, documents were discovered showing that in the sixteenth century Basque mariners had been sailing to a place in the New World they called Terranova – just 50 years after Columbus 'discovered' the Americas. 'Terranova' was subsequently identified as a tiny settlement on the coast of Labrador, on Canada's Atlantic seaboard, now called Red Bay.

In 2015 I drove up to Red Bay from Newfoundland, to the place where the red, white and green Basque *ikurriña* now flies alongside the Canadian maple leaf. Red Bay was an outpost for the processing of whale blubber. The intrepid Basque sailors made this perilous journey every spring to hunt whales and render their blubber into oil, which was used in lamps and paint. The men who produced the oil were like modern-day oil-rig workers, putting up with hardship, danger and social isolation for the sake of *reales* in their pockets and to keep the lights on at home.

On the journey across the Atlantic, they filled the holds of their ships with roof tiles and barrel staves. The tiles were then used to roof 'try-houses' – kitchens-cum-furnaces where the blubber was rendered into oil – and cooperages where the staves were assembled into barrels that were then used to transport the whale oil back to Spain.

The stony beaches of Red Bay are littered with fragments of terracotta roof tile fired in northern Spain in the 1500s. They provided key evidence that identified modern-day Red Bay as the sixteenth-century Terranova. Yet no one in Red Bay had any idea what they were till archaeologists came poking around in the 1980s.

I met a local woman in her fifties who remembered playing with the sea-smoothed 'red stones' as a child and thinking they were just, well, stones that happened to be red. The kids used them like chalk, to draw on boulders and pavements. All the time, and for hundreds of years before that, the tiles were telling a remarkable story but no one was listening.

In our field, we were doing our best to listen but the stories were tantalisingly broken. Manni found a piece of Hampshire border white ware, made on the Hampshire–Surrey borders from the fourteenth to the sixteenth century. Then 'a bit of medieval – typical: overfired inside, underfired outside. Two colours.' The sun glinted off a piece of glass, blue-black with a bloom of yellow across it: part of a Georgian 'onion bottle' (i.e. onion-shaped) that had probably held wine. Manni's conclusion: 'This is a multi-period settlement without a doubt.'

We talked in a meandering way about stuff, as detectorists (and surface artefact collectors) do. Manni was due to start university in Germany the following year – not to study history or archaeology as I had assumed, but chemistry. His passion for and knowledge of the past were so manifest that this surprised me.

'Archaeology and history aren't my interest,' he said. 'My *village* is my interest.'

Manni is of mixed German–Cuban parentage. 'I'm half and half,' he went on, 'I don't feel I have a nationality or a home. But I feel rooted here. I've had the most stability here.'

I asked him if that meant he felt at least *kind of* English, rooted as we are among all these tokens of England's past. For detectorists can't help but build a connection to history that they did not have before, even if it's of the most simple kind, such as the mnemonic for remembering the kings and queens.

'I've got big problems with nationality,' he replied. 'The village is *not* England.'

This comment helped me realise that I had been over-thinking my own dilemma over where I 'belonged'. The options, as far as I was concerned, had been specific and literal: Wolverhampton, where I was born (hence my lifelong allegiance to Wolverhampton Wanderers, an attempt at some kind of belonging), or South Yorkshire, where I spent formative primary-school years; North London, South-west London or rural Hampshire, where I'd spent my adult life. My gut feeling was: 'none of the above'. Sometimes I felt that this made me footloose and sophisticated, a 'citizen of everywhere', but mostly if I was honest it just left me feeling a bit lost.

Manni said his sense of connection was not to a place precisely but to something else. To explain, he picked up a triangle of yellowish glaze, pointing out where a medieval potter had smoothed the clay into shape: 'That's why I like pottery. Someone, six hundred years ago, ran their finger along there. And somewhere on the planet their descendant exists. The wealth of information that's locked in that object . . .'

The information locked in our village concerns the precise route of the Roman road or roads that passed near it. Manni had been on this case for a while now. Pete Welch reckoned he might have cracked it. That was why I had been so keen to get on to 'Roman Ridge', the field that he claimed contained a telltale breadcrumb trail of road-related Roman artefacts from hobnails to potboilers.

Then Pete told me that the farmer had put a turnip crop on there to feed sheep through the winter. The window had opened and shut without us being able to squeeze through. This news would have dismayed me a few weeks before. I had been hanging on for the moment when that field became available. But now I had met Manni, and he had his own permissions and possibilities that pertained to the road and a possible settlement or villa.

We got the map out and looked at the evidence. The idea was that the village was a 'black hole'. An equal distance to the north and south were Roman villas, marked as such. On the 'centuriation' principle, of roads and farm plots set out in a grid, you could expect something significant to be on our doorstep. Right in the middle of this zone of possibility Manni had some new permissions.

'I found a Roman coin and a lot of Roman pottery *here* – maybe ten to fifteen shards,' he said. 'Then to the south, by a very nice lady's paddocks, I've found a lot of *opus signinum* . . . it's enticing because there's lots of Roman all over the shop. It's just boiling it down, trying to find where the original settlement was.'

These fields awaited, but after the field walking it was my round, as it were – my turn to invite Manni out. This brought me back to the permission problem. I decided that there had been an unconscious grandiosity in my wishing to detect on the land of the gentry. Sally and Rob had found their wonderful sword belt hanger in a paddock belonging to a relative, not an abandoned medieval village. There were plenty of paddocks round here and I knew the people who owned them. My permissions had been staring me in the face.

Our immediate neighbours kept two horses and had three paddocks. I knocked on their door. Neighbour David answered. A laid-back, retired maths teacher, he hadn't known I'd become a detectorist and seemed surprised and amused by the information. But he was amenable to the idea. 'What happens if you find treasure, though?' he said.

'Fifty–fifty. But I won't. It's not about treasure. It's the little things. Everyday things.' Afterwards I suspected this made me sound like a conman, me knowing something he didn't and trying to put him off the scent.

'Put the holes back, won't you?' he said.

Manni came along with his own detector and we detected on the first paddock one bright autumn morning. The initial embarrassment at outing myself as a detectorist had faded, but that was partly because I had been playing away, free of the stares of people I knew and lived near. Now it returned.

It was embarrassing to admit, but I had over the years attempted to cultivate a bit of a local reputation as an enigmatic writer type. Why had neighbour David been amused by the idea of me becoming a detectorist? Because it showed I was a much more run-of-the-mill character than I pretended to be. I was a fraud!

Togged up in detectorist gear, with digging tool over one shoulder and machine in the other hand, I had to negotiate a corridor of jeopardy that ran from our driveway, a hundred yards up the lane, to the neighbour's paddocks. Perhaps, if I kept my head down as an acquaintance driving or walking down the lane went by, I might pass as a BT Openreach engineer, or a tree surgeon, with Manni (in camouflaged cut-offs) my apprentice? (Manni, by the way, a third my age and twice as grown up, didn't give a toss about such stuff.)

But the situation didn't arise, the lane was clear. I felt relief as I climbed the fence into the first paddock, though the danger didn't end there, as public footpaths ran either side. But then – switching on, setting the ground balance, adjusting the headphones – you disappear into the detecting and lose your ego somewhere in the grain and possibility of the earth.

This paddock, of a couple of acres, occupies a swelling hillside that flares into a dazzle of buttercups in the spring – a sight that every year my body waits for and buzzes to. According to the tithe map of 1839, the land belonged to a 'G. Stevens', who also owned the house that David and his family now occupy. Abutting it is our orchard, which Sarah Prior then rented from a D. Stevens (presumably a relation).

At first it was iron coming up, including big horseshoes. David came out to see what his land was giving us and seemed amused by the trawl of sizeable junk, as if it confirmed the harmless pointlessness of the hobby. Manni didn't rate these early signs. I felt relaxed and confident even though I was getting nothing decent. We discussed shifting on to paddock number two before long. As he leaned back on the fence, munching a baguette, I got a sweet signal.

Like many good finds, it gave itself up without a fight – it was in the first clod I scooped, no more than four inches down.

'Hey! Buckle!'

Manni came over and, based on the D-shape and the dark green of the metal, pronounced it 'post-medieval'. By anyone's standards, this was not 'hedge fodder'. I put it in my finds pouch and, feeling warmly happy, continued sweeping.

Presently we moved on to the next paddock, where Manni found a buckle of his own – probably not as old as mine – and I found a heavy knob for a door or cabinet. We called it a day after a couple of hours. I didn't even think about the possibility of being spotted as I swaggered back down the lane. The buckle was monopolising my thoughts.

It was a 'Post Medieval copper-alloy single-loop buckle, dating to c.AD 1500 – 1650', according to the PAS database. I could establish this with such certainty because the buckle was almost exactly the same in shape and dimensions as examples on the website that carried this description. There were many such buckles; it was far from rare. But what puzzled me was that none had been found in the South-east or central southern England. They came from Buckinghamshire (×2), my home town of Doncaster in South Yorkshire, Lincolnshire,

North Lincolnshire, Derbyshire, Worcestershire, Cornwall (×2), Cumbria, Suffolk, Denbighshire and North Yorkshire – places far from Hampshire, Surrey or Sussex. An obvious conclusion was that the person who had lost it – a man I had been thinking about from the second the buckle came out of the ground – was, like me, not local. (This is not necessarily the case – the data could just be skewed in various ways that are frankly too boring to go into but this is what I wanted to believe: I had found a soulmate across the centuries.)

The find spot was just off the course of a footpath that led down off the hill, coming from a hamlet with a manor house and church and going nowhere in particular. Was he an itinerant hawker of haberdashery to the remotely domiciled?

There is a story among detectorists that the reason so many buttons are found in fields is that farmers used to use old, discarded clothes as mulch or to inhibit weed growth. In any case, buttons are always falling off clothes. You expect to find them. But what about buckles? These are also found frequently – Kris came up with one on my first outing in Kent; I got the pin, or chape, of a Georgian buckle in Norfolk before this one – but I couldn't imagine the circumstances in which they might be inadvertently mislaid. This was because I associated them with trouser belts, and if you lost the buckle from your trouser belt, you'd soon know about it because your trousers would fall down.

My post-medieval buckle prompted a more general thought: how was it that items got lost for detectorists to find centuries later? Most of it was accidental loss, coins being the prime example. This in turn means the objects must be small and portable, easily carried but also easily mislaid. And in many cases they were lost while people were travelling and therefore unlikely to go back and look for them. The sites of markets, fairs, battles and trackways are all obvious places.

This man and his buckle had been on that path on the hillside. Maybe he had stepped, or guided his horse, just off it to rest and enjoy the view. The view would not have included our cottage, as I had made a point of studying eye lines and angles after I pulled the buckle from the ground and started to build a story around it.

The cottage had existed then – the core of it dates from the late fifteenth century – but it was obscured behind a shoulder of hillside. However, depending on the time of year, he might have seen wood smoke rising from the chimney. He might have been on his way there, or just left it. And then he lost a buckle without noticing.

What I did know was that the buckle had offered a point of interplay for my imagination. When I looked at it, I did not see, or at least saw past, an object that was, according to the Portable Antiquities Scheme (PAS) database, 'D-shaped/sub-rectangular in plan with concave sides . . .' and so on. It became a cipher for thoughts and feelings about time and place and my status within them. It wasn't just this buckle of course. It applied to all finds because they all fired my imagination in some way.

But the buckle had a quality the others, so far, didn't. I had found it on land next to my own. The person to whom it belonged had had some sort of relationship with my cottage four or five hundred years ago – even if that relationship only extended to glancing at it in passing or seeing smoke rising over trees. This gave the buckle a power in my hand, as if it were a time-travelling pill that was mine alone to swallow.

Chris in Norfolk had raised the idea of 'home turf', the possibility that you stood a better chance of finding good things on land that was familiar to you. It was true that I had never felt so comfortable nor confident as in that stint of detecting on the neighbour's paddocks. Two of three paddocks remained to be searched. I couldn't wait to go back. I knew I would make worthwhile finds, that they were waiting for me.

The weather closed in with a series of rainy, windy days that shook the remaining leaves from the trees. Manni and I had agreed to go back on the neighbour's paddocks when the weather improved and meanwhile I had work to do, writing about the ancestor worship of the Vietnamese, the way a family house will have – in pride of place – a shrine to their forebears. As I wrote this, I looked at my sandwich box of metal artefacts on the corner of the desk. The collection was small but growing. If it were found in the ground in five hundred years' time – and the plastic box would last far longer than that – what would archaeologists make of it?

An October morning dawned bright and mild, and I made a snap decision to detect on my own, Manni having gone off travelling for a couple of weeks. After a quick stroll up the lane to do my neighbours the courtesy of renewing their permission, I was back on the paddocks, this time concentrating on the second one that sloped up from a steep bank behind their house. Their horses, a big grey and his neat little sidekick, were now grazing on the field where I had found the buckle. As I climbed over the fence into paddock number two, they watched me with a look of prick-eared amazement before resuming more important business.

The initial harvest of iron didn't put me off. At the high point of the field, I paused for a biscuit and a cup of Thermos tea and ploughed on, attempting a rough to-and-fro system. At the end of my next line down, the low point of the paddock, I had a sweet signal. It was a coin. Definitely not a hammered, too big and uniform for that. But still . . . my hopes rose as I tried to brush off the mud. Then I saw Britannia, sitting on her shield.

It was an old penny. I remembered them from my childhood – cascades of them in the 'Penny Falls' arcade games on Doncaster Racecourse during St Leger Week, giving me such early swoons of addictive hope. My paddock penny had the honour of being the first coin in my portable finds pod, where I slotted it in a slit of the duck-egg-blue foam rubber.

On I went, reasoning now that due to gravity the low point of the paddock was probably the area to concentrate on. Up next came a button with a convex front, nearly as big as the penny, with a loop on the back. As I was spraying it with water, David the neighbour appeared at the fence.

'Any luck?'

'Just got this button,' I said, holding it out. I hadn't made a good job of removing the dirt. The button looked grey and nondescript and David didn't look impressed. 'Got a coin a few minutes ago,' I added.

His ears pricked up at this.

'Shall I get my Spink?' he said. Spink – both an auction house ('founded 1666') and a publisher of reference books – is *the* authority on British coins and David had a copy of their *Coins of England and the United Kingdom*. He was, it turned out, a coin man.

I said a book wouldn't be necessary, it was just a common-or-garden penny, maybe 1950s. Soon after this, I retired for the day, feeling content. The return had not been spectacular but I had felt a oneness with the land I hadn't felt before. The finds had come easily as if wanting to be found. And I had barely covered a third of this second paddock. There was so much more to sweep.

Back at the cottage I used toothbrush and water to clean up coin and button. Both ambushed me. The button was far from nondescript. As I brushed gently under water, a pattern emerged and I saw traces of black lacquer around the edges. At first I thought it was military – I was still keen to establish a direct connection between the environs of the cottage and the Battle of Cheriton – but the pattern, incised in gold, was surprisingly free-form. Some sort of exotic plant? The face of an elephant?

The pattern reminded me of an uncharacteristically wry description of a 'tombac' button on the PAS database: '. . . an abstract incised design which may be intended to represent a flowering plant, but manages to convey the impression that the engraver was either drunk or had never seen one . . .' My button was dressy, not military; decadent, not formal. It was a button from the frock coat or cloak of an eighteenth-century dandy, a man about town – a so-called 'dandy button'. What was an urban poseur doing in a muddy backwater like this?

Leaving the button to dry on a piece of kitchen towel, I turned to the coin. I had assumed it to be mid-twentieth century but when I flipped Britannia over I saw not the smooth-shaven profile of George VI, or even the youthful Elizabeth II, but what looked like a Roman emperor, with a laurel wreath on his head. For a moment I thought I had found a Roman coin and that idea is not so ridiculous – the figure of Britannia, the Roman personification of these Isles, first appeared on British coins in the time of the Emperor Hadrian, the second century AD.

Then I made out a date beneath the bust: 1827. The guy in the greenery, aping the imperial grandeur of Ancient Rome, was George IV, as depicted by the engraver William Wyon (who was also responsible for the likeness of the young Victoria that persisted on her coinage until she was well into middle age). The 1827 penny is classified as 'rare'. Those in 'extremely fine' condition sell for a few thousand quid; an 'uncirculated' specimen would cost several thousand pounds.

I assumed at first that this was because only 1.5 million were minted in 1827 (the figure for the year before being nearly 6 million). But fewer – about 1 million – were issued in 1825, yet these are classified as merely 'semi-scarce', with an 'extremely fine' specimen worth only £250. Something else had to account for the rarity of the 1827 penny.

After some virtual pinpointing in the slippery earth of the internet, I discovered that most if not all of the 1827 mintage was intended for circulation in the penal colonies of Tasmania. There is also speculation that while in transit, in wooden crates in the holds of ships, the coins were badly corroded by saltwater, which further accounts for the rarity of 1827 coins in good condition and their consequent high value.

So what condition was my coin in? Pretty good, possibly 'very good' in the official classification – which would make it worth about £150. But as with any found object, its value did not lie in the amount it might go for on eBay. The coin was a story, the story of where it came from and how it got there. It was minted in copper in the Royal Mint, in the year in which William Blake died, and remained in circulation for 43 years. It conceivably went to Australia in a crate and came back in a pocket. It fell out of a pocket.

The reference to Australia's penal colonies reminded me of the fate of two former occupants of the cottage. Three years after the 1827 penny was minted, Thomas Budd and his son William were convicted of sheep stealing and sent to Botany Bay for eight years. Most convicts stayed when they had completed their sentence, not having the means (or possibly the inclination) to return. What about Thomas and William? Was it in one of their pockets that the penny returned?

When I first had the idea of taking up metal detecting, I was prompted by the whispers I was starting to hear, rising like morning mist from the landscape surrounding the cottage. The whispers were growing bolder and merging, creating a keening soundscape in the folds of fields. When I went walking, taking the paths of our man with the buckle, the incongruous dandy, a prodigal son, I felt I was slipping through time circles.

In Siem Reap, Cambodia I had bought a tourist book featuring illustrations of the famous Angkor sites as they are now, interleaved with painted overlays of how they looked at the height of their use and power. Flicking the overlay back and forth enables the imagination to build a picture of how it used to be. On my walks now my mind was forever flicking the overlays back and forth, seeing the field systems and the pedlars.

The neighbour's paddocks drew me back. It was rich ground, it wanted to yield to me. On the third visit I found a small dark disc, smaller than a 5p piece. First thing I did, the mud still thick on it, was flip it over to check there was no loop on the back, make sure it wasn't a button. No loop. I brushed mud from one side. There appeared to be patterning or lettering on both sides, though I couldn't make any of it out.

The object went in the finds pod and I detected for maybe an hour more but have no recollection of what I found. I just enjoyed the lazy swinging, and the delayed gratification. As I was about to pack up and walk back down the lane to investigate my little find, David came out and asked me how I was doing.

'Think I've found an old coin,' I said. 'Can I borrow your Spink?'

7

MY SANITY FOR
A HAMMERED

Under running water, I used a toothbrush to brush the rest of the mud off what I had already decided was a hammered. *Shit!* The markings – whatever they said, and I would need the spiffing new magnifying glass with inbuilt light I had recently upgraded to in order to read them properly – were incised, not raised. There was no kingly head in profile. But my groan of frustration turned up at the end into a quaver of curiosity. Not a hammered – I'd learned to live with that in any case – nor even any kind of coin, but *something provocative,* freighted with story nonetheless.

This is what showed up under the magnifying glass, the letters and figures crowded on to the little disc in the same configuration on each side:

$$S \quad P$$
$$6 = 9$$

It seemed to be a token of some sort, quite crudely done, very much local and homemade. Tokens were 'a bit of a mystery' according to one of my local Finds Liaison Officers (FLOs) when he replied to the picture I sent him. He said that 'these sorts of farm token [for so he identified it] probably reflect social and economic practices which have long since been forgotten.' They are thought to have been used as a substitute for small change in remote areas (like Romney Marsh), especially in the late Georgian period when there was a shortage of low-value copper coins. They were also used as tallies for piecework by farm labourers or as counters in local shops or taverns, thereby tying people into their local economy and maximising the profits of local farmers and businesses.

He couldn't shed much light on the one I had found, beyond the fact that it was probably later than Georgian and made of brass, and that the initials – S P – were presumably those of the issuer or landowner. 'The function of the other numbers [6 = 9] I do not know,' he wrote. Still, it was an exciting response because, far from dousing my original hope, it had if anything reinforced it.

My belief, from the moment I set eyes on those initials, was that SP was Sarah Prior, the woman who lived in the cottage in the mid-nineteenth century and seems to have had her fingers in multiple local pies. According to the tithe map of 1839, Sarah owned a 'house garden plot' (our current cottage), a 'field' and a 'hanger', both for arable use, and rented a 'plot' also for arable use. The map shows that men who owned or rented land in the locality outnumbered women by about eight to one and of the handful of female landowners Sarah was the biggest, the rest tending to own just domestic plots.

Sarah did not farm the field where I found the token, but she did farm two fields abutting it. It was perfectly plausible that a token issued by her had found its way over the fence and into a field farmed by another. It was also consistent with my idea of her that she would have been sufficiently business-savvy to bother having tokens made and paying her workers with them.

For periods in the past, the cottage was run as an alehouse. Was this in her time? Was Sarah, in addition to being a farmer, also a landlady? When her farmhands knocked off at the end of the week, did they then slope straight round to Sarah's parlour to spend the tokens she had just handed them in the fields?

In my mental picture Sarah was ahead of her time, wearing the trousers, bossing her neighbourhood, even (if my previous speculation was correct) enjoying the attentions of a toyboy lover in the form of stepson Henry Prior. Feeling an affinity, for some years now I had been in the habit of talking to her headstone in the village churchyard whenever I walked to the village shop. The token went some way to hardening up my hope for the person she had been.

This was part of a bigger picture that fed into a certain self-serving narrative about the cottage: it attracted and nurtured singular characters. After we bought the place, I discovered that in the late 1960s the cottage had been owned by an Australian artist, Loudon Sainthill, who designed sets for the Royal Opera House, and his partner Harry Tatlock Miller, 'book seller, art critic and leading member of the avant garde scene' (says Wikipedia). Our neighbour and friend, who grew up in a house near the cottage, told us that this gay ménage in the heart of the conservative shires of the 1960s had scandalised the local farmers and retired army bods.

She remembered that original Picasso prints had hung on the walls, there were wild weekend parties attended by reprobates from

London and the whole rackety household was presided over by a 'Chinese manservant'. I privately suspected that this latter detail was an embellishment too far, though I was happy to repeat it.

Then I got hold of a biography of Loudon Sainthill that mentions Harry's 'Hong Kong-born houseboy'. It also describes a decor not so different from the one we have created with bric-a-brac from our travels. In these exotic surroundings, Loudon would apparently work on his 'personal folio of homoerotica'.

My go-to leisure activity may not have been quite so racy, but I felt Loudon's spirit around the beamed and low-ceilinged rooms, as I did Sarah's, and I warmed to both. I even fantasised about inviting them to dinner at the long table in the kitchen – far more interesting company even than David Bowie, or the Queen, and I reckoned they would get on like a thatched cottage on fire.

The night after I had found the 1827 penny – the one minted exclusively for Australia's penal colonies – I had a dream that conflated this find with my early obsession with digging in the ground till I broke through into Australia (I'm not sure where that came from or what I expected – maybe a kangaroo bouncing, startled, into South Yorkshire). In the dream it was as if I had struck oil – the hole gushed forth a geyser of 1827 pennies. I did not relate this dream to my partner, who already thought I was becoming obsessed with metal detecting. 'I'm getting a bit worried about him,' she had taken to remarking drily to friends.

The respective narratives spun by coin and token bedded down nicely in my growing sense of belonging to this small green valley. And there they would have stayed but for another encounter with the local historian Jane Hurst at the Curtis Museum in Alton. I had gone there to see if I could follow the fates of Thomas and William Budd once they had been packed off to Botany Bay. If I could prove that one or both subsequently returned to this neighbourhood, it was a reasonable bet that my penny had travelled back with them.

Poised like a tiny organist in front of a cathedral organ, Jane stared up at a huge screen as she riffled through databases. And it soon emerged that my original information, taken from that unpublished history of the cottage, was inaccurate. On 26 July 1830 at the Summer Assizes in Winchester, 44-year-old Thomas Budd was sentenced to death for stealing a sheep (it is incredible that sheep stealing was a capital offence, but it was) from a field at Chawton owned by William Edwards, a butcher. Thomas's 17-year-old son William was also indicted, but 'acquitted on the plea that he acted under the influence of his parent' (*Hampshire Chronicle*).

Thomas's death sentence must have been commuted because on 11 October 1830 he was among prisoners removed from the County Gaol in Winchester to the prison hulk *York* in Portsmouth Harbour. The hulks were decommissioned or captured warships used as overflow prisons. Shorn of masts, machinery and any form of creature comfort, they were mere deathly husks where disease was rife and the mortality rate high.

Four years after Thomas's arrival on the *York*, some of the Dorset labourers and proto-trades unionists known as the Tolpuddle Martyrs were also banged up there prior to transportation, having been stitched up in what amounted to a show trial at Dorchester Assizes.

In the early nineteenth century, a Frenchman, Ambroise-Louis Garneray, was held as a prisoner of war on the hulks at Portsmouth and painted several panoramas of the harbour. They show the floating clinks lined up like black cabs outside London's King's Cross station. In this grim place Thomas's trail went cold – or I thought it did. We could find no record of him arriving in Australia, nor of dying on the hulk. And had he survived the passage and served his time, would he really have come back?

Once again, my confirmation bias seemed to have led me up a garden path, and it was about to propel me along another one. On my way out of the cottage I had picked up the 1827 penny to show to Jane, then at the last second decided to bring the 'farm token' too. Studying it under a magnifying glass the size of a frisbee, she seemed sceptical that it was a token. And later that day she emailed me to say that she had identified it as an eighteenth-century 'coin-weight'.

Through the 1700s, silver coins were being so badly 'clipped' that they were often traded by weight rather than face value. For this you needed an accurate weight measurement. Traders bought these weights blank from wholesalers and put their own stamps on them. There are plenty of these stamped coin-weights on the Portable Antiquities Scheme (PAS) database and many are marked 'S' and 'D', the traditional Roman abbreviations for *solidi* and *denarii* (i.e. shillings and pennies).

Jane thought that 'SP' could be a variation standing simply for 'shillings' and 'pennies'. What was more puzzling was the '6 = 9'. This almost certainly meant '6 shillings and 9 pence' but how to account for such an apparently arbitrary amount? Time for a deep dive into the furthest ocean trenches of the internet.

I opened a bottle of red wine and for an hour or so finned about in the waving sea grasses of numismatic websites. Then, just as I felt I was getting the bends, I hit on an obscure paper entitled 'Provincial coin-weights in the eighteenth century'. This told me that '6s. 9d' was the equivalent in weight of a 'quarter-moidore', a moidore being one of a family of Portuguese coins (another being the Johannes or 'Joey') that were widely circulated in Britain and mainland Europe in the mid-eighteenth century.

Moidores are referenced by contemporaneous writers such as Daniel Defoe in *Robinson Crusoe*, Jonathan Swift in *Gulliver's Travels*, Voltaire in *Candide* and, more than a century later, by John Masefield in his famous poem 'Cargoes', featuring that 'Stately Spanish galleon' loaded with 'Topazes, and cinnamon, and gold moidores'. Absorbing this information, I felt traitorous towards Sarah Prior, as if I had just traded her soul for a shipful of stolen treasure.

Before the first storm of the winter, I took a break. This was to be the longest journey – by distance or time – I had done since the time before Covid-19. Then, on that other side, I had travelled intemperately. In a four-week period in 2014, for example, I caught nineteen long- and short-haul flights: to Indonesia, the American Deep South and the Netherlands.

In order to write essentially superficial travel articles, I trampled all over the face of the earth in my big carbon boots. Yet in another sense, my feet barely touched the ground. My thoughts scarcely skimmed the reality of the subject matter, let alone dug down into it. There is little or no verticality to this kind of rushed exploration, which is often little more than ticking off countries on a bucket list. (I do not have a map of the world on the kitchen wall covered in coloured pins, but people do, people do.)

Metal detecting, I was beginning to realise, is all verticality and, at its most meaningful, locality. Everything you unearth is found by you alone; is by definition unique, not written or experienced before or anywhere else, by anyone else. And if it's on your home patch, well, then it's talking to you directly, placing you in a continuity of existence and experience. My five-hundred-year-old soulmate whose buckle I found saw the same land and stars from the same perspective as me, and that idea was altogether novel and thrilling.

For now, it was a different perspective I was seeking. From Wessex I drove up through Mercia, along highways lined with huge distribution warehouses that looked like pieces of ill-fitting sky, to Northumbria. My initial idea had been just to enjoy the change of scenery. The Covid-19 era had locked us all into small plots, in our heads as in our surroundings. I needed to break out for a while and planned to walk on the beaches of Northumberland. Then I found a contact for the Scottish Detector Club, which organises days out near Edinburgh.

Club member Alastair Hacket, who is also a former president of the National Council for Metal Detecting (NCMD), and Linda Adams, the club secretary, responded warmly to my emails. Linda invited me to a Sunday dig near a village in East Lothian, so I chucked the metal detector in the boot with my little travelling case and extended my trip north of the Scottish border.

Linda wrote: 'The fields are very close to the medieval village and also where they burnt witches! (Potential pocket spills from people jeering at the accused witches)'. In the decades preceding the Salem witch trails of 1692–3 in the new colony of Massachusetts, people (men as well as women) were being tried and burned for witchcraft in Scotland – and the county of East Lothian was, as it were, a hot spot. Over a period of about 250 years, some 2,500 Scots were murdered for being 'witches' – an historic injustice for which the Scottish First Minister Nicola Sturgeon issued a posthumous apology shortly after my trip north. 'They were accused and killed because they were poor, different, vulnerable or in many cases just because they were women,' she said.

I drove up on the A1, the former Great North Road, a journey I must have done a hundred times from the 1980s to the early 2000s on visits to my parents in South Yorkshire. I would break the journey north of Peterborough, either at a hamlet called Water Newton (for a leg-stretch) on a loop of the old road above Peterborough, or at a funky little place about 15 miles north of that called the Ram Jam Inn (for a bacon sandwich).

Once, at the Ram Jam, a fellow punter mentioned that 'blokes with metal detectors' were finding a fortune in Roman coins at 'that old Roman town down the road'. He meant Water Newton, which I hadn't realised was the site of a Roman garrison town called Durobrivae, where Ermine Street crossed the River Nene.

But Water Newton, so deathly quiet yet so close to the noise and fumes of the A1, had always had a timeslip quality for me – its mellow stone houses, the church with a Roman coffin outside, the water meadows and river and the fact that I never saw a soul when I nosed around.

In 1975, a hoard of Roman silver vessels and plaques bearing Christian symbols were unearthed by a farmer's plough at Water Newton and recognised as significant by a local detectorist. The Water Newton Treasure, now in the British Museum, is regarded as the earliest known collection of Christian silverware in the Roman Empire. It was presumably following its discovery and the attendant publicity, in the lawless late 1970s and 1980s, that the looters mentioned by the guy in the Ram Jam moved in and hoovered up, and there were organised rallies there in the 2000s in which many other objects are thought to have disappeared.

Beyond the Ram Jam (now derelict, awaiting probable demolition) the A1 crosses the River Trent, which by the Middle Ages (and on various measures) had been generally accepted as marking the border between the South and the North of England. The river rises in Staffordshire and hardly knows which way it's going for much of its 170-mile progress to the Humber estuary and the North Sea.

When I was 11, I crossed it from the north side in a Hillman Minx driven by my dad and I feel I never went back, at least not as the same person, for I was uprooted from my South Yorkshire housing estate and replanted in a single-sex boarding school deep in the Sussex countryside.

I feel now I was a proxy in my parents' thwarted dreams, a social mountaineer on their behalf. They wanted me to be the respectable gent my mother's father really hadn't been, become the solicitor my father had aspired to be rather than the cement salesman he was. Their problem was that they could not afford private school fees, so they found a charity school that looked the part – ivy on the old walls, etc. – but cost a pittance.

The school uniform was adapted from Tudor garb; many of my fellow pupils were the sons of vicars or from broken homes, mostly from London and the South-east. Though these lads took the piss out of my northern accent, they weren't toffee-nosed, far from it – just bewildered like me. To the end of our time there we had the camaraderie of the marooned about us, as if we had been turfed out of the lifeboats of secure childhoods and washed up on the shore of a quarantine island.

Homesickness, like seasickness, can make you want to die. The journeys home, from south to north, were like moving back into sunlight after being trapped underground. The journeys in the other direction, back to school, were trudges to the gallows. Home and school, north and south, short and long vowels were warring realities that I'd never really resolved. I didn't, as they say, know whether I was coming or going. Any sense of belongingness I may have had evaporated many years ago over the dark and tree-fringed waters of the River Trent.

On a newspaper assignment in the 1990s, I accompanied a Scottish folk musician called Norman Chalmers to the outermost of the Outer Hebridean islands, St Kilda, which was evacuated of its last human inhabitants in 1930. Among those last to leave had been Norman's ancestors and I stood with him as he contemplated the roofless house where they once lived. Breaking the silence, I asked him wistfully what it felt like to be able to pin down your past so precisely to a set of stones and a blackened hearth.

'I feel lucky to have such a defined place that I come from,' he replied, 'a strong rock in my sense of being. I don't have ontological anxiety about where I fit.'

It had taken me another 25 years and a pandemic to realise so explicitly that I probably did have such anxiety.

On its original route, the Great North Road passes the house south-east of Doncaster where my family moved from Wolverhampton when I was five and where I first felt affinities for old buried things that metal detecting was now rekindling. The name of this neighbourhood, Bessacarr, has a Norse suffix, -carr (meaning watery brushland), and the wider area is full of other -carrs. Torksey, the place where the Viking 'great heathen army' overwintered in the ninth century, whiling away the long damp nights by making their lead gaming pieces, is 20 miles away.

The Great North Road at this point was built over a Roman road that took a kink near our house, diverging from the modern route beneath a widening, swelling grass verge – an *agger*. I seemed to have always known about the Roman road. If we drove past in a friend's car, his dad would be sure to say self-importantly, pointing at the verge, 'Know what that is?' and, just as surely and self-importantly, I would aim my tomato of prior knowledge at him before he could take his bow.

Brought to life by school trips to Roman York, the Romans buzzed around our childish imaginations. A friend with a particularly vivid one said he had found a centurion's helmet in his back garden, though he was unable to produce it (to be fair, he also claimed his granddad was a big game hunter in Africa who had caught the lion that roared at the beginning of MGM films). The local museum had lots of Roman pottery and coins on display – some of the *mortaria*, beakers, jars and flagons having been made in kilns near where my primary school stood – and I enjoyed gazing on them on midweek mornings after attending the verruca clinic next door.

My ever-expanding collection of verrucas was a ticket to Roman times. I acquired them at will in the town's municipal swimming baths, through which thousands of schoolchildren and their pestilential feet passed every week, and to my secret pleasure they necessitated a weekly visit to the clinic on my own, on the bus, in school hours. This trusting arrangement enabled me to steal time.

After the procedure – which involved a scalpel and purple ointment painted on with a brush – I didn't go straight to the bus stop on my burning feet, I sneaked into the museum where I made for the Roman galleries. And there, always solitary and uninterrupted, I gazed for several minutes on these cabinet-bound memos and puzzles. My batteries thus charged, I then caught the bus back to school down the Great North Road.

Some 175 miles north, in the wilds of Northumberland, the A1 gives up the pretence of being a modern highway and takes on a high road to nowhere feel. The traffic thins out, dual carriageway narrows to single, the route sways romantically, dipping down to the sea. I felt the reality of moving into another country and time frame.

For a period in the Dark Ages, Northumbria, the Anglo-Saxon kingdom 'north of the Humber', extended well north of the boundaries of present-day Northumberland, as far as the Firth of Forth. This *was* another country, not so much compared to England as to my adoptive backyard of ancient Wessex. The more I delved into the soil of these isles, the more I thought in terms of the ancient place names and boundaries – it's not, after all, as if they have disappeared from use and view.

Northumbria is the name of a university and a police force, West Mercia is also a police force, Wessex is, among other things, a fictional literary landscape and a water company, and East Anglia is still East Anglia. In an interview on *Channel 4 News* concerning the spread of a Covid-19 variant, a Welsh GP and academic named Dame Helen Stokes-Lampard said, without missing a beat, 'Omicron doesn't respect

Hadrian's Wall or Offa's Dyke.' In historical contexts, 'England' – a word that didn't come into use until the late ninth century – and 'Scotland' – first used somewhat later – are just useful labels.

In an email, my new Scottish detectorist friend Alastair Hacket had pointed out that Scotland's history of occupation was very different from that of England and that the range of metal-detecting finds is correspondingly different. 'Detectorists in Scotland are generally envious of their English counterparts,' he wrote to me, 'since there were no Roman towns in Scotland – the Romans were almost exclusively a military presence – and few Roman coins and artefacts are therefore found.'

He added that 'evidence of Celtic tribes is also very hard to find compared with England'. Bronze Age likewise – though that hadn't stopped Mariusz Stepien, the Pole I had heard about at Detectival, unearthing the remarkable Peebles Hoard in June 2020.

It turned out that Mariusz was a member of the Scottish Detector Club and when I reached the site of the dig on a Sunday morning there were rumours that he would be turning up. It was a crisp, cold morning with dustings of frost in the hollows and steely sunlight. The field, a mile or so from a small village, was about 40 acres – powerlines down the middle, a burn along one edge, scattered wind turbines to the north and distant views to the west of the low Pentland Hills.

I correctly identified Linda as the muffled and beaming figure who was hailing each arrival and stopping for a blether with them. She told me later these gatherings are as much about the social as about the search.

'I'm constantly getting updated on whose dog is due puppies, whose grandmother is about to head into a care home, who's building a new shed,' she said.

Linda hooked me up to Alastair Hacket and within five minutes of arriving on the field I felt welcomed and included. Alastair, a retired local government official, was a gentle, dapper man who fell straightaway into knowledgeable talk on metal detecting and local history. But he had some disappointing news.

'Hammered silver coins are difficult to find in Scotland,' he said in reply to my confession that I was yet to find one and that everywhere I went, on every outing with my machine, I hoped that this would be the day my luck would change.

Furthermore, he went on, the hammereds that *are* found north of the border tend to be English, though Scotland minted its own coins.

'Alexander or later – it's nice if one of those turns up,' he said, 'but I've been detecting for 25 years and the number of hammered coins I've found is probably less than a dozen.'

This is probably due to relatively light population density, the fewer number of coins issued and the likelihood that in any case in remote areas official coinage was used less than farm or trade tokens.

Still, Alastair's lack of success in the hammered department put my own into perspective and I was reflecting that maybe I was being too hard on myself when he keyed his phone into life and swiped up visions from a numismatist's wet dream, if they have such things – row upon row of hammereds neatly displayed in cabinets in apparently endless variations and multiplications. They belong to an English friend of his.

'When I saw them, I thought, *My God* . . .' said Alastair. 'Then again, he lives in Peterborough, so he's got the stuff on his doorstep.'

My desperate hope had been that I might find a hammered or two from the purse spills that Linda had waved tantalisingly in front of my imagination. Waiting for the off at 9.30am, I peopled the field in front of me with crowds of straining rubberneckers so turned on by the spectacle of freshly cremated crone that they didn't notice the coins loosed from their flapping garments.

Before setting off for Scotland, I had looked up the village in the Survey of Scottish Witchcraft and discovered that in 1662 a young villager called George Lacost was one of a 'large number of people denounced by James Welch' for attending a 'meeting of witches' in a wood near the village. Deemed too young to stand trial, George was still put in prison – but not before denouncing others.

As I pulled on my boots by the gaping boot of my car, I asked my next-door neighbour if he knew roughly where in the field the witch-burning site had been.

'I think it was over the other side,' he said, pointing. 'Just before that wind turbine there's a drop-off and a bend in the river. That's where they burned the witches – so they say. It's marked on the OS maps, the old ones anyway. They tend to take that kind of thing off the new ones.'

When the time hit 9.30am, I stepped out and swept towards the corner of the field nearest to this point. Alastair's comments about the dearth of hammereds in Scotland had doused my fire a bit but now the hope revived – just a half or a quarter, please, a delayed dividend of the burning sport! That hope shrivelled almost immediately. From the outset I had a sense of the field being an alien place – not personally hostile, for everyone was very friendly, but almost illegible/unintelligible.

Every field chunters and chatters through the headphones, but this chatter was faint. I thought back to what Chris had said in Norfolk, about familiarity. Maybe it is to do with the 'ideomotor effect', the unconscious impulse that directs the finger on the ouija board or the hands holding divining rods. In the case of metal detecting, you sweep more efficiently and diligently on your home patch because you feel more confident – something like the home advantage that is so evident in football. And I was a long way from home.

At any rate, within five seconds I had a bad feeling about this field. I knew it would yield nothing no matter how long I stuck at it (and though I was wrong about this, the find I did make, presently described, still felt against the grain). After an hour the only signal I had had that was even vaguely promising was a moo tube. Then I ran into a man with a trim beard who pushed up his beanie hat on his forehead and caught my eye.

He wanted me to say, 'Any luck?', so I did.

'Three coins and a button,' he shot back. 'The coins are corroded but I'm chuffed. Shows there's stuff in there.'

'I'm getting nothing,' I replied.

'Aye. Someone else said that. Usually it's me but not today.'

Well, bully for you, I thought.

Now I was beginning to rethink the day – knock off early after lunch, perhaps. Contemplating an afternoon watching football on TV back at the hotel, I worked out a curved route back to the car for my packed lunch that looped round one of the telegraph poles. And, just on the other side of the pole, I registered a crisp-as-a-Granny-Smith bleep with an ID number of 95.

Boof! I was in there, reacting with an instinct I barely knew I had developed. Quick scoop of the new high-tensile spade, a big clod, scan of hole and clod to determine whereabouts of the target – now in the clod, not the hole – a truffle in the clod with the carrot, the earth breaking open and there, embedded in the sundering, a large green disc. A coin?

There was a moment of trepidation as I flipped the disc over to see if there was a loop on the back. Nope. Definitely coin. A flutter of the heart. Not modern, far too big, and heavy. It was badly corroded but I recognised it from my hours spent reading *Treasure Hunting* mag. The giveaway was the raised rim, which gave it its nickname: cartwheel penny. It was the trophy item Digger Dawn had gifted her little girl with autism; the coin Dean had hoped to find on Romney Marsh. It wasn't a hammered, but it was a minor milestone for detectorists.

Alastair confirmed its identity five minutes later when we convened by the cars for lunch.

'A great find, in the context,' he said.

He meant because so far the field had been disappointing and other people had found little of interest. Was there a note of envy in his voice? I liked to think so.

Cartwheel pennies, and twopenny pieces, were made over just two years, 1797–8, but all bear the date 1797 – a very fine year for visions, as it happened. Samuel Taylor Coleridge wrote his trippy 'dream fragment' 'Kubla Khan' and the people of Hastings in Sussex were treated to projections of the French coast hovering over the chimney pots, the result of a freakish conjunction of hot and cold air and its prism-like effect. The cartwheel coins were all too tangible.

The idea behind them was to provide literal value for money in the form of money worth exactly the value of the copper it was made of. The penny weighed an ounce, the twopence piece two ounces. The thickened rim was intended to make them more difficult to counterfeit but just added to their unwieldy quality.

Now, as then, they seem immediately ridiculous, a design-too-far like the brick-sized mobile telephones of the yuppie era. Too heavy for loose change, they were mocked as 'cartwheels' and eventually used or modified as tokens or gaming pieces rather than currency. Even in my little coin tub the cartwheel sat there foolishly, like a Great Dane in a puppy basket. As 44 million cartwheel pennies were minted, they are hardly rare, but this one had made my trip north worthwhile.

Over sandwiches, I felt a spasm of envy when told that someone had found a 'quarter hammy', and a detectorist called Anthea Skea – with a Galloway accent so soft I mistook it for English – gave me an update on Mariusz Stepien: apparently he had gone to London for the weekend. She also let drop that despite the scarcity of Roman coins in East Lothian, she herself had found one and would be happy to show it to me later, seeing as I was staying in a hotel in the village where she lived.

On the afternoon session I ran into two young Spanish men detecting together – Sergio from Toledo and Víctor from Asturias. They had cycled over from Edinburgh, where they worked in a fitness centre and a children's home, and said they had taken up metal detecting during lockdown as a reason to get out in the countryside. In Spain, they said, the activity was confined to looters of the *patrimonio* and had 'super-bad fame'. They opened a carrier bag to show me the day's haul – a jumble of muddy rust-red iron but they looked as pleased as Punch.

Smirking at this swag bag of crap, I asked loftily what their best find was so far in their fledgling detecting careers. 'Coin of 1629,' said Sergio.

I digested the implication of this date.

'So, a hammered,' I concluded gloomily.

Sergio's association of metal detecting with looting is a common view across mainland Europe, where the activity tends to be either more regulated than in the UK or illegal. There are practical reasons for this. The terrain of the old Western Front across northern France and Belgium, and World War II sites further east, is littered with unexploded ordnance and every year the plough brings a fresh harvest of bombs and bullets to the surface. But, more widely, a philosophical argument holds sway against the idea of individuals just walking off with old stuff and sticking it on their mantelpiece.

One (British) archaeologist put it this way: 'The view is held, especially in countries where metal detecting is illegal, that you wouldn't have just anybody being a brain surgeon – they've obviously got to go to university and be educated and know what they're doing. So they say that unless you're a professional archaeologist you can't do any archaeology whatsoever. That includes metal detecting.'

In the United Kingdom, the PAS and Scottish Treasure Trove allow a compromise that seems more pragmatic. It has led to the scene then in front of me in East Lothian, of ordinary people, with garden sheds and frail grandparents, seeking the gloss to their lives of finding talismans in the soil. Though not so many, as it happened, this parky Sunday.

By mid-afternoon our hopes were tempering down as we and our machines cast ever-lengthening shadows in the low sun. A sudden flurry of sleet decided me to wrap it up. My sole post-lunch find had been a buckle from a horse harness, but the cartwheel penny was the business even if news of the Spanish lads' hammered had taken the wind out of my sails (and after all, if metal detecting teaches you anything it is the acceptance of failure, along with its bouncy sibling, surprise).

Anthea said she would see me in half an hour outside my hotel. She turned up on foot holding a small box containing her coin. Roman finds are not unheard of in Scotland. In 1919, on a hill called Traprain

Law – seven miles from the village where I was staying – archaeologists found not just a Roman hoard but the largest hoard of Roman silver yet found, inside or outside the Roman Empire.

It contains over three hundred pieces of hacksilver – literally hacked-up silver – that was once exquisite jewellery and tableware from the households of Roman aristocrats. Coins found among them date the probable burial of the hoard to those desperate days that heralded the Dark Ages, when the Romans were jumping ship and leaving Britain to devour itself.

One theory is that this phenomenal wedge of loot was used by the Romans as a bribe. Traprain Law was an Iron Age hill fort that was probably the capital of the Votadini tribe until the early fifth century and remained occupied after that date. When the Romans invaded Scotland under Emperor Antoninus Pius in AD 139, the local people fell under Roman control. Two decades later, the Romans decided that keeping the Scots pacified was more trouble than it was worth and withdrew back to Hadrian's Wall, cutting a deal as they left.

Under this deal, so the theory goes, local tribal chiefs agreed to operate as borderland enforcers for their erstwhile masters, keeping the peace in the wild lands above Hadrian's Wall and preventing raids across it. The quid pro quo was regular bungs of bullion, which they could exchange or melt down and use in their own beautiful creations. In another excavation on Traprain Law, archaeologists found a Pictish chain necklace made from Roman silver.

During their invasion of Scotland, the Romans built a fort at Inveresk, outside modern-day Musselburgh. Two altar stones found there were quarried near Anthea's village. In 1985, when she lived in a house a few doors down from my hotel, she was weeding in her garden when she found a copper coin that she took to be antique but thought little more about. The coin lived in her dressing-table drawer until four years ago, when Anthea took up metal detecting in her retirement and realised that coins were storytellers.

She had it checked out by Scottish Treasure Trove, who confirmed that it was a Roman *sestertius*, dating from AD 134–8, with a bust of the Emperor Hadrian (of Wall fame) on the obverse and the figure of Salus, the Roman goddess of (to use a current term) 'wellness' on the reverse. Anthea lifted it from its box and held it to the fading daylight. Hadrian has the lantern-jawed profile of an old-school centre-half. The outline of Salus is indistinct but she is apparently feeding a serpent coiled around an altar from a *patera*, a ritual vessel.

These details are confirmed in a document from Scottish Treasure Trove. But Anthea's coin, like many a compelling storyteller, could be an unreliable narrator. The expert also raised the possibility that the coin is not original, minted in Rome, but a 'contemporary copy' made locally at roughly the same time as the real ones (common in copper alloy *sestertii* of the first to the third centuries). It could even be a 'modern copy', made from the sixteenth century to the present day as a replica or to deceive collectors – like the fake pharaonic figurine I saw being knocked up in Egypt. Either explanation would account for Hadrian's resemblance to the former Chelsea hard man Micky Droy.

When she discovered that her coin is or could be Roman, Anthea thought back to the day she found it in the garden – in that dull pre-detectorist era when objects held little fascination – and convinced herself that she could have been sitting on a Roman hoard. So she knocked on the door of the present owners of the house and asked their permission to bring her detector to bear on their lawn.

'They said, "Oh no, you can't dig up our garden",' she said, shaking her head. 'I wouldn't mind, but I was being nosy the other day, so I had a look through the fence at the back – and the garden's a tip!'

Two days later, I was back at my desk at the cottage, looking up information on cartwheel pennies on my laptop. The box with my finds in it sat on the edge of the desk. I slid it towards me and unclipped the four edges. Inside, trapped in slits of custard-coloured foam rubber, was my meagre haul of buttons, gaming piece, dress fastener, coins, buckles and so on. Lifting the Stanley knife I had retrieved from my DIY drawer (where it lies in near-solitary confinement), I cut an extra-big slit and added the cartwheel penny from East Lothian.

The 1827 penny that may have been to the penal colonies and back was a plum, I had to admit, but otherwise it was a pretty feeble return for all the work I had put in. Norfolk Chris or Kent Kris would find more, and better, items than this on a single weekend. 'It's not about finds,' Digger Dawn had told me. 'Yes, a find makes it better, but if you found something every time you went out you wouldn't have the same joy, would you?'

That was all very well but I felt much more childish than that, foot-stampingly needy in fact. I *did* want something every time I went out. That something was a hammered.

After I had ordered my metal detector and subscribed to *Treasure Hunting*, but before I had done any actual detecting, I read an article in the magazine that idealised my view of how it could and should be. The article was headlined 'The Hidden Valley Treasures' and in it a Wessex detectorist 'of 40 years' experience' called Mark Vine described the extraordinary finds he has made over the years on land attached to a seventeenth-century manor house in a corner of Dorset that is remote even by Dorset's standards of Hardyesque remoteness.

There were pictures of many of these finds, all of which seemed in fine condition – a twelfth-century lead 'textual amulet' often used in burials (placed on the abdomen and containing 'words of power'); Roman coins and brooches; a Tealby penny, Henry VIII groat and James VI of Scotland silver quarter merk (the equivalent of one English shilling, from the late sixteenth/early seventeenth century); a gold George III guinea; seventeenth-century bronze spurs inlaid with silver; a Bronze Age gold bead. Much more.

But it wasn't just the extent and quality of these finds that captivated me. Without precisely identifying the manor house and location, Mark painted a vivid picture of its dramatic history when it was the home of the Sydenham family, who supported the Parliamentarian cause in the Civil War.

Thomas Sydenham was a physician who wrote *Observationes Medicae*, a standard textbook on clinical medicine and epidemiology for two centuries. His eldest brother, William, distinguished himself in various battles against Royalist forces in Dorset and after the war became a close aide of Oliver Cromwell. Mark had written a book called *The Crabchurch Conspiracy* about William Sydenham's military exploits, and provided the inspiration and lyrics for an album of the same name by Dorset-based 'rebel gypsy folk band' The Dolmen.

This synergy of place, history and objects struck me as the recipe for detecting heaven and prompted me to contact Mark via *Treasure Hunting* magazine. My approach was a shameless fishing exercise for an invite to The Hidden Valley, and Mark was decent enough to oblige.

He promised to fix up a day for me to come over. All he had to do was clear it with the current owner of the manor house, a peer of the realm whose family had owned it since the early nineteenth century.

I heard nothing for a while. Then Mark sent me an apologetic email explaining that the owner did not want a stranger on his land – but that all was not lost. 'I have another estate in Dorset a bit nearer to you,' he wrote. 'It also happens to be the childhood home of the wife of Colonel William Sydenham. A beautiful Jacobean house.'

The present lord of the manor, Sam, was happy to have me apparently and Mark said he'd had three hammereds out of a field there recently – one Elizabeth I and two medieval. Aware by now of my obsession, he added: 'It's just a matter of time before your first hammered. And it's a wonderful feeling when it comes up.'

It went quiet again on the Wessex front. Then, a couple of days after I'd got back from Scotland, Mark hardened up the arrangement for the Jacobean house to a date and time.

'I've taken the liberty of inviting the greatest Dorset detecting legend of them all to join us,' he wrote. 'Mike Clark is his name, he's an old Poole fishing skipper and he has found some of the greatest treasures imaginable.'

The following week, in a dawn of frost and sunshine, I drove west to within six miles of Dorchester and turned into a driveway by a gatehouse and church. Waiting for me was a red pick-up that I then followed down the driveway, twisting between green fields, to a house of many windows and chimneys, with Flemish gables: Warmwell House. In front of the house an immaculately striped lawn unrolled to a hidden ditch that created an invisible join to the surrounding pastureland.

Though we had been in touch for weeks now, I had not set eyes on Mark till the moment he unfolded himself from the pick-up. He had long rock-star locks and out on the gravel he clapped me on the back and inducted me seamlessly into his comfort squad of wry middle-aged maleness. As well as Mike the old salt, there was stentorian-voiced Jon Dixon, known as The Preacher because he plays one (with uncanny conviction, apparently) in the English Civil War enactments they put on, and, standing proprietorially apart, Warmwell's owner Sam in loafers and with swept-back hair.

'Well, best of luck chaps,' said Sam, 'and whatever you find today I can guarantee it won't be as old as *this*.'

Strolling behind our parked vehicles, he pointed out an ammonite bigger than the hubcaps of my car, embedded in the end of a low wall: a *titanites giganteus* from Dorset's Jurassic Coast.

Sam disappeared through a double-arched loggia and back into the seventeenth century. Warmwell House was built on the site of an earlier manor by John Trenchard, the MP for Wareham, in 1618. There was a link, Mark told me as we walked back up the drive to our first field, between this house and The Hidden Valley he had written about in *Treasure Hunting*: it was John Trenchard's daughter, Grace, who had married William Sydenham.

Ever sleuthful, Mark had also spotted connections between both families and the Victorian novel *Moonfleet* by John Meade Falkner, set in the netherworld of eighteenth-century Dorset smugglers. The novel's young hero is called John Trenchard, the heroine Grace; 'Blackbeard's ghost' is the ghost of a character whose CV resembles William Sydenham's, having been a colonel in the Parliamentarian army and Governor of Carisbrooke Castle on the Isle of Wight, where

Charles I was imprisoned. In *Moonfleet*, 'Blackbeard' was rumoured to have stolen a diamond from the king.

'Was William Sydenham suspected of doing the same?' mused Mark. 'Is this a lost legend from that time?'

We turned off the driveway through a gate and crossed a field to the pasture we'd been allocated for the morning. Behind us was the church where John Trenchard was buried, ahead a sweep of pastureland and copses. This was all familiar terrain to Mark, who pointed at the next field over.

'See the corner of that wood? Never found any Roman there. All medieval. Then the other week my friend finds this phallic Roman pendant. He didn't know what it was, he was going to throw it away. I said, "What do you think it looks like?" He said, "It looks like a knob!" I said, "Yeah – that's what it is!" '

We talked about hammereds – the good chance I stood of finally finding one. I'd heard that before but let myself hope. Jon said ruefully, 'If there's a hammered in a field, Mark will find it. If there are a hundred hammereds, I'll manage to steer a clear path between the lot of them.'

Mike had offered to lend me his spare machine, which was a top-of-the-range XP Deus and to buy new would cost five times what I paid for my Q30. It would have sounded churlish to refuse. His detector picked up objects much better than mine, offering accurate signals and discriminating out most rubbish. But I was secretly annoyed, and would have preferred to stay in my comfort zone, because it takes time to learn to operate a new machine and I'd only just learned to read my own.

Now I knew I'd have to go back to detecting-by-numbers, deliberating over every action and signal. It would be like swapping my little hybrid for a supercar and expecting me to just jump in and drive at 300mph. I'd end up in the ditch. Sure enough, for the first hour I had a wobbly time. My targeting was often inaccurate, as bad as the early days, and I was wasting time digging ugly compound holes. At least, thanks to the machine's inbuilt discrimination, I wasn't hitting iron.

A small ball came up that Mark said was a pistol ball; then a slightly bigger ball from a small musket, both post-medieval, 1600–1800. Then a sliver of aluminium that, for a heady half-moment, I thought was a half-hammered. But I still didn't feel comfortable and was looking forward to the post-lunchtime session when, I had decided, I would politely revert to my own detector.

Meanwhile, I was enjoying the being-there. The low sun sparkled across the thick grass and brightened the Portland stone of the distant manor house. Rooks racketed in the fringe of woodland. I parked machine and digging tool in the lambda position – I was getting good at it by now and a bigger digging tool helped – and took some pictures of the arrow-shaped shadow they cast, pointing towards the house.

Then I looked over to see Mark resting on his knees over a hole while his upper body did a little jig. It was a coin but not a hammered. I walked across and Mark held it up: a big, bold, highly detailed thing with a frog-green patina.

'Sixteen ninety. Very unusual, I'd say. I *love* that.' He tossed it in his hand. 'Really chunky.'

The date was significant. It turned out this was an example of the brass, copper and pewter coinage issued to the Jacobite forces of the deposed James II during his war in Ireland against William III, William of Orange. The coins were known as 'gun money', as they supposedly came from melted-down guns, though other objects, such as church bells, were also used.

The idea was that following James's victory the soldiers would be entitled to redeem these base metal coins for silver ones. They even bore a month as well as a year of issue, to enable their phased replacement. But there was no victory. In 1690, the Protestant 'King Billy' sent the Catholic James packing at the Battle of the Boyne, the event still contentiously celebrated every year by the Orangemen of Ulster, and the coins became anomalies – not only hapless wallflowers whose silver knights never rode to their rescue but the only British coins ever to bear both year and month of issue.

Mike and Jon were on their own trips in far corners of the field. Mark said they'd all start heading back to the cars for lunch in 20 minutes or so. I resumed my sweeping without much conviction. I just wanted to reach half-time, then swap to my own machine and my mouth was thinking about cheese-and-pickle sandwiches. Then: a signal that I somehow knew was right, something that could not be bettered, like a penalty lashed sweetly into the top corner.

These spot-on signals happen, if at all, just once or twice a day. I had learned to savour them, take my time in the digging, for a great signal does not necessarily translate into a great find – it could just as likely be a moo tube or ring pull. Still, those moments of anticipation are an experience in themselves, worth lingering over. I removed my gloves, rubbed my mouth, took a swig of water, focusing on the target spot that I had scuffed with the toe of my boot.

Deep breath.

I slid the sharp tip of the digging tool into the earth about six inches off the bullseye and methodically worked the head of the tool around it till I had almost but not quite closed the circle. Then I levered up the big plug of earth I had sculpted till it was tipped upside down and, sitting there on the grass, looked like a large Christmas pudding. I knelt and stabbed the carrot into the pudding.

What followed took less than a minute. The target was in the clod, not still in the hole: a small disc. Fragile, some revealed silver. I peered, tried to spray off the mud but my muddied glove only re-smeared it. I found a tissue and rubbed. A cross on the silver. A cross!

A cross. I paused, took breath. Then I called over to Mark.

'Hey! I'm not saying anything but . . .'

He sensed the moment and hurried over. Took one look and raised his smiling face.

'Well done! A very nice hammered.'

'Sure?'

He hugged me. Handing it over, I almost dropped and lost it, my fingers panicking with the precious cargo on their tips. Even now there was room for Mark to row back on his diagnosis. I watched his face anxiously.

'I can't get the dirt off to see the date . . .' he said. 'But yes, there we go. I'd say Tudor.'

We put in another 15 minutes of detecting before lunch – dreamy, floating minutes for me. As we all funnelled back towards the house for our sandwiches Mike caught up with me.

'Well done, mate.'

'That's Dorset for you,' said Mark.

Back by the cars, we perched on the low wall alongside the giant ammonite and I unscrewed the top of my finds pod and lifted out the hammered.

'Oh, very nice,' said Jon. 'Definitely a Lizzie.'

He meant Elizabeth I. How did he know?

'Back pattern. Instead of a long cross, you've got a shield. But the head is the big giveaway.' I looked again. I could see the cross and the shield but the obverse, where the head should be – a likeness created by the Chief Engraver of the Royal Mint from his own master portrait – looked blobbish, detail-free.

Replacing the coin in the foam rubber, I anticipated the process of getting to know Lizzie better back at the cottage. The next day, with the help of my new magnifying glass and a copy of Spink's *Coins of England and the United Kingdom*, borrowed from neighbour David, I confirmed the coin as an Elizabeth I silver half-groat. I could make out the crown and the neck ruff but, disappointingly, the face remained a smooth mask, as is often the case with coins of Elizabeth I. (There are various possible explanations for this: that they were rubbed for luck; they were defaced by people who didn't like her, perhaps because she was a woman; or it's just general wear-and-tear. The truth is probably all of these.)

Then, trying to capture a good image of the half-groat with my iPad camera, I placed it on a sheet of A4 on a smooth kitchen surface and positioned my head torch to apply a strong side light, creating contrast and relief. The effect was startling. The bony ridge of her nose, her hooded eyes and pursed, determined mouth – Gloriana, the Virgin Queen, lived again.

Meanwhile, sitting on the wall in winter sun, I was feeling a rare contentment. This affable old Wessex crew had welcomed me aboard as if we were lifelong friends and the banter was flowing around me and occasionally, as if by chance, also spilling from my own mouth. For the first time, I felt a full part of the world of earth sifters and message collectors. Mark showed off his other find of the morning, a silver poesie ring with an inscription that was impossible to read without a magnifying glass.

Jon pretended to have a go anyway: ' "This ring . . . belongs to . . . Jon!",' he said, and mimed putting it in his pocket.

Then, as he passed it on to Mike, a bit of the ring fell off and we all got down on our hands and knees to search the gravel for it, probing with a carrot. But it was gone, prompting Mark to reminisce about a previous escapee – another piece of genital-themed jewellery, a Saxon phallic pendant.

'I think it might have gone down the back of the sofa – and then the sofa went to the dump,' he said.

All the time, I was thinking about my hammered. Who had it belonged to? The coin was contemporaneous with the beginnings of the present manor house. Whoever owned it would have seen the meretricious new edifice with its fashionable foreign-influenced façade taking shape across the meadows. If they could open their mouth to me now, would I understand the words that came out? Equally, would they understand my syntax, vocabulary and accent when we attempted to converse? What was the last item purchased by my half-groat? Idle thoughts that ran through me like sips of wine.

'It doesn't matter now what happens for the rest of the day,' I said to Mark. He smiled indulgently and I realised I was telling him something he had learned 25 years ago.

For the afternoon session we went on a new field, where the grass was thicker, and I went back to my own machine. My experience with the Deus supercar detector had set me thinking. Was it a coincidence that I had found the hammered with it? Or did it show just how crucial your kit was? Were there all these phantom finds out there, in Sussex and East Lothian, Hampshire, Gloucestershire and Norfolk, with my name fading to nothing on them? Impossible to know the answer to those questions, but I felt a stubborn loyalty to my modest Q30 and had no plans to upgrade. Whatever we found together, I'd be satisfied, I told myself primly.

In any case, none of us had any luck on the new field, so we went back on the old one after a while. But my concentration had gone; I can't even properly recall what I found that afternoon – a button and a buckle, I think, along with junk. My mind was endlessly retreading the unlikely path that had brought me here, through lockdown and adjusted horizons, and savouring the new status that finding the hammered had conferred on me. Blow me but I had just become a proper detectorist!

As the shadows lengthened, a pair of green wellies appeared by the lip of a hole I was digging (that turned out to contain an iron spike). I looked up at a swathe of green tweed.

'Any luck?' said Sam from above the tweed line, then added hastily. 'Show me later, show me later. You must come in for tea.'

As we trooped off the field, Mark told me that in the final half-hour Mike had found three hammereds.

'That's why they call him a legend,' he said.

Catching us up, Mike explained it thus: 'I was doing lines and *for some reason* [my italics] I decided to veer off.'

Afterwards I asked Mark about this. Had Mike been suggesting that something else was going on beyond his conscious control, some force that directed him off-piste, away from the rational system of searching he had devised for himself, towards those tiny, long-sunk beauties? Or was that all bollocks?

'Not bollocks at all, mate,' said Mark. 'Intuition, I believe, plays a big part in detecting. You can often start off with good intentions as to doing lines, but I often get drawn to an area of a field and something just tells me to concentrate on it, and I get results.'

We intuitive souls left our muddy boots in the loggia of Warmwell House and padded across the tiled hallway, past a nest of riding boots, into the dining room. The long table was big enough to seat ten and the walls were lined with portraits of Sam's bemedalled ancestors and an imaginary pastoral landscape (featuring a youth wearing nothing but a blue sheet) in a gilt frame by a seventeenth-century French painter, Gaspard Poussin.

It turned out that to top up the coffers Sam let out his beautiful gaff for grand weddings and society parties – 'which is perfect, as it was built for entertaining,' he said. On these occasions Mark, Mike and Jon provided the security, keeping on the acceptable side of boisterous the revellers cavorting across dewy lawns under summer moons. Now Sam ferried in mugs of tea and a plate of shortbread biscuits, and brought out a tray of more than 40 detecting finds from his fields that the lads have given him over the years.

These included a Roman trumpet brooch, several hammereds, lots of Roman coins (all from the third century AD) and a bow-like 'La Tène'-type Iron Age brooch (La Tène being a site in Switzerland where similar objects were first found). But the most resonant object was the personal seal of a previous owner of Warmwell that Mark had found in 2017 and given to Sam as the most appropriate custodian. It was an oval brass lozenge with the bust of a bewigged gent on one side and the intertwined initials 'JR' on the other: John Richards, the local squire in the late seventeenth and early eighteenth centuries.

'He seemed to spend most of his leisure time drinking, hunting and, sadly, hare coursing, so I suppose that was when he lost the seal,' said Mark.

According to one local historian, Richards also liked to stage cockfights and was 'by all accounts . . . bigoted and unpleasant'.

When conversation stalled momentarily, Sam said quietly (and it could have been a line from an M R James story): 'Do you know the story of the Warmwell Prophecy?'

Richards's predecessor as owner of Warmwell was John Sadler, who inherited the house through his marriage to John Trenchard's daughter Jane. Sadler was a prominent Parliamentarian figure who had served as Oliver Cromwell's personal secretary. When he retired to Warmwell after the Restoration, he was, said Sam, 'apparently much disordered of his senses and was having visions'.

One vision took the form of a man with a loud voice who appeared in his bedroom and 'had great things to tell him'. Ordering his servant to bring a pen and paper, and to summon the local minister as a witness, Sadler recorded what the vision told him.

'This is a facsimile of what they wrote down,' said Sam, pointing at a framed document in a window bay. 'The original is in the British Museum.'

The document is an affidavit written by the minister, Cuthbert Bound, entitled: 'A prophesy related by Mr John Sadler, late of Warmwell in the county of Dorset, who was a very learned and pious man, in the yeare after the return of king Charles the Second (1661).'

The 'prophesy' included plausible foretellings of three momentous events: the Plague of 1665 ('that there would die in the city of London soe many thousands . . .'); the Fire of London in 1666 ('. . . and the time that the city would be burnt downe, greate parte of it, and that he saw Poles [St Paul's] tumbled down . . .'); and the ill-fated Monmouth rebellion of 1685 ('. . . there would come three small ships to land to the West of Waymouth, that would put all England in an uproar, but it would come to nothing').

Sam said there is a 'fair possibility' that the room he sleeps in is the one where John Sadler claimed the phantom soothsayer appeared to him. He said he does not feel the presence of ghosts, but he ventured this observation: 'Life is full of mysteries.'

8

THE SEMI-CIRCULAR FEATURE

Then I got Covid, which left me feeling, like John Sadler, 'much disordered of my senses' for a week or so. As I was lying in bed with several digging tools embedded in my skull, I received an email from Kris the Kentish bleeps addict. I'd been trying to get him over for a day or two's detecting on my new permissions. The idea fitted with his new incarnation as a detectorist with wheels – he'd customised a van to sleep in and was planning to make 'on the road' videos featuring visits to detectorist buddies in other parts of the country.

In preparation for this branching-out, he had posted several mini-films of him converting the van and trialling nights out in it. I was fascinated by these videos. They were not about metal detecting at all, or even, in the end, about how to be a man in a van. They were about something I couldn't quite put my finger on.

In the videos he lined the interior of the van with thermal wrap, built a bed platform and stuck a crash mat on it for a mattress. On the roof he attached a solar panel for powering his portable power unit, which in turn charged his detector, drone, phone and laptop. There was carefully thought-out space for both domestic and detecting gear. Finally, he rigged the cabin with coloured lights and festooned it with stickers so that it looked like 'a Seattle underground rock club from 1988'. Then he took it on the road.

Lying in it in the dead of night, in the middle of nowhere, he pretended to be happy but didn't look it. It felt like an unconscious confessional, but of what I wasn't sure. On one occasion there were noises outside that frightened him and he suddenly seemed so lonely and bewildered that, watching him, I felt my eyes sting with tears.

We arranged for him to drive over from Kent and park in my driveway. My idea was that we would detect together during the day and in the evening he would retire to his van (there'd always be a bed on offer in the cottage, incidentally, but I knew he wouldn't take it) where I would join him for a session of chatting and (the ace up my sleeve) drinking Scotch. That way, I'd get to the bottom of the van business and discover the real Kris beneath the bearded bonhomie of his videos.

It was pure curiosity on my part. Ever since our first meeting, when he'd talked of the zone that metal detecting can take you to where you become nothing and no one, I'd wondered what demons he was hiding from. Mention metal detecting and most people still roll their eyes and snigger, in that patronising way I'd been guilty of myself, as if detectorists were just objects of fun and butts of jokes rather than real people. Kris was a complicated character, and detecting was a key element of his make-up, with the van a recent addition. It was a question of how it all fitted together.

But he kept postponing the trip over to Hampshire because, he said, the van was playing up. The latest email said: 'So, this past week has been a nightmare re the van . . .' I was starting to suspect that, sensing my curiosity, he was backing off and making excuses.

Manni, the committed field walker and in-denial detectorist, also got in touch via email: 'I was searching the Hants environment records and saw this behind your house. It's an undated semi-circular feature.' He had attached a link to the Historic Environment Record (HER) page, a map showing the location and an aerial photograph revealing an unmistakeable arc of darkening in the green field.

The spot was familiar, just the other side of the hill that rose behind the cottage. I had walked past it a thousand times and failed to notice any shape in the ground. I wanted to tip myself out of bed there and then and stagger up the hill to see how unobservant or otherwise I had been all these years – was there a visible ridge that I had missed? But I could barely make it as far as the bathroom, so I continued to stew in my own sweat, escaping in flights of fancy about the semi-circular feature and what it might be concealing.

The glow of finding the hammered had not worn off. It was still warming my soul even as Covid was chilling my bones. But my yearnings – what detectorists call their bucket list – had not worn off either, just redirected themselves. Roman (anything) was on the list, but the outlines of Bronze Age and Celtic worlds were also rising invitingly in my imagination. Closing my eyes, I saw round thatched huts on the hill behind the cottage, and campfires in the otherwise coal-black night.

After two days confined to bed, I felt well enough to decamp to the living-room sofa. As I dozed with the early evening local news on the TV, the words 'metal detectorists', 'Iron Age' and 'hoard' penetrated the fog of my Covid headache. Three detectorists had found 'almost three hundred' Iron Age coins in the New Forest in Hampshire. 'The three began searching the site after seeing a circle in the ground on Google Earth, which they suspected was a sign of a Celtic dwelling,' said the reporter.

Yikes! The TV now had my attention. The big, jolly head of the TV historian Dan Snow appeared. He was helping the St Barbe Museum in Lymington raise the £37,500 funds required to buy the hoard. He said it was important for it to remain 'close to the place where it was found, and maybe near the descendants of the men and women who buried it'. An archaeologist sitting in front of a bookshelf said that the discovery of the hoard had forced a re-think on the local history. 'We used to think the New Forest was a blank area,' he said.

The hill behind the cottage was no more of a blank area than that spot down the A31 in the New Forest had appeared to be. A semi-circular feature had been staring up at us all along. Our feature was on high ground. Safe. Long views. Could be Iron Age, or later. Or earlier. It *made complete sense* that it could be something significant. In fact, within five minutes I had convinced myself we were practically sitting on top of a mini Danebury Hill Fort.

Sitting out my isolation period, I could only plan and dream. The immediate and obvious problem was that Manni and I would need permission to detect the 'undated semi-circular feature', and that I was pretty sure the owner of the field it was located on was none other than Farmer Quad Bike.

It was out of the question for me to approach this farmer, as robust views had been exchanged between us over my inadvertent trespass and we did not part on good terms. My initial thought was that I could send Manni off to knock on his door instead, without filling him in on the background, but I decided this would be cowardly. Then I thought to double-check the ownership of the field and discovered that I had been mistaken. It belonged to a couple who lived in a house called ——— Farm on the road that ran along the base of the hill to the south-west.

Researching this couple, I discovered that they were keen golfers. I knew nothing about golf but considered whether, in my pitch to them, I might throw in a golfing analogy along the lines of detecting offering a similar (maddening, addictive) mix of hope and frustration. In the end I decided to just walk over there, introduce myself as a long-standing neighbour and turn their heads by showing them a couple of the finds from my neighbour David's paddocks.

The isolation period ran out and I was quick out of the blocks the following morning. Walking up the hill, past the spot where I'd found the buckle, I felt out of breath. But then I reached the location of the semi-circular feature and forgot about the tightness in my chest. How could I have failed to spot it over all these years? Under its blanket of grass and clover, a ridge was clearly visible, curving out towards the patch of woodland behind the cottage, following the same line as a bank of trees some 30 yards in front so that they were like a pair of spaced brackets:)).

The line of trees formed a natural belvedere beyond which the final shallow breathings of the South Downs faded to a hazy horizon. When the valleys were covered in forest and there were any number of hostile people out there intent on caving your head in and nicking your bear skin, you would feel pretty safe in this high spot. What a permission this could turn out to be!

Walking down the other side of the hill towards ——— Farm, I rehearsed my patter to blackbirds rustling about in the base of the hedgerow. Through the glass panels of the front door of the farmhouse, I could see an old OS map framed on the wall, and below it a carved wooden bench with armrests at either end that looked as if it could once have been a church pew. I took these as promising signs. In the glass itself I spotted my reflection – hair combed, chin shaved, my features set in a tone of respectful neighbourliness. Ready as I'd ever be, I rang the doorbell.

No answer, but there were signs – an open side door, a gardening trug – that people were close by. I finally tracked them down to the stableyard behind the farmhouse. An elderly lady – Mrs Smith – dressed in no-nonsense country garb cruised towards me.

'Sorry to bother you . . .' I said, and launched into my spiel.

She listened with a polite pretence of interest, then summoned Mr Smith, who appeared round the corner with his hands full of horse-related equipment. And we all got on swimmingly.

The Smiths did indeed own that field and had had no idea that a feature of possible archaeological significance was located on it. When I showed them a print-out of the HER record they said, 'Well I never!' Mr Smith said that he had always enjoyed the long views from there and that a neighbour claimed to have once seen the spire of Salisbury Cathedral from that very spot.

This struck me as unlikely – the cathedral is 40 miles due west – but then I remembered that driving east along the high chalk ridge of the Hog's Back in Surrey a few weeks before I had been able to see the London skyline of Canary Wharf, The Shard, etc., a comparable distance away.

Even before I produced my goody bag of finds, the Smiths seemed happy with the idea of me and my detecting buddy (I also asked on

Manni's behalf) giving their field the once-over. They even invited me on to the paddocks behind the farmhouse.

Then I got out the old buckle, the dandy button and the rare George IV penny and touted them as examples of the kinds of finds we might make, explaining that the decorated button had once been attached to the frock coat of an eighteenth-century swell or dandy, hence the name.

'No idea how it got to be in such an out-of-the-way rural spot,' I said.

'Chap out hunting, I expect,' said Mr Smith.

I hadn't thought of this. Of course! *Chap out hunting!*

The rain came and the forecast was poor for several days. Manni and I fixed on the first day of half-decent weather to do the field with the semi-circular feature. The day before, with the rain still falling in a fine drizzle, I went for a walk around the neighbouring fields and as I was crossing a plantation of young trees spotted the unmistakeable silhouette of a detectorist going about his business.

My first thought was that it was the same one I had met all those years ago, the one whose sandwich Bertie had eaten. My second thought was proprietorial – how dare someone else detect in my neck of the woods? I veered off the footpath towards him and, seeing me approaching, he called out, 'Can I help you?'

'I'm a detectorist too!' The phrase, I was surprised to note, came out naturally.

As I got nearer, I realised it was not the same person I'd met before. This one was taller, bulkier, with feathery hair like a 1970s footballer.

'Found much?' I said.

Not really, was the answer: 'A horseshoe, a billhook.' (I wasn't sure what a billhook was but nodded as if I was only too familiar with them.)

When I said I'd only been detecting for a few months, he launched into a lengthy bout of mansplaining – a mode of communication that evidently came so naturally to him that a female audience was optional.

'It's all about the *grrr* and the *bing*,' he said as I tried in vain to tell him about my paltry but precious haul of buckle, penny and dandy button I'd found nearby. 'And it's no good sweeping like this', he said, swinging his coil like a priest with a censer. 'They do say, "Keep low and slow. Loooow and sloooow." Like soooo . . .' As I walked off, he said, 'Remember the *binggg* . . .'

'What a boring twat he was,' I said to Manni the next morning.

It was a fine morning for finding an Iron Age hoard. Before departing east, the rain had rinsed the sky a glacial blue. A quarter moon hung low over the woods behind the cottage and the sun was illuminating avenues of cobwebs across the field containing 'the feature'. Far away, someone was shooting rabbits or crows.

After 20 minutes I had found two shotties and a moo tube. Then Manni called out.

'Pottery! Iron Age!'

I said to myself, *I knew it!* This field was the business. He came running over and held out two small dark shards.

'Sure?' I said.

'And I'm getting a good signal underneath. Could be an Iron Age hoard!'

We ran back. Manni knelt and dug furiously. I patted my pockets for my phone, turned the camera on ready for the moment. His shoulders slumped, he shook his head. It was a ploughshare. Reconsidering the potsherds, he said he thought they might be Roman, not Iron Age. And even then only maybe.

We continued, sweeping across the semi-circle of the ridge and the slopes to either side. Water was sparkling in a natural depression that formed a dew pond. It all felt so right, as right as I'd known it. The sense of things being down there was palpable. I kept anticipating those diamond-sharp signals that make your heart race – the dopamine hit of the beautiful find . . . but for the next hour or so we found nothing except more moo tubes.

When we next ran into each other, Manni had evidently been rethinking our Iron Age assumptions.

'I wonder if we could have something even older up here. Stone Age. Because they made earthworks and didn't leave a trace. I might have found a Stone Age arrowhead.' He held out a small, sharp shard of semi-translucent ochre flint.

'Hey, remember the Neolithic scraper,' I said. Was this the place it had washed down from, over the millennia?

The rest of the morning was about as lively as a straight line on a heart monitor until we sat down for sandwiches on the stumps of trees among the natural belvedere. Twenty years ago, on a summer night of a full moon so bright it threw hard shadows across the greyscale fields, three of us came up here with a bottle of wine and moonbathed, like the man that Thomas De Quincey came across on one of his nocturnal Lakeland walks, 'apricating himself in the occasional moonbeams'.

Manni pointed me west with his finger to Roman Ridge.

'See the pylon and the row of houses, the field behind that with the woods above?'

The field was long and straight, below a wooded crest, above the boggy valley. A logical route for a road to take. High in the sky, the sun-flecked speck of a passenger jet just missed the moon on its silent passage from Paris to Dublin or Copenhagen to New York.

A thought landed with a thud in my head. I was going to share it with Manni, then decided that talk of my dead dust would not interest a lad with so much of his life still to live. The thought was a good one though, solid as St Kilda: I'd be happy to be scattered here, in the mysteries and the long views. I just needed to tell my partner before I forgot (which I have remembered to do, so that bit of afterlife housekeeping is settled).

In the afternoon I finally got something that looked promising as it sat there in the hole – what Chris would call a 'round in the ground', a coin. Brushing off the soil, I recognised it immediately.

'Lizzie!' I bellowed to Manni, who hurried over.

'No way!' he said.

I held it out: 'Lizzie the Second.'

This was a joke I had heard another detectorist tell. I'd found a 1962 penny – not even the year of the Beatles' first LP, just their first single.

Shortly afterwards, Manni made the find of the day, a small coin that he confirmed later to be a Charles II farthing. That was a good return for him, but I felt short-changed. As the sun dropped, the outlines of old field strips became visible in the low light. I swept past a solitary half-opened daisy. A fly buzzed past my ear. Manni got a conical piece the diameter of a saucer with a nipple-like protrusion and a serrated edge – one cup of Boudicca's brassiere? A 1930s doorbell? As the sky turned the cold pink of a good rosé, we agreed to pack it in, leaving two-thirds of the field still undetected.

The day had not gone according to plan. I had had a *feeling* about that field. I had been so sure it would be full of plums and happy to surrender them and I'd been wrong. Either my intuition had malfunctioned or the whole idea of detectorists having a sixth sense was indeed bollocks. On the other hand, the field had been telling me *something*, because it made me want to have my ashes scattered across it. And there was plenty of it still to check out.

I had the slightly nutty idea that maybe a field gets annoyed when a detectorist rocks up presuming to know its secrets, so it decides to play hard to get. I had already found a possible provenance for the Neolithic scraper. I needed to get to know the field even better, show it patience.

Manni went off to Leipzig for a few months to brush up on his German, which put the field in mothballs till he returned – as he was the one who had spotted the semi-circular feature, it would be breaking an unwritten code for me to go on it alone. His absence also meant that exploration of his promising Roman permissions in and around the village would have to wait.

Meanwhile, I accepted an invitation from the Smiths to detect on the five acres of paddocks behind their house. The first field felt gagged from the first second. Almost all land chatters, the mineralisation of the soil forming a background crackle like the murmur of a half-full pub and the objects grunting and howling like half-cut punters. And then occasionally a perfectly formed sentence flows out of this muddy soundscape and you know that the past is trying to gain your attention.

But today there was nothing. Even quieter than the field in East Lothian. I moved to the top where a gap in the hedge gave access to another of the Smiths' paddocks. Here I had a cup of tea and a digestive biscuit, reflecting on the loneliness of hearing nothing. Even drunk mumblings are better than the indifference of silence. Then I reset the ground balance – minimising the chatter of mineralisation, the better to hear the good signals – and plunged into the fresh promise of green.

Within seconds it was as if the landscape had been unmuted. The grunts, squeaks and, yes, *bingggs*, came thick and fast. Over the following 20 minutes I found: a buckle, with some age to it; a section of horse harness; a numbered cattle tag that had once been clipped to a sheep's or cow's ear; a moo tube (just the one); lots of boats; and a small oblong plate with a solitary scrolled upper-case L incised on it, thus: $\mathscr{L}$.

Hedge fodder really, but my spirits were lifted. Then, as I was detecting alongside the boundary of a garden attached to a bungalow, a dog I had not spotted barked at me, giving me such a fright that I dropped my digging tool, which got entangled with the cord of my headphones, which in turn wrapped itself around my legs and brought me down like a textbook rugby tackle.

The detector, which I had somehow managed to keep hold of, was now squawking and spluttering in public and I realised that the headphone cord had been yanked out of its socket. From my horizontal position, I peered across the tufted grass at a small black terrier behind the garden fence who was staring back with a look of amazement, struck dumb, after his initial barkfest, by the phenomenon of a human being keeling over then starting to emit strange noises.

When I had recovered my natural poise, I discovered that the headphone cord had been ripped from its plug. The cans would need replacing – an opportunity to upgrade to cordless, which I did on the phone later that day. The new headphones came with a dongle that plugged into the socket and a strip of Velcro to secure it to the shaft of the detector – 'so it doesn't dangle,' explained the man down the line from the metal-detecting shop.

'Ah. To prevent dongle dangle,' I said.

There was a pause before the man replied, 'That's *funny*. I'll remember that.'

I gave the new headphones a run-out in the orchard – the first time I'd detected in there since my very first day as a detectorist. Last year's nettles had died back, so I scoured around the areas where they'd been, enjoying the novelty of not having the headphone cord trying to trip me up. The orchard was immediately chatty, though it wasn't making any sense. Then a strong signal cut through. I hadn't expected to find anything – this was just a quick spin to test the new equipment – and when I turned up, from just under the surface, a flat piece of irregular shape, I assumed it was junk.

Back in the cottage I brushed off the mud and an incomplete piece of decorative metalwork appeared, with an incised six-petalled flower and other curves and loops on it. I went down the now familiar route of photographing it and sending the image to a couple of buddies, whose opinions tallied, and cross-referencing their diagnosis with examples on the Portable Antiquities Scheme (PAS) database. This led me to a near-identical example.

It was a furniture fitting, specifically the 'escutcheon' or protective plate behind a drawer handle, and it dated from 1600 to 1700. Perhaps some rickety old sideboard had been chopped up for firewood and its metal bits chucked in the orchard. Apart from General Gordon of Khartoum, this was the first object I had found that related directly to the interior, domestic world of the cottage. But its relative smartness puzzled me. I'd understood that pre-nineteenth century the cottage was a bit of a bumpkins' hovel, occupied by several families (there are still two front doors and two garden paths of old brick, with signs of a third, bricked-up door). A history of the local village even records the vicar visiting a woman living in the cellar. What were they doing with a fancy bit of furniture work like this?

My local permissions were coming thick and fast now. One – a set of paddocks owned by friends – bordered the field (owned by you-know-who) where in 1845 a gold Bronze Age torc was ploughed up. Having passed through various pairs of local hands, it was sold at Sotheby's in 1925 to the Royal Cornwall Museum in Truro, where it is now on permanent display. The proximity of this new permission to the find spot of the torc had me dreaming of more ancient objects than I had found so far. Even gold!

For my first outing there, I decided to invite my partner. After I asked her for a new, bigger digging tool for my birthday, she had taken to expressing concern for the person I was becoming. When the new headphones arrived, she had caught me parading around in them in the kitchen with what she said was an inane expression on my face, a spectacle that she believed justified her worry.

'Come and see what all the fuss is about,' I said. 'And if you get bored, you can pop back and have a cup of tea with Louise.'

'When, not if,' she replied.

We did it on a Monday morning. Farmer Quad Bike was ploughing the next field, pursued by a wheeling flock of seagulls. After an uneventful hour, we shared a cup of tea from the Thermos and watched a hare run across the paddock. I then told her the hare-related Boudicca story. To her credit, she did not slope off back to see Louise but stuck it out for another hour. Over the two hours I found nothing but junk and a 1971 penny. As we trudged back to the car, she broke the silence by saying in a vague manner, 'No, I *can* see how you could get hooked on it . . . well, *I* wouldn't get hooked on it . . .'

My haul of potentially significant finds had been so meagre that I had not arranged a face-to-face meeting with the local Finds Liaison Officer (FLO), Jenny Durrant, to register them with the PAS. But I had been saving them up, always noting where and when I found anything I thought might make the grade. To pin down the find spots, I had used the 'what3words' app, which divides up the entire surface of the globe into three-metre (ten-foot) squares (57 trillion of them!) and gives each square an address expressed in three random words.

This is not as precise as a ten-figure grid reference using longitude and latitude – which is theoretically accurate down to the square metre – but is still pretty good and vastly simpler. It also generates strange poetry-like fragments reminiscent of David Bowie's cut-up method of lyric writing that he took from William S Burroughs: 'translate.alley.carpeted' is in a field in North Wales; 'traded.lend. punchy' is part of a street in Aberdeen. Each find is thus immortalised in a flicker of verse.

After turning up the furniture fitting, I finally felt I had accumulated some items worthy of half an hour of the FLO's time. We arranged a meeting at the offices of the Hampshire Cultural Trust on the edge of Winchester, housed in a former riding stables at the end of a lane chopped off by the cutting of the M3 motorway. And there it was, in a large room of boxes and wide tables, that I laid out five objects for Jenny to inspect, muttering that I believed they all passed the basic test of being pre-1700 but adding, 'There's nothing earth-shattering, I'm afraid.'

Representing the very acme of my metal-detecting career to date, the items I had chosen were: buckle, dandy button, Viking gaming piece, furniture fitting and hammered coin. Not all of them had been found in Hampshire – the coin was from Dorset, the gaming piece from Norfolk – but FLOs are happy to record out-of-county finds. I had placed each in a grip-seal bag and I now spread these across the table.

Wearing a flowery mask and almost-matching flowery top, Jenny examined each, occasionally passing them under a magnifying glass. This was a tense moment for me. I had got used to these finds being what I had decided they were, based on similar finds on the PAS database but also, I had to admit, on an element of wishful thinking. She would be putting them through the official identification process but made an initial examination as we sat there – and it was a relief to find that my suppositions seemed more or less correct.

She also clarified some confusions – as to why so many buckles are found by detectorists, for example. Assuming these were primarily belt buckles, I had imagined trousers falling down on a regular basis and the fields of yore being full of peasants waddling about like debagged prep-school oiks. But Jenny pointed out that there was more to buckles than trouser belts – clothing, baggage and horse fittings would have been festooned with them: 'You'd have straps and attachments on your clothing – trousers buckled at the knee, for example, and you might not notice if the buckle fell off.'

The button, with its slightly off-kilter decoration, seemed to intrigue her.

'It's a debased [i.e. rather crudely done] flower motif – I'm pretty sure that's a thistle design. Very, very stylised,' was her preliminary verdict.

On the other hand, the hammered Lizzie – this tiny silver disc that more than any other object I had found beckoned me across the centuries and, so far at least, defined me as a detectorist – merited scarcely a glance.

I had been worried about the gaming piece. Was confirmation bias yet again skewing me towards a glamorous but false ID – Viking chess! – when all along it was just a lead weight? Jenny hesitated, saying there was an ongoing debate on the subject.

'Where did you find it?' she asked.

'Norfolk.'

To my silent joy, this answer tilted her towards 'gaming piece'.

The furniture fitting, she said, belonged to a piece of 'middling status'. So what was it doing in a humble country abode, where the furniture it was part of may have stood on a dirt floor?

'Was the cottage associated with a landowner?' she asked.

Probably, was the answer – the oldest deeds we have, from the end of the nineteenth century, show it then belonged to a local estate. Apparently, in such a feudal set-up, the toffs sometimes deigned to hand down household items that had seen better days – as wedding gifts, for example.

Knowing that I was a rookie detectorist, Jenny also found time to discuss wider, philosophical issues. As she said, when I bought the metal detector there was no requirement for me to register as a new user, nor did it come with any information on the legal requirements and ethical responsibilities.

'There's nothing that says you've got to get permission, that you can't detect on scheduled monuments,' she said. 'It should be a simple thing to do, I don't know what the resistance is from the manufacturers.'

That said, Jenny was anxious to point out that she was not one of the old-school anti-detectorist archaeologists.

'Without them, I wouldn't exist, the role of the FLOs wouldn't exist,' she said. 'Metal detectorists have revolutionised our understanding of history in this country. The sorts of things that are found on archaeological excavations are not the sorts of things that are being found by metal detectorists. The finds that detectorists are making have completely altered our understanding.'

One simple example: Roman coins have enabled the accurate mapping of where the Romans went and settled. Then think about all the wonderful hoards (not just Roman) of the last 30 years, generating endless excavations, research papers, grants, books, exhibitions, lecture topics, TV programmes – apart from anything, we've been keeping the academics busy!

Jenny said she also understood the buzz and addictive dimension of the hobby: 'That sense of discovery, of finding something buried in the soil and holding it, touching it for the first time in hundreds of years – I call it the magic moment. And that is really special . . .' I sensed a 'but' coming, '. . . but what frustrates me is when that is kept to the individual or their small group, for approved friends and acquaintances.

'I strongly feel that heritage belongs to us all. It's not an individual, private thing and I think that's where the difference between archaeologists and detectorists comes in, that detectorists – this is a massive generalisation, I'm aware of that – are much more in it for the sort of individual experience and enjoy being out by themselves in a field in a space and connecting with that moment, whereas archaeologists are much more about telling the bigger story and how that can help us *all* understand that field in that space.'

Her distinction and reservations made me feel uncomfortable. However much I had learned about the wider implications of the hobby, and despite possessing what I liked to think of as a reasonable sense of social responsibility and a fast-improving historical perspective, it was still the 'magic moment' that floated my boat – the instant, individual gratification of it.

'Has any good treasure come in recently?' I asked Jenny as I was leaving.

'A hoard of Viking silver ingots,' she said. 'And Bronze Age gold. Lots of Bronze Age gold comes up in Hampshire. Which is quite nice.'

Driving home between Hampshire fields, I imagined all the torcs out there, awaiting my touch.

A couple of days later, I watched the first episode of the new series of a long-running TV show about archaeology. A team of middle-aged, middle-class people in lumpy T-shirts sweated heavily under summer sun as they dug a very long trench, carting the soil away in millions of buckets, then spent endless hours on their hands and knees, scraping away at the exposed undersoil with ridiculously small trowels.

Detectorists are sceptical of such programmes, believing they are edited to make sure a metal detector or detectorist rarely if ever creeps into shot even though they are widely used on archaeology digs. Now they mentioned it, I could see this might be the case. Certainly, the overall impression conveyed is that archaeological finds are made exclusively in trenches by archaeologists and volunteers with trowels, on official digs usually sponsored by a university department – whereas the truth, even allowing for the fact that metal detectors find only metal objects, is that 90 plus per cent of archaeological finds made in any given year are made by detectorists.

By the first commercial break, our friends in their sweaty T-shirts were looking increasingly hot and bothered and had not found so much as a Roman hobnail. On the other side of the adverts, the archaeologist in charge, sporting a fetching linen sun hat, announced that the trench was in the wrong place – they would need to fill it all in and start again.

'Hey, mate,' I found myself shouting at the telly, 'you should take up metal detecting!'

9

WHERE THE BODIES
ARE BURIED

I was now a cheerleader for the tribe. When I took up the hobby, I'd been selective in who I'd mentioned it to, but I had reached the out-and-proud stage. Metal detecting was part of the routine of my days and I let the subject emerge naturally in conversations with my (middle-class) friends and acquaintances.

If they sniggered – which most of them did, with horrible smirks – I'd ask them why they found it so funny. One friend said, 'That's a new one on me.' He meant, metal detecting wasn't cycling (becoming a MAMIL, a Middle-Aged Man In Lycra, was considered a more acceptable form of middle-aged crisis management), or birdwatching, or beekeeping or even, for crying out loud, golf.

The gear in the porch was seasoned and muddied, I had dedicated detectorist clobber hanging on pegs there and every time I walked past it on my way to the garden or the car it beckoned me out on to imagined fields. For the next outing, I needed wellies too. I'd had a new permission earmarked for when Kris got his van together and came over, but then he invited *me* out, and I was relieved because I'd been getting paranoid that he was avoiding me – that I was too weirdly nosy, and too much of a crap beginner, to share detecting days out with.

I felt honoured to be included in this gig. It was an exploration of the foreshore of Portsmouth Harbour and on the ticket was Kris's fellow YouTuber Simon, who posts hugely popular videos of mudlarking on the Thames under the title Si Finds (when I mentioned in an email to Manni that I was going mudlarking with Si Finds, he replied, 'The Si finds!?? Lucky you, I'm a fan of his, haha'). I felt, courtesy of Kris's patronage, I was being parachuted directly into detecting's elite echelons.

Kris and Si were making a video together and hoping for naval/ military stuff, the harbour and dockyard being arguably the most famous nexus of maritime history and lore in the world. For me, it was an opportunity to detect for the first time on the edge of sea and land – as well as perhaps finding time at the end of the day for a guided tour of Kris's van.

Britain's foreshore, defined as the land between mean high and mean low water, is mostly (but not entirely) the property of the Crown Estate, which grants a 'permissive right' for metal detecting on it, without need of formal consent. But on the Gosport side, the public infrastructure of fences and walls around the mouth of Portsmouth Harbour conspires to imply that this territory is out of bounds and dangerous – and it *is* treacherous without a mud pilot to guide you along the shingle spits and steer you clear of the sudden sucking sloughs of river clay.

Kris had arranged for just such a guide, a black-clad mudlarking detectorist called Rich who, it turned out, knew where the bodies were buried. It was a breezy late winter Saturday of scudding clouds and for around five hours, straddling the mid-afternoon low-tide time, we had this watery, ambivalent realm to ourselves.

Rich, having the spirit of the urban explorer about him, had recommended bringing an extendable ladder to lower on to the foreshore from a gap in the railings at a certain vulnerable point (he emailed map and photograph to identify the spot). We decided instead to access it from the end of a tidal creek a mile or so inland. We would rendezvous with Rich halfway up the creek, by a culvert he identified as a bottle dump, and he would lead us back to the harbour.

The creek was a ship's graveyard. At one time or another, dozens of smacks, tugs, ferries and Royal Navy vessels had been sailed up it and either broken up or scuttled. A website called The Derelict Miscellany has an apt description of the scene: 'Along the backwater shore they lie, bleached whalebone wrecks garlanded with sea-slime, berthed in black mud.' The mud and Swarfega-green slime were alien and off-putting to me. I was used to chalkland and pasture, solid earth under my no-nonsense hiking boots. I knew where I stood with them. Now I was wearing cheap invertebrate wellies and I was slithering, all at sea.

For the first time, I had to set the search mode of my machine to 'Saltwater' rather than 'Field'. This filters out the chatter caused by increased conductivity and high mineral levels in the water, but the tones and ID numbers are completely different.

'What do I listen out for?' I wailed petulantly at Kris.

'The good signals will sound like Sweep,' he said, referring to the canine half of that anarchic duo of TV glove puppets, Sooty and Sweep. He demonstrated by sweeping his machine over his metal spade. The detector made a familiar reedy squeak. We bent double with laughter. 'Who doesn't want their metal detector to sound like Sweep?' he said.

'Did Sooty ever say anything?' Si mused. We agreed that he didn't.

Sooty let his magic wand do the talking and his catchphrase – 'Izzy wizzy, let's get busy' – was spoken by a man with his hand up his back. Si's catchphrase, which he articulates himself, has echoes of Sooty's: 'Let's get some luck in the mud!'

As well as mudlarking the Thames foreshore, he and his mate Steve explore the mudflats of the estuary as the Hovercraft History Hunters. His well-crafted videos, combining a sense of adventure with some bizarre finds (such as a dump of thousands of old London lampposts and street lamps) attract hundreds of thousands of views.

From the Essex–London borderland of Upminster, Si has a matey on-screen persona and, like Kris, is warm and easy-going off-screen as well as phenomenally knowledgeable on the tokens and clues of the past.

'It's good to find another YouTuber,' Kris had told me a little wistfully. 'It can be lonely, making videos on your own.'

In this world of land and sea, and the gradations in between, your targets are not just buried in the ground – in this case, mud, silt and clay – but up on the surface, half-embedded in the glutinous top layers and shrouded in slime and seaweed. And they are not just made of metal. We were also on the search for bottles, earthenware jars, pottery and clay pipes (there was a clay-pipe factory at Portchester, north of the harbour, in the early nineteenth century that had a government contract to supply Portsmouth Dockyard) – which meant we were looking with our eyes as well as our machines.

With his finds bucket and dry bag, Si was in his element, quartering the creek with mud-tuned eyes. Despite wearing his 'Darth Vaders' (waders), Kris felt, like me, 'freaked out' by the unreliable medium we were struggling through and the thought of what might lie beneath. 'Remember *Stand by Me*? he said, referring to the scene in Rob Reiner's coming-of-age movie in which the kids are covered in leeches as they splash along a riverbed.

But then we reached the culvert and bottle dump, where we were to wait for our guide Rich before proceeding towards the harbour, and I began to relax into the mudness of it. The signals – those comical Sweep squeaks – were refreshingly sharp and easy to identify compared to the often ambiguous signals on dry land. I pulled out another 2p piece and a cigar-shaped lead fishing sinker. Then a gold bullet.

'Bloody hell! Hey! Gold bullet!' I shouted.

The others gathered round. It unscrewed in two places and was a replica of a .303 round. 'Something "vapey"?' said Kris.

'What do you call those things you shove up your bum? Suppository!' suggested Si. Then we noticed it had a hole at one end to loop a chain through – it was a pendant of some sort. It went in my finds bag pending later investigation.

The mud was becoming strangely attractive. Glistening black and eggy smelling on the surface, it gave way within a few inches to a dense grey-blue clay. Blundering around in it and enjoying the textures, my feet stuck fast. Both wellies were deeply sunk. I couldn't face the ignominy of having to request help and tried to extricate myself with as little fuss, and as much dignity, as possible, hoping Kris and Si wouldn't notice.

Tugging on the right leg, I lifted foot and welly clear and planted them gratefully on a slab of concrete – but at the expense of the left foot sinking even deeper. 'Errr, guys . . .' I said. Kris came to my rescue while Si filmed it on his phone. My left socked foot sprang from the welly and hovered as if of its own volition as I teetered. Mud and clay – black and grey – were flying everywhere. I had not been this mud-splattered since I was about three. It was proper cool.

At this point Rich appeared, rounding the mudbanks of the headland that lay between us and the harbour. Bang on time. Beanie hat pulled down on his forehead. Quietly authoritative. He had the mudflats and foreshore laid out in his head like a Middle Eastern souk. Instead of kilims and lanterns, spices and jewellery, it was broken bottles and crockery there, pipe stems and bowls there, lead shot and bullets *there* . . .

'Any hammereds at all?' ventured Kris. When Rich shook his head, I was relieved. With no possibility there was no pressure.

Before setting off for the harbour, we loafed around the culvert. Si was digging for bottles. He turned up half a dozen in two spadefuls. There were plenty of Shippam's Paste bottles, probably because the factory had been down the road in Chichester. I pocketed a perfect specimen that had been lying on the surface. Wide-topped and vertically ribbed, with SHIPPAM'S emblazoned diagonally across it, it was another reminder, after Sooty and Sweep, of childhood: of crab paste smeared thickly on teatime bread. Later I would use the Shippam's bottle as a vase for small spring flowers.

Having a dig myself, I came up with a bottle of standard lozenge shape with sloping neck, embossed thus on front and sides: 'SCOTTS EMULSION'; 'COD LIVER OIL'; 'WITH LIME AND SODA'.

I held the top to my nose. After possibly a hundred years, the bottle still harboured the viscous smell of fish oil.

A variety of bottles was now arrayed at jaunty angles in the mud. Should we take them home? 'I'd have all those but she wouldn't let me,' said one. The others agreed – their wives had reached the limit of old bottles they would permit to cross the threshold. Someone found an old wooden rolling pin and waved it around like Mr Punch.

We had become four silly boy-men playing in mud and casting music-hall aspersions on our other halves. I thought back to Kris's mention of *Stand by Me* and felt a sudden bond of gentle maleness with these strangers. The moods and patterns of boyhood we had clicked into felt all the warmer for being totally unexpected. And they kept on coming.

From the bottle dump, we followed Rich back towards the harbour, sticking to the shingle as far as possible. When we came to a narrow inlet, he advised against just leaping from one bank to the next – the mud looked firm but could be deep and treacherous at this point. Instead, we crossed on the slippery, sloping deck of a boatwreck, a manoeuvre that was tricky in itself. Beyond the ribs of a half-dissolved wooden hull that looked like the salvaged Tudor warship *Mary Rose* – the real thing lay barely a mile away across the harbour – Si ventured away into grey mudland and, sounding alarmingly like an Enid Blyton character, called out, 'Ginger beer!'

It was easily missed, a sand-coloured stoneware bottle lying on its side and three-quarters submerged. Lifting it, he revealed the name Mumby – the soft-drinks manufacturer Charles Mumby who operated from a shop in Gosport High Street in the mid-nineteenth century. The local connection was much prized.

'Happy with that!' said Si.

And so we loitered and circled in mudlarking fashion till we arrived at the mouth of the creek and were hit between the eyes by the panorama that unfolds there. Having spent the previous two hours peering no more than six feet in front of our noses, we were unprepared for the sight of sister aircraft carriers HMS *Prince of Wales* and *Queen Elizabeth* docked bow to stern at the Naval Base across the harbour, their officially grey hulls and superstructures looking more like a camp shade of teal in the afternoon sun.

Maritime history lay about us.

'See the mast sticking up there?' said Rich, pointing beyond the deck of the *Prince of Wales* to a filament, thin as saffron, against the sky. 'That's the *Victory*.'

Ahead of us, a shingle spit curled out to a tidal island called Rat (or Burrow) Island, its eroded banks festooned with red notices: 'Ministry of Defence Property. Keep Out.' At our feet, railway tracks stretched off into the slime, the remains of a railway once used at low tides to transport superfluous explosives from the old armaments depot in Gosport to Rat Island to be blown up in safety.

While Kris and Si went off fossicking on their own, Rich escorted me along the spit to Rat Island. Though the signs warned us to keep out, we kept to the tidal side of them, in that intertidal space where no one could get us. A police launch was bustling about the harbour. At one point it appeared to shadow us, as if trying its best to think of a reason to turn us back. But we were on the right side of the tide and the law.

The fencing around the island that reinforced the message of the keep-out signs was new, said Rich – possibly put there after homeless people tried to camp there during lockdown. This reminded me that as we made our way around the creek to the bottle dump we had passed the blue tent of a homeless man, carefully located in the safety zone of the foreshore. A mountain bike was parked next to the tent, in a poignant echo of the hatchback in the suburban driveway.

The mud bubbled and oozed beneath our boots. We were treading on smoothed brick, cockle shells and black seaweed. 'You'll see the graves soon,' said Rich. 'I don't want to be morbid but they do make you think.'

On our right, the raised shoreline of the island steepened into shingle cliffs that had been eaten into by the tides. At their base were three, possibly four slots where coffins and bodies had been found. An old car tyre lay in one of the empty graves.

'They were uncovered a few years ago in bad storms,' said Rich. 'Probably Napoleonic prisoners of war.'

We contemplated them in silence for a few seconds, me thinking along the lines that Rich had invited me to, about time and fate. Then I noticed, near my right boot, the stem of a clay pipe and wondered absurdly if the pipe had belonged to any of the men whose graves I was now looking at. I stooped to retrieve the partly charred, nicotine-yellow cylinder and swivelled to place it in the bag I kept over my shoulder – to discover that the bag was no longer there.

I looked around me, I looked between my legs, willing the bag to stop its tricks and reappear. I asked Rich if by any chance he had seen the bag recently. He hadn't. Reality asserted itself. Somewhere along the route we'd taken from the end of the creek to Rat Island, as I stopped to dig or take photographs, I had put it down and not picked it up again.

My initial reaction was to just give up on the bag. After all, I reasoned, it contained only the day's finds – two bottles and that strange gold bullet, basically. The bag itself was a smelly old canvas pouch I had found in a cupboard 15 years ago. And it would be almost impossible to spot – if a team of camouflage experts had been tasked with producing a colour scheme indistinguishable from the foreshore of Portsmouth Harbour, they could not have improved on my bag in its current condition, the original sand colour having been taken to another level with spatters of mud and clay.

But then, checking my pockets, I realised my electronic car fob was also in the bag. There could be no question of giving it up graciously to the incoming tide. In that moment the day changed complexion, from the mellow hues of nostalgic adventure to the crimson of panic and time ticking down on disaster. Making my excuses to Rich and trying not to look severely panicked, I started to retrace my steps along the shingle spit. I was now on a race against the tide.

My first thought was that I must have put it down when the four of us paused at the mouth of the creek, while arranging a plan for later and then splitting into two groups. But there was no bag there. Or was it there and I just couldn't see it – like the Great Potoo, a bird I had failed to spot in Brazil owing to its remarkable resemblance to a dead tree branch? I scoured the shingle and mud with my eyes, willing the bag to appear. It really wasn't there. I now had no choice but to go back along the creek.

With the tide on the turn, I struggled along at a half-trot in my cumbersome wellies, deciding that the next likely spot was a section of harbour wall where I had paused to watch Si pull his ginger-beer bottle out of the mud. It wasn't there. Paranoia kicked in at this point. What if somebody had found the bag, rummaged in it and found the fob? It wouldn't be hard to work out where the car that belonged to the fob might be parked. Or the perp could simply stroll around all the cars parked in Gosport, zapping the fob till the right car flashed and beeped. I thought back to the warning of a friend from Pompey on where to leave the car. 'Remember, this is *Gosport*,' he'd said darkly.

All thoughts of finding time to talk to Kris and inspect his van were now out of the window. My sole mission was not so much to find the bag as to get back to the car and guard it from the predations of The Gosport Bag Snatcher. When I reached the inlet that we had crossed on a wrecked boat, I decided to ignore Rich's original advice and save time by leaping across.

Mistake. My feet sank deep on the other side and there was a split-second when I was stuck fast and an embarrassing scenario flashed through my mind, involving the swiftly rising tide, a circling helicopter, a fireman barking incomprehensible advice through a megaphone and a growing band of sniggering onlookers.

That evening, I ran a scalding bath and spent a long time soaking away the mud and fear of the day. I'd managed to extricate my feet from the mud. The canvas bag had been on the top of the brick culvert, next to the bottle dump. The car fob was still in it. I'd even had time to do some more detecting (finding a real bullet and some sort of flywheel) and when I met up again with the others I pretended that the temporary loss of the bag had been a minor interruption. Disaster averted by a wave of Sooty's wand.

There are two phases to a journey – the actual doing it, in real time, and the re-experiencing of it through recollection, with photographic prompts and retrospective research. As I sat wrapped in my dressing gown, glass of wine on the go and relief still pumping through my veins, I thought back to the graves we had found on Rat Island and opened my laptop.

In 2014, a series of winter storms uncovered several old graves on the south-east side of the island that contained human remains. Archaeologists removed the bodies for examination and three years later returned to conduct a thorough investigation of the area, an exercise that yielded more bodies. Over the two occasions, the skeletons of at least nine men were recovered.

This was no surprise to locals, as the island was rumoured to have been a burial site for Napoleonic prisoners of war. But the excavations of 2017 revealed a different angle and as I hunched over my screen, digesting the implications, it dawned on me that this story had started in the very house where I was sitting. The apparent synergy spooked me a little.

The archaeology project on Rat Island was called Exercise Magwitch – after Abel Magwitch, the good convict in *Great Expectations* who escapes from a prison hulk. This fictional ship was moored in the Medway or Thames Estuary but the focus of the research into the bodies found on Rat Island was the stagnant fleet of hulks that once floated in Portsmouth Harbour and which Charles Dickens would have known about from his close associations with Portsmouth.

The remains retrieved from the island graves were all men, aged from young adult to late middle age, and though it was not possible to date them accurately, the burials probably took place from the late eighteenth to early to mid-nineteenth century. This fits the theory that the men could have been prisoners of war, from the American War of

Independence or the Napoleonic Wars, but the evidence points in another direction: that the men were prisoners from the hulks.

Cholera, dysentery and typhus were rife in these hellholes and inmates dropped like flies. The tidal Rat Island, besides being a short boat ride away, was an appropriately inaccessible place to dispose of disease-ridden corpses. There are various nineteenth-century references to the island being a prisoners' cemetery, and on an OS map of 1858, the south-eastern section of the island, where I saw the exposed grave slots, is identified as the 'convicts burying ground'. Exercise Magwitch concluded that there are likely to be many more graves of convicts from the hulks as yet undiscovered on Rat Island.

There is at least one person buried there whose identity can be verified, through contemporaneous reports in the *Reading Mercury*. His name was Charles Morris Jones and he was a convict on the *York* prison ship – the same hulk in which my predecessor in the cottage, Thomas Budd, was banged up. On 3 February 1831, Charles, who was described as a 'genteel looking young man', died aboard the *York* and on 7 February 'was buried on Rat Island'. The details and timeline of his case are close to Thomas's.

On 3 March 1830 at Berkshire Assizes in Reading, Charles was found guilty of theft (of money, from a draper's shop where he worked in Abingdon) and sentenced to death, commuted to transportation for life. In mid-May he was transferred to the *York* where he was joined five months later by Thomas Budd. Nine months after that, still awaiting transportation, Charles died. Did Thomas also die on the *York*?

As Jane Hurst, my friend at the Curtis Museum, established, there is no evidence of this but it is far more likely that a record would exist of Thomas having made the voyage to Australia. In the course of the

50 or so years that the hulks were in service, hundreds of convicts must have perished without their details being properly recorded. Charles Morris Jones was just a rare if not unique exception.

On a website dedicated to the history and culture of Portsmouth, someone called Roger White has posted this comment in relation to an article about Rat Island and Exercise Magwitch: 'My 4xgt grandfather, George Larby, died of pleurisy on the convict ship *Briton* in Portsmouth Harbour on 11 Jan 1842 (he was sentenced to transportation for stealing a large ham, no doubt to feed his wife and 9 kids in Farnham). No burial place has been found. I fear a place like this was his final fate.'

The question for me was, when I stared at those grave cuts on Rat Island, was I looking at the last resting place of Thomas Budd, who also stole to feed his family; or if not, did his body lie extremely near, in the frangible ochre cliffs? And what forces had led me to that place anyway? When Kris invited me to Gosport for a day's larking on the foreshore, he didn't know about my association with Thomas Budd or the graves on Rat Island. When Rich led me across to the island, he knew nothing about me full stop. Now the strands of the story were intersecting right here in my kitchen, humming in the cobwebby spaces above my head.

The published findings of Exercise Magwitch feature a photograph of a skull recovered from one of the graves. Upper and lower teeth on the left-hand side are worn away to form an oval notch where the convict habitually lodged the stem of his clay pipe. I reached for my finds bag and took out the pipe stem I had found near the graves. It brought the fellow home to me – brought them all home, for a moment, from the hell of the hulks.

On this reflective note I was about to go to bed when I spotted in the finds bag the gold bullet. As I unscrewed it into three pieces, the uneasy thought occurred to me that it was the kind of macabre receptacle a Russian agent (on a visit, say, to see Portsmouth's famed Spinnaker Tower, which is even taller than the spire of Salisbury Cathedral) might keep his Novichok in.

The truth – which I found online in one click – still left me feeling queasy. It was a 'gold bullet cremation urn pendant designed to hold a token amount of a loved one or pet's ashes, ensuring that there is always a part of them held close to your heart'. (The web page extolling its many qualities was laid out in bullet points. Was this a designer's in-joke?) I had brought home a small part of a dead person (or animal).

Once I knew this, I didn't want the cremation urn pendant in the house but nor could I put it in the wheelie bin, to be carted off to landfill. For the sake of respect, I decided I would have to wait till my next trip to the seaside when I would return the bullet to the ocean – possibly for another mudlarker or beachcomber to find, though such a fate would be a horrible parody of the Buddhist concept of *samsara,* the endless cycle of death and rebirth. Before taking care of that bit of business, I revisited the idea of finding Roman – grubbing for grots, sifting for *sestertii,* whatever it took.

10

THEY'RE JUST BITS OF METAL!

This mission took me to Wiltshire. On the day in late February 2022 when Russian tanks started rolling into Ukraine, I parked my car on a suburban street in the market town of Devizes and rang the doorbell of a corner house with a campervan parked outside. The door was opened by a man called Dave Crisp. With his white hair and goatee, and a certain air of being at ease in his own skin, Dave could be an old rocker; a onetime member of The Troggs, say (I could picture a youthful Dave singing 'Wild Thing').

A contact had put me on to him and I figured out that if anyone could point me at Roman it would be Dave. Being a late middle-aged working-class English bloke, Dave is typical of detectorists. They belong to a demographic who have come to believe that their lives are of scant interest to anyone else because no one has ever showered them with praise or curiosity. And so their stories remain largely untold, and I would not blame them if a certain bitterness hides in their soul.

Dave's story took off one morning in April 2010. He has an aversion to detecting in the rain but the day he had off from his job as a hospital chef was set for unseasonably dry, warm weather. So he decided to return to a group of fields he had permission on near Frome in Somerset.

On two previous visits to the same permission he had found, and reported, a dispersed hoard of about 50 *siliquae* – small fourth-century Roman coins – that had probably been scattered by the plough. Such a hoard would represent a lifetime high for most detectorists and that was the case with Dave at that point. In archaeological terms they are notable but not Premier League – the Portable Antiquities Scheme (PAS) now records more than 50 Roman coin hoards a year.

The *siliquae* he found were mostly near the surface on the second of two grass fields that he had been crossing to reach his real goal, a field that had been ploughed and rolled ready for seeding. On this latest outing, he couldn't believe there'd be anything else in the *siliquae* field – one hoard was unusual enough – and was determined to finally get on to the ploughed-and-rolled.

A detectorist, as I had already noticed, is always 'on'. As Dave made his way from the car to his chosen field, he was nevertheless sweeping studiously as he went. And crossing the *siliquae* field, following his nose as he always does, he picked up a 'funny' signal.

'It worries me sometimes – supposing I'd turned left instead of right?' he said when we sat opposite each other across a table in his back room. 'But that's what life is, isn't it? It's all about decisions that you *didn't* make.'

He still can't believe the luck involved in this.

'Maybe we've got something in our heads that's primeval that makes you as you go into a field think, *Yeah, that bit's where I'm going today*,' he mused. 'Maybe that's all it comes down to and the detector is just a modern extension of our senses.'

Dave had been metal detecting for 22 years. He knew there was something big and deep beneath his coil and he was pretty sure it was iron, such as a ploughshare. 'But at the back of your mind you think, *Supposing it's not . . .?* Something at the back of your mind says, *Dig it!'*

He cut his usual neat divot, seven inches square, and flapped it back on the uncut side. Nothing in the divot, no change in the signal. He dug down six inches, nothing; another six inches, passing into gluey yellow clay that meant he was now in the subsoil. He was more than ever sure it was iron. Then he turned up a small piece of pottery, which he recognised as Roman black burnished ware, a cheap pottery that was easily broken and used for basic items of everyday use.

Beyond it, he prised up a lump of clay with a grot stuck to it. Knowing that a single coin at that depth would hardly produce the signal he'd received, he kept going, now sweating slightly and not just due to the spring sunshine.

'Then when I turned the second piece of clay up, I had about 20 of them stuck in there,' he said. This was the moment he froze, breathed deeply and let out a shout of joy to the heedless hedgerows.

He assumed it was a cache of coins like the first, this time lying so deep it hadn't been touched by the plough. The presence of the black burnished ware made him think it was probably a small 'legionary's money pot', which a soldier had buried at an easily remembered spot – under a tree, for example – while he went off 'to kill all the Scots or whatever'. Maybe this legionary had been killed himself; at any rate, he never came back to reclaim it. Dave had now found not one but *two* hoards – an extremely rare achievement. But he had no idea what he was really standing on the edge of.

It's what he did – and didn't – do next that makes his case so famous in the world of archaeology. He didn't keep digging. He didn't bring in a couple of mates with extra-big spades and some heavy-duty sacking. He didn't speed-dial some dodgy coin dealer down in Eastbourne. Dave Crisp played it by the book, to the point where his exemplary behaviour is cited by archaeologists as the template for responsible metal detecting.

After allowing himself that little shout of triumph, he filled the hole back in. Then he called the then Finds Liaison Officer (FLO) for Wiltshire, Katie Hinds, so that the archaeologists could take over. Katie, as it happened, was now my near-neighbour in Hampshire, taking a break from full-time archaeology while she looked after a new baby. I had found her by chance, through an email daisy chain that started in Edinburgh and passed down through Cumbria, and she was the one who put me on to Dave Crisp. When we met over midday cups of tea, in a real-ale pub popular with winter curry nighters and summer bikers, she cited Dave's case as one of the highlights of her career to date.

Recalling that fateful phone call, she said that Dave had pulled her leg, pretending he was calling about the *siliquae* he had found the previous week, then casually letting slip he'd found another hoard. Having informed her colleagues over the county border in Somerset – where the hoard was found – Katie came back to Dave and asked for the coordinates of the find spot.

Though Katie didn't remember this, Dave told me that he replied, 'On your bike! This is my hoard and I'm going to be there when you dig it up!' What he feared was that, having done the (literal) spadework, he would be sidelined as Basil Brown was in the Sutton Hoo dig in favour of the professionals with lots of letters after their names. At this point in the story Dave veered into unexpected territory.

As Katie had already told me, Dave is the poster boy of the metal-detecting community as far as archaeologists are concerned. But Dave doesn't feel reciprocally warm towards the world of archaeology, even if he gets on well with individual archaeologists such as Katie. For him, archaeologists are institutionally anti-detectorist.

'They have this thing about everything's got to be done the right way,' he said, 'which is understandable, but they say it's got to be done by *archaeologists*. We get a lot of heat still from archaeologists. There are fanatics who'd rather have objects rot in the ground than have us dig them up.'

As we talked in Dave's house in Devizes, a ginger cat peering through the glass door periodically from the garden, there was a shout of 'Sorry I'm late' from the hallway. This was his friend and detecting buddy Gary Cook, with whom he runs the annual Rodney Cook Memorial Rally, a charitable event to raise money for the cancer centre at Bath Royal United Hospital where Gary's late father was treated.

Gary is the sales director of a plumbing company and a former carpet fitter. Bouncing into the back room, he said in a stage whisper, 'He doesn't like to talk about his hoard' – a jokey catchphrase among Dave's mates. Then, impassioned and forthright, he picked up and doubled down on Dave's theme.

'We're always having to deal with the fact we're classed as treasure hunters, or tomb robbers – or scumbags,' he said. 'Just because I didn't go to university, just because I don't have a degree, I'm nothing. But thanks to people like Dave I can now pick things up and say, "Oh, that's a Roman buckle." Does that mean I know less than a 25-year-old who's just done his degree in archaeology?'

The latest trigger for their resentment was an article in a magazine called *The Searcher*, a rival publication to *Treasure Hunting*, headlined 'Is there any such thing as a good rally?' The author was Professor Michael Lewis, the Head of the PAS, based at the British Museum – a man they both knew, describing him as 'a lovely bloke' even as they took issue with his point of view.

In the article, Michael Lewis was keen to make clear that he was not anti-detectorist, acknowledging that 'many of the most important [archaeological] finds of recent years have been made by detectorists . . . and these have transformed our understanding of the past.' His problem was that finds made by detectorists are not always properly reported, and this has been especially true on rallies where FLOs who attended were overwhelmed by the sheer volume of material – the reason why the PAS has now stopped supporting these mass events.

Reading this, the full implications of what I had glimpsed in the Finds Recording Tent at Detectival began to dawn on me. Michael was arguing that it was time for rally organisers to do their bit and use some of their profits to employ a properly qualified team on the day to 'triage' finds, and finds experts to record them on the PAS database after the event.

However, as rally organisers themselves, Dave and Gary felt they were being scapegoated – especially as all the proceeds from their rallies go to charity and they don't make a penny in profit.

'Is it the metal detectorists' fault that PAS is so successful it can't cope?' Dave scoffed.

The issue also had a personal angle because they'd had a disagreement with Michael over their most recent event.

It took place on land owned by a farmer who would not allow precise find spots to be recorded. (This is the landowner's prerogative – perhaps he feared the information would encourage nighthawks to embark on speculative looting sprees across his fields.) For Michael, this meant that any objects found on the rally had next to no archaeological value – as he put it in the article, 'Once that [find spot] information is lost (disarticulated from the find), then it becomes just "another" find – another coin, brooch, buckle, strap-end, token, etc.'

Better, in that case, not to hold rallies on land where find spots cannot be accurately recorded.

Dave and Gary said they were acting within the PAS guidelines, so any dissatisfaction Michael felt should be directed back at himself and the scheme he is in charge of. They also emphasised that they're passionate advocates of the PAS themselves (Dave has an astonishing 1,400 finds recorded on its database).

'It distresses us very much because it always feels we're being pushed back by the academics,' Gary said.

He and Dave told a story that sums up the state of play. A well-known archaeologist who appears frequently on TV documentaries turned up at an event organised by a local radio station and they spotted him looking over the tray of finds they had brought along. As he walked away, Gary called out, 'So what do you think?' The well-known archaeologist turned round and replied dismissively, 'They're just bits of *metal*!'

Gary was incensed, pointing out that, as each object had been scrupulously recorded with the PAS, thus helping to build a historical picture of the locality, they were far from worthless. Instead of jumping to conclusions, he suggested, archaeologists like him should engage with detectorists. By failing to do so he was perpetuating the problem. They both knew the problem he was referring to – those traces of bad odour between the two camps that just won't disperse, whatever breezy disinfectant is brought to bear on them.

Given this depth of feeling, it must have been tough for Dave to take a back seat on his new discovery in that Somerset field, but that's what he was obliged to do once he'd reported it. Still, he insisted on being there when the excavation took place, so it was arranged for Dave's next day off from his chef's job a week later.

For a whole week the hoard remained in the ground and Dave fretted about it being found by someone else, someone not so scrupulous about doing the right thing. He knew this fear was absurd – it had lain undisturbed for more than fifteen hundred years and would survive intact for another seven days. But just in case, he buried a decoy above it – a big horseshoe, so that anybody who happened to be illegally detecting in that particular field and picked up a signal from the hoard would dig down, hit on the horseshoe, mutter a curse about big iron and be on his way.

At 8am on the appointed day, he turned up on site with his grandson Aaron to meet Katie, her Somerset counterpart Anna Booth and an archaeologist, Alan Graham, hired by Somerset County Council to carry out the highly specialised and delicate excavation. He showed them the 'radiates' (cheap coins minted in the third century) and the fragments of black burnished ware he had found so far and they agreed that they were probably looking at a small hoard in a pot.

So the archaeologist got to work, cutting a large square hole around Dave's original divot, levelling it off and cleaning it out with obsessive neatness while Dave shuffled about impatiently. And slowly a different story began to emerge from the claggy subsoil. The black burnished ware was, in Hitchcockian terms, a MacGuffin. It was just a bowl that had been inverted and used as a lid on a much bigger pot. As Alan painstakingly removed the sherds of bowl, the top of this larger pot appeared and, within it, coins stuck together in a green encrustation.

Scraping around the outside of the big pot with his trowel, Alan revealed a vessel that just seemed to get bigger and bigger as the sides continued to slope outwards. And Katie's ambitions for what it could be were also growing.

'I remember the point where we got down to what we felt was the maximum diameter, just as the curve of the pot started going down again, and we measured it and I knew there'd been a hoard of similar-dated coins that was the largest known Roman coin hoard found in Britain,' she said.

This was the Cunetio Hoard – of 54,951 coins, found in 1978 near Marlborough in Wiltshire, in a pot and a lead container – and Katie knew that the pot that had contained most of the coins of the Cunetio Hoard was on display in the Wiltshire Heritage Museum in Devizes because she used to work there.

'So I rang up the receptionist and I said, "Can you just nip into the Roman gallery and measure the Cunetio pot?"

'It was a very similar measurement and we went, "Oh my goodness – this is going to be big." It was at that point we got very excited. I rang up

Roger Bland, who was then Head of the PAS. Then everyone from the British Museum wanted to come and visit.'

And Dave himself?

'As it got bigger and bigger, inside I'm going, "Wow! Yes!" But on the outside I'm very laid back and I'm going, "Yeah, not bad . . ."' he said.

Dave's big pot was, he said, the size of a beer barrel. It took three days to spring it from its Somerset strongbox. This was the period of maximum vulnerability. Caches of the magnitude that this promised to be are typically valued at hundreds of thousands of pounds, so by rights a team of truncheon-packing heavies in helmets and stab vests should have mounted a night-time vigil over the site. Instead, it was down to Dave and his teenage grandson Aaron (as it was for Mariusz Stepien with the Peebles Hoard).

'I phoned my daughter and the family brought out a tent and sleeping bags, some food, and we literally slept right next to the hole – put a couple of sacks over it and some cardboard,' said Dave. There was moonlight and moonshadow, and a sense of Roman gods watching over them.

Over the following two days the coins were removed in layers, each layer placed in a mushroom box, then bagged up and labelled. The hoard filled 60 bags and weighed 160 kilograms (353 pounds) – 'Two of me!,' said Dave, patting his stomach. It was impossible to say at this stage how many coins there were but they knew it had to be one of the biggest-ever coin hoards, that it represented an important moment in modern archaeology and the history of metal detecting. There was also uncertainty about the coins themselves. It looked like they were all radiates (coins of everyday usage) but you couldn't tell for sure because they were stuck together and covered in green gunk.

'On the third day,' said Dave, 'I arrived just as they were taking the last few out of the bottom of the pot. Once they've taken the pot out of the ground, once you've held the coins in your hand for the last time, all the excitement is over. The archaeologists have gone, the coins have gone up to London in a big van, the farmer's gone back home to his cows, they've filled the hole back in – subsoil, topsoil, grass – and me and the boy are standing there going, "Oh, is that it?"

'And it really is it, because you're not going to see those coins again. Now it's down to somebody else. Then I'm thinking, *Oh, there's always tomorrow. I can come out tomorrow.* So me and the boy get in the car, I drive out of the field, he locks the gate and we drive away. And that's the end of the story. Except it wasn't was it?'

Dave Crisp's hoard was assigned the name – taken from the town nearest to the find spot – by which it is now known throughout the world of archaeology: the Frome Hoard. It comprises 52,503 coins, making it the second-largest cache of Roman coins (just 2,448 coins short of the Cunetio Hoard) ever found in Britain and the largest found in a single container. It has cast new light on Roman Britain in the second half of the third century AD. And it is renowned in archaeological circles for the exemplary way in which Dave behaved as soon as he realised what he could be dealing with, for it enabled archaeologists to properly excavate for the first time a hoard of such a size.

Previously, comparable hoards had been nighthawked or, at best, removed from the ground before the finder reported them. It's even possible that the Cunetio Hoard may have been two separate hoards, in which case the Frome cache is the biggest yet found, not the runner-up – not that Dave is nickel-and-diming over it.

Framed on the wall of his kitchen is a page from the *Daily Express* showing him kneeling by the hoard hole wearing sunglasses and looking modestly chuffed with himself. Above him, over four decks, is the following headline: 'Minted . . . the cook who found £3.3m of Roman coins in a farmer's field'.

The newspaper made up the figure of £3.3 million. The Treasure Valuation Committee subsequently valued the Frome Hoard at £320,250, the sum it was purchased for and which Dave shared 50–50 with the landowner.

'Changed my life, yeah, the money changed my life,' he said. Coming up to retirement, he'd been wondering how he was going to live on his state pension. This wedge of Roman – half of it at least – became a nest egg. Changed things too in that a chef from Chippenham Hospital became a celebrity – appeared in the papers, did TV and radio interviews across the world, featured in an episode of *Digging for Britain* with Professor Alice Roberts, 'got a lot of bonus points from all the archaeologists because I did it by the book'.

The coins were subjected to a lengthy process of conservation at the British Museum before taking a brief bow in Frome Library and going on temporary display in the British Museum as part of the campaign to raise funds for the Hoard's public purchase under the Treasure Act. It was eventually acquired by the Museum of Somerset in Taunton with the help of the National Heritage Memorial Fund and other bodies.

The coins date from the third century AD and are almost all radiates, so-called because of the radiant crowns worn by the emperors featured on them. British Museum staff took 12 weeks to sort them into the different emperors – about 30 in all, spanning the years from AD 250 to 290 and ending with the usurper Carausius, who set himself up as emperor of an independent Britain and northern France and in AD 293 was bumped off by his accountant (which presumably he didn't see coming).

Thanks to stratigraphy and a subsequent geophysical survey of the site, all sorts of things have been established about the Frome Hoard that would never have been known if Dave had just rocked up at Katie's door with a load of bags.

The cache was buried at an auspicious spot, on high ground, next to an ancient watercourse and just below its source (this probably also accounts for the presence of the *siliquae* hoard, which Dave found close by). There was an extensive settlement a few hundred yards away. The pot was put in the ground empty, then filled up with the coins.

This seems to have happened in one go rather than gradually. This is evident from the fact that the newest coins were halfway down the pot, and seeing the pot *in situ*, said Katie, the coins 'did indeed look like they had been poured in in separate batches, from the way they were lying'.

The whole set-up was an odd way of burying money for safekeeping and the consensus is that the Hoard was a votive offering made by people from the nearby settlement, each person waiting in line before chipping in with their twopennyworth to appease the gods of harvest, or war. 'Perhaps the next year they got a bumper crop of cabbages,' said Dave.

But the Frome Hoard is not an entirely open book. Among the many thousands of grotty radiates were just five rare silver *denarii,* in excellent condition, of the renegade Emperor Carausius – prestige dosh that you might not want to squander on your little wheeze of celestial bribery. Dave has one idea of how they got there.

They were in a leather purse, tucked well away – in a top pocket, or equivalent – from the small change going in the pot. But then the purse slips into the pot unnoticed as a person bends over the hole in the ground (I have lost my glasses in the Thames this way) to make their contribution to the pot. A person spends the next week fretting that they've had their pocket picked. The leather purse spends the next seventeen hundred years rotting away to nothing. The coins remain, glinting among the grots, fresh as the day they were minted.

I asked Dave if they'd let him keep a coin, just one out of the 52,503 – I'd pictured a soft-hearted conservator looking over their shoulder, then palming him a tiddler. He looked shocked: 'No no no.'

Hanging on the kitchen wall next to the framed page from the *Express* is a digging tool presented to him by fellow organisers of the Rodney Cook Memorial Rally in thanks for his dedication to the cause. It is engraved with that Hoard-related, affectionately mickey-taking catchphrase, 'But I don't like to talk about it.'

In the intervening years, white-haired Dave has become the *éminence grise* of metal detecting. He contributes articles to *Treasure Hunting* magazine, he gives talks, accompanied by cabinets of his finds. He unstacked some of these on the kitchen work surfaces for me to see. They are the usual dusty, shyly thrilling mix – of coins, buckles, lead weights, crotal bells (used as rattles on horse-drawn wagons), thimbles, bridle mounts – of which my two plastic sandwich boxes are an embryonic version.

And he still goes out in the fields whenever he can.

'You coming out with us this afternoon?' Gary asked me.

'Definitely!'

I had persuaded myself that I wanted to meet Dave to hear his account of how an 'ordinary bloke' – a hospital chef – made one of the greatest archaeological discoveries of modern times. It goes to the heart of the stand-off between metal detecting and archaeology – how the man in the street can trump the prof in his trench. But I had to admit to a less noble motive.

Dave had found 52,503 Roman coins *in one go*! I had yet to find one Roman coin in about fifty goes. Was there a proportional element to the pleasure one might derive from finding a stack of stuff as opposed to a single example? Did Dave feel 52,503 times more pleased with himself than if he'd found one coin? I'd settle for one. If I could persuade the man responsible for finding more Roman coins than anyone else alive to take me detecting, he should be able to fix that.

Dave has an extensive portfolio of permissions stretching across Wiltshire and Somerset. He wondered aloud to Gary where they should go: 'Maybe on the Roman?' He didn't mean *the* Roman – that's off-limits. He meant a field where they know there are Roman coins to be found because they've already found several there.

I couldn't believe what I was hearing.

'Sounds good to me,' I said, 'I'd really like to find just one Roman. You found 52,000 – in one go!' I tried not to sound too pathetically grateful.

'It was just one signal,' Dave said modestly.

Gary gave Dave a lift in his van. I followed them out of Devizes and into a landscape that felt, when I saw it for the first time 30 years ago, as if it had been in my head all along – a feeling that had been spreading, like sunlight, over other landscapes recently. I followed Gary's car through Avebury, with its circle of standing stones and mysterious cone of an ancient man-made hill, then he turned off the A-road and threaded up towards the pillowy softness of the North Wessex Downs.

On that first visit, Avebury was the starting point of a walk I did along part of the Ridgeway, the prehistoric trackway that runs from the Dorset coast, up along these Downs and eventually to the Wash. A few years ago I returned to the area to write a newspaper article about an archaeological site called Marden Henge, the third of Wiltshire's 'super-henges', the others being Avebury and Stonehenge (and a 'henge' being a prehistoric, usually circular earthwork).

These chalk hills are embossed with thousands of years of human civilisation – the hilltop swells of Iron Age hill forts, Neolithic burial mounds, Celtic field systems, not just the Ridgeway but the earthwork known as the Wansdyke, which probably marked the boundary between the Anglo-Saxon kingdoms of Wessex and Mercia.

A few years ago, Gary Cook made his best find out here – a Bronze Age 'bivalve' axehead mould, now on display in the Wiltshire Museum in Devizes as part of the country's finest collection of Bronze Age artefacts.

He talked about the axe-head mould as we made the transition into detectorists, having parked in a muddy layby between two vast seeded fields. What intrigued him was that the mould had been made by and was the precious possession of an individual he described as an alchemist.

'That's why I prefer artefacts to coins – they're more personal,' he said as he pulled on his waterproof leggings. 'And wouldn't it be great if one day I found an axe head that fitted the mould?'

Gary hung back, having to make a couple of work calls to cover his back, while Dave led the way across the narrow lane and into the

'Roman' field. It looked like green corduroy and, being indivisible from the fields beyond, appeared to stretch for a good mile towards the Downs themselves. The downland flanks were creased with field systems and along the ridgeline stood clumps of beech trees, looking like footballers in a pre-match huddle. Above, billows of grey-bellied clouds hung in the cold blue sky of a February afternoon.

As I trudged in Dave's gumboot prints, I thought about what he'd told me that morning: 'When you go into a field, sometimes you make a plan and other times you just wander and go where the metal detector takes you.' Was he going to wing it or study it today? The field rose into a gentle dome. On the top, he told me, was where he and Gary had had luck with Romans. 'Slow down when you get up there,' was his advice.

So we set off, detecting parallel, a good 30 yards apart. And I couldn't help sneaking glances at the man, absorbed in the moment in his green waxed jacket and yellow gloves; an unruffled deliberation to his technique, a professorial air emphasised by the white hair. Entirely in his element. How an 'ordinary' person – a person society perceives as ordinary – isn't.

I got a couple of early good signals. Both moo tubes. But I was digging more than Dave, I noticed. I felt lucky. I began to imagine the Roman I might find. I'd like it to have detail and rarity, to impress Dave and Gary as a token of my competence. Next up: an offcut of folded aluminium, followed by the base of a Coca-Cola can and an iron spike. As we neared the top of the hill, our paths converged. Dave paused, lifted his headphones clear of his ears.

'Any luck?'

I wrinkled my nose. 'Moo tubes. You?'

He shrugged. 'Junk.' Then he added: 'A find is a bonus. A good find is a good bonus. But keep going. This is the area.'

I liked our exchange. It was man-to-man and contained both wisdom and optimism. We veered apart again on our separate tracks.

It was Dave's contention that there had been some sort of settlement or camp up here. I dwelled on the idea that as the Romans sat around in their rough fabrics and clanky metalwear their eyes would have been drawn to the Downs and the already-old human traces across them – the ghosts were well embedded even then. This thought led on through warm thickets of speculation and I was feeling the truth of Dave's homily, about a find being merely a bonus, feeling content just in the being-here. Then I saw that he was coming over with an outstretched hand.

'That's what you're looking for,' he said. Perched on his finger ends was a small, green, featureless disc: a grot. He invited me to sweep the coil of my detector across it to note the ID number and signal so that I knew what to look for. This changed the game. Dave was leading the horse to water. I felt both energised – I had something specific to aim for – and nervous: would I find it in me to drink?

Three hours later, my best find – my only find apart from junk – was a musket ball. Dave and Gary found six or seven Roman coins each, on and around the crown of the field. On the way back to the cars they were sympathetic.

'If you didn't walk over it, you didn't walk over it,' they said, diplomatically, forgetting that between them they had managed to 'walk over it' about 14 times. I was trying hard to be content in the not-finding.

As we stood by our cars in the dusk, stripping off boots and khakis, Gary handed me one of the Roman coins he had just found, saying, 'Here – a memento of the day.'

I was touched – as well as embarrassed to think that he felt sorry for me. 'I'll pretend I found it myself,' I said, only half-jokingly.

'We won't tell anybody any different,' said Dave.

Then they talked about the nose they have developed over the years for finds that don't quite smell right, the lengths to which some detectorists will go to cheat. The type of detectorist they call 'planters' will turn up at a rally in order to plant an object they have found illegally, on a scheduled monument or on land where they didn't have permission, then claim to have just found it – the purpose being to establish a legitimate provenance for it. Planters are looters by another name.

'Bringers' also pretend they have just found items they have actually planted, but they are essentially harmless.

'They do it for the glory so that they can be the centre of attention for five minutes,' said Gary. A bringer will bring along a really nice thing – a piece that they have previously found themselves, or even bought on eBay – and pretend, with elaborately staged celebrations, to dig it up. This struck me as the equivalent of cheating at golf – sad, sneaky and funny all at the same time.

There is, or was, a sub-genre of planters and bringers. They said that at some rallies they used to attend the organisers would give away a brand-new metal detector for the 'Find of the Day'. This was stopped when they realised that people were smuggling along pre-found objects in order to win the prize. (This is just plain sad.)

When I got home and looked at Gary's Roman properly, I was even more touched, as I realised that he hadn't given me one of his real grots but a coin with some detail to it. As I squinted through the magnifying glass, the prominent brow and right ear of a Roman emperor rose into focus. He appeared to be wearing one of those wiggly earpiece cords in his ear, like the thick-necked security men who flank POTUS on public walkabouts – a detail presumably representing the crinkliness of the emperor's hair.

I hadn't expected the grot to have a personality. Who was it supposed to be? To find out, I resigned myself to waiting till my next meeting with the FLO. Then I thought of Katie, the former FLO who lived in the next village. Would it be cheeky to ask her – like calling on a doctor you'd met socially to show them the fungal outbreak in your armpit?

It turned out the process of coin identification was the one part of her former job Katie really missed ('armpit fungus' would have been an impatient detectorist hassling her for an immediate verdict on his finds). I dropped the coin off with her and received an email two hours later.

'It is a nummus [a *nummus* being a low-value copper coin of the late Roman period] of Magnentius or Decentius, I think Decentius, as the inscription seems to read [. . .] CEN [. . .] but it is quite worn. It could be a contemporary copy, as the true coins are usually larger and copies are smaller (and common).'

The coin dates from AD 351–3 when Decentius was 'Caesar' of the Western Roman Empire, having been appointed by his brother Magnentius who had usurped the position of Emperor. The brothers' power grab was short-lived and they committed suicide (separately) in southern France in AD 353.

*

The week after I went to see Dave Crisp, I had planned to go to the British Museum to see its latest major exhibition, 'The World of Stonehenge'. While I was there, I had also hoped to grab a quick chat with Professor Michael Lewis, the Head of the PAS, about archaeology and metal detecting. Turned out there was yet more synergy in the air over these two visits.

When I arranged to meet Dave, I had no idea that he would know Michael Lewis and have a particular beef with him that went to the heart of the bad feeling between archaeologists and detectorists. Angling to go out with Dave on one of his permissions, I little suspected he and Gary would take me deep into Wiltshire's mystical Stonehenge-flavoured landscapes. To complete the 'meant' feel of this BM visit, when I emailed Michael he suggested that as part of our conversation he should take me in to see the Stonehenge exhibition, as he wanted to show me a couple of objects in it that had been found by detectorists.

We met in the pillared entrance hall of the BM. It was before opening time and the only sounds, before we got yacking, were the muffled echoes of footsteps on concrete-and-marble flooring. Dave and Gary were right, Michael is a nice bloke – more matey student than pontificating prof. He was under no obligation to see me but, sensing my curiosity – or perhaps just wanting to get me off his back – he found the time.

We sat on a bench in one corner and talked around the mutual antagonisms between academics and hobbyists. Michael reckoned politics had a lot to do with it.

'Most archaeologists tend to be to the left of centre, whereas most detectorists tend to be to the right,' he said.

This was something I had suspected was the case without having tested it by asking too many leading questions – afraid of being disillusioned, on my own terms; of disillusioning others, on theirs.

One detectorist told me he wouldn't otherwise be seen dead with some of his group, one of whom he described as a 'gammon' and a 'racist'. Yet when they get together they occupy a common ground that is located in a passion for old, found objects and a willingness to circle the wagons against their common enemy, the archaeologists.

On the face of it, my own background – private school, university degree (not in archaeology) – is more 'archaeologist' than 'detectorist', yet I was developing a tribal loyalty to us unassuming hobbyists and the way we can feel marginalised and looked-down-on by the academics. My days in the field with these unfashionable middle-aged people had made me wonder if I wasn't seeing in them the person I might have been without the parental intervention to have me socially engineered into someone posher. As if they were me in another life.

'I'm not saying that politics matters *particularly*,' Michael went on, 'but it adds to this thing of "university-based versus man-in-the-street", this feeling of, "Well, we're different, aren't we? We do archaeology in a different way, we think politically differently, we've had a different education, maybe a different upbringing . . ."' He added that he, and many archaeologists, hardly deserved an elitist label, having come from ordinary backgrounds and gone to state secondary schools.

He confines his battles to the small patch of soil that is the find spot – hence his disagreement with Dave and Gary over holding a rally where the farmer would not allow the finds to be accurately recorded (for fear of encouraging nighthawks on to his land).

'There is no middle ground in metal detecting,' he said. A detectorist is either adding value to the sum of archaeological knowledge by recording where he found an object, or taking value away by failing to.

This brought up a related bone of contention. A detectorist likes – *loves* – objects for their own sake, while suspecting archaeologists of only caring about the context, the wider story they tell. Dave, for example, said of the archaeologists who got so excited about the Frome Hoard, 'They wanted the *information* from the coins, they're not really interested in the *coins*.'

Like that self-important telly troweller at Dave and Gary's rally who dismissed the tray of finds as 'just bits of metal', there are some purists who don't approve of the 'fetishising' of objects that in archaeological terms are unremarkable. As Michael said, my Lizzie half-groat (of course I had slipped this into the conversation) is of little interest to an archaeologist, beyond the find spot that is, because so many are found. But it means the world to me. And I do like to get it out and wave it about.

Some hardline archaeologists would like to deprive me of this modest pleasure, believing it wrong for private individuals to have their own little collections that they can bring out and handle, taking pleasure from a tactile privilege afforded no one else bar museum professionals. Michael is firmly on the side of the object lovers. He gets it, he said. But then what happens to these dusty aggregates of historic artefacts when the owner dies? They enter an afterlife of uncertainty.

At this point, sitting in these sepulchral surroundings of pillars and echoes, I had the feeling commonly described as 'someone walking over your grave'. Thinking forward to my own death and its aftermath,

I pictured some junior relative drawing the short straw of family obligation and having to sort through my belongings (to his undisguised irritation: 'Why me?!'). The old CDs are definitely going in the skip (Fairport Convention! WTF?) but then in the next drawer down is a series of plastic sealable boxes with weird old stuff in. Not gold or jewels, though, nothing valuable here surely. He hesitates. Fuck it. Skip.

Michael led me through the ground-floor shop of the British Museum, past the replica Sutton Hoo helmets and Stonehenge-shaped candles, to a little-visited gallery with a display case of finds recorded by the PAS. In other words, objects found by detectorists. If the purpose of the display was to highlight the merits of the scheme and acknowledge the role of metal detecting in modern archaeology, it could have been more impressive.

Besides being tucked away as if for minimal exposure, there were only a handful of objects, including a gold medieval brooch and some finger rings. My eye was caught by a caption card detailing items from 'a Viking hoard found in 2015 near Leominster' – the hoard looted by Powell and Davies. I'd have loved to see in the flesh the gold bracelet and the crystal pendant in its harness of gold but only gaps were there because 'This case is in the course of arrangement'.

By contrast, 'The World of Stonehenge' blew me away. It wasn't really about *Stonehenge* – the stones, the icon, the view from the A303. There were no scale polystyrene models of the kind that feature in the spoof 'rockumentary' *This Is Spinal Tap*. Instead, it told a story of prehistoric beliefs and thought patterns through beautiful objects made and found across the British Isles and Europe.

One of the most astonishing is the Nebra Sky Disc, made of gold from Cornwall and bronze from central Europe in around 1600 BC. The arrestingly strange pattern on it – highlighted in gold against bronze that has turned green – shows the sun or the full moon, a crescent moon, possibly a 'sun boat' (in which to sail to the heavens), and the star cluster of the Pleiades, and represents, according to the accompanying textual information, 'the oldest known material depiction of cosmic phenomena in the world'.

It is a work of mind-blowing sophistication that embodies both an extraordinary knowledge of the infinite world and a sublime sense of beauty, and it's no surprise that the British Museum chose it to be the image of the exhibition, its green-and-gold face appearing on posters throughout London and beyond and on various bits of merchandising in the museum shops.

What the exhibition did not mention is that the Nebra Sky Disc was found by detectorists, near the town of Nebra in the former East Germany, in 1999. The detectorists were nighthawks, just two among many who took advantage of the lawlessness that followed the collapse of the GDR to go on looting sprees across archaeological sites. The Disc was part of a Bronze Age hoard that disappeared into the recesses of the black market. It was recovered a couple of years later in Basel in an elaborate sting operation fronted by the state archaeologist of Saxony-Anhalt, Harald Meller.

But Michael Lewis's focus was not on the Nebra Sky Disc. In the exhibition's low dawn-of-time lighting, he whisked me straight past it to a case containing a gold, ribbed, round-bottomed beaker that had been crumpled by a plough: the Ringlemere Cup, found by detectorist Cliff Bradshaw near Sandwich in Kent in 2001.

'I was the FLO in Kent at the time,' Michael said. 'I got a call from Cliff and he sent me a picture. He said, "I know what it is, it's a Bronze Age cup, because I've got a book with the Rillaton Cup in it." '

The Rillaton Cup, flat-bottomed and uncrumpled but otherwise similar, was excavated in Cornwall in 1837. There it was, sitting next to the Ringlemere Cup in the display cabinet.

The caption explained that the vessel found in Kent is probably round-bottomed because it was a chalice, designed to be kept on the move by being passed from hand to hand in spiritual ceremonies (I experienced something similar in Ladakh, India, drinking a barley hooch called *chang* from a ceremonial silver cup; I'm happy to report that intoxication resulted). In 2012, the Ringlemere Cup featured in an episode of the TV documentary series *Britain's Secret Treasures* – incongruously enough, sharing star billing with guest contributor Bill Roache, the actor who played Ken Barlow for about a million years in *Coronation Street*.

Being a man of self-professed deep spirituality and psychic powers, Bill was thrilled to hold this mystical and mysterious symbol of deep history. He cupped the Cup with eager hands and, feeling the heat rising through the thin, highly conductive gold membrane, exclaimed excitedly, 'It's getting really hot . . .!'

The other object in the Stonehenge exhibition that Michael singled out for having been found by a detectorist was a gold sun pendant, in the shape of a partial solar eclipse, found in the Shropshire Marches, the ancient lands that straddle the Welsh borders, in 2018 by an experienced detectorist. The 'rays' of the sun on the surface of the pendant are represented by triangular panels, each incised with fine lines running in alternating directions that were making it dazzle and shimmer in its spotlight. To replicate such an effect today would probably require laser-guided micro-engineering, which is why Michael Lewis mouthed that question-of-amazement, 'How did they do that?'

Three thousand years ago, said the caption, the pendant was 'cast into the sky before it sank into the gloom of a pond dotted with water lilies'. Did the British Museum have someone crouching pond-side to witness the moment? This word picture sounded like poetic licence, but – as one of the exhibition's curators, Neil Wilkin, told me afterwards – it 'draws on the environmental archaeological analysis/ excavation at the site . . . after the sun pendant's discovery.' There was nothing whimsical about this detail. It was down to knowing and analysing the find spot.

The Shropshire Sun Pendant is an object of such exquisite beauty that it was currently threatening to glow a hole in the glass case trying to contain it. Abandoning a certain degree of professional cool, Michael got his phone out and took pictures of it from different angles, muttering, 'If you're saying we're not interested in *objects* . . .'

As I left the British Museum I spotted a coin dealer's shop on Great Russell Street and dropped in on an impulse to ask them about my rare penny. 'I found this 1827 penny—' I began.

'What, in *this* country?' interjected the masked numismatist.

When I said yes, his eyebrows shot up, so I explained that I knew the story about the 1827 mintage having gone to Tasmania and he confirmed it.

'I was going to say,' he said, 'it's rare to find one here.'

'How rare?'

'Pretty rare.'

At this point, having piqued his curiosity, I couldn't resist detaining him further with the story of Thomas Budd – the version in which Thomas didn't end up in a hastily hewn grave on Rat Island, Gosport but instead survived the prison hulk, was transported to the penal colonies, served his time and, Magwitch-like, returned to his old stomping ground with at least one penny and a hole in his pocket.

'Nice little story, that,' observed the numismatist.

Of course I hadn't been hiding in the hedge when the rare penny dropped in the Hampshire field. And I had no find spot evidence or any other data to back up this version. But if it is not true, I know this tale of homecoming has a truth all its own.

11

THE END OF THE EARTH

It had been almost a year since I'd gone online to order my metal detector and in doing so reordered my life. Spring was giving England's moth-eaten winter clothing a dusting of vivid green and we had lit our last fire till October in the old inglenook. With most fields off-limits due to crop growth – and the Iron Age field inaccessible due to cows – it was closed season for metal detecting. A good time, then, to do some more beach work and while I was at it return that gold bullet to the ocean.

I put it in a pocket of the canvas bag and set off for Kent, where Kris had invited me on to some promising coastal sites. We met again at that Brewers Fayre pub on the outskirts of Dover and this time passed through its jaunty portals, hooking up with two of his detectorist buddies: Billy – wiry frame, goatee and flat cap, known also as Merlin or 'the man who sits on mushrooms'; and Steve – ex-army, runs a scrapyard, manner of a shy bear about him.

Steve turned out a pocketful of grip-seal bags, each with a find in it. In front of us – among the pint glasses and my plate of polished-off haddock and chips – lay things the quality and rarity of which would grace the most prestigious museums and I was convinced I would never find if I metal detected for 30 years: gold hammered coin, Roman figurine of Mercury in his little winged cap, gold quarter stater of the Iceni tribe, Bronze Age spearhead . . .

Finally, a piece of lead with that chewing-gum look to it: a papal bulla of Leo III, AD 795–816, deep in England's Saxon history, when Kent was annexed by the Mercian Kings Offa and Coenwulf, and Charlemagne became the first Holy Roman Emperor. Where Steve found it is on a more-or-less direct route from Dover to Canterbury.

'That is the earliest papal bulla found in England, so I've been told,' muttered the man who runs a scrapyard.

'He's a jammy twat!' said Billy gleefully.

Feeling relaxed, among friends, I realised that I now had enough of a backstory as a detectorist to tell my own stories, so I described, with a show of seasoned cynicism, the Pompey mudlarking expedition – how that police launch had followed us along the foreshore just desperate for us to step over a line so that they could bust us (there was no actual evidence for this but it fed into a certain anti-authoritarian, outlaw mentality we detectorists like to cultivate without actually being outlaws – nighthawks excepted).

Billy offered a little saying that is apparently typical of his little sayings: 'Hope flies high in the sky and it's got no legs, so it can't land, so you can't get hold of it.' He added vaguely that he thought this might be a Chinese proverb.

'You've lost us there, mate,' we said.

Kris was in reflective mood, and after Steve had stuffed the plastic bags and their extraordinary cargo back in his pocket and he and Billy had pushed off into the night, he went back over his career.

'I was a good youth worker,' he said. 'I was really good at getting kids off the streets and off the drugs and into positive pursuits. I literally saved lives – pulled two kids off the railway tracks.' He also played bass guitar in a band called Hot Buttered Muffin that was well known on the local circuit. 'Mark King was a fan of mine – from Level 42?' he said.

He talked wistfully of his friends who followed conventional career paths and now have mortgages and architect-designed houses while he's still renting in his mid-forties. 'But I couldn't have done that, the corporate life is not for me,' he said. 'It kills something inside you.'

I asked him about the van. By now I had seen it close up and admired its blokeish self-sufficiency, concluding it must be a womb substitute, or a capsule for firing himself into his own outer space. I wanted to draw him out but he played down its significance. He said it was just a vehicle.

After a night in the Premier Inn by Dover Harbour, listening to a ship's foghorn honking like a lovelorn walrus, I was back at the pub car park to rendezvous with Kris and another two of his detectorist mates, Simon and Luke – like many of us, middle-aged men with downcast eyes and a no-frills air about them that reminded me of a line from *Brighton Rock*: 'With immense labour and immense patience they extricated from the long day the grain of pleasure.'

In our hotchpotch of wagons, we set off in convoy for Reculver, on the north coast of Kent near Herne Bay. Beyond Reculver's clusters of static homes lies a palimpsest of English history of which the most prominent features, balanced precariously on top of crumbling cliffs, are the twin towers of a twelfth-century church. The rest is below ground or has been lost to the sea, as has the Anglo-Saxon monastery that predated it. Around and about it are the stone walls and grassy undulations of a Roman fort named Regulbium.

To reach Reculver, we drove across the marshy flatlands, covered in frothy green umbellifers, that once formed the Wantsum sea channel. This separated the Isle of Thanet from the rest of Kent in Roman times but had silted up by the medieval era. At the southern end of the Wantsum, at a place called Richborough, at least some of the massive Roman invasion force of AD 43 came ashore and established a heavily fortified supply base that grew into a major port. This was the Dover of the Roman occupation, in the land described by the Roman poet Horace as 'the end of the earth'. The fort at Regulbium – Reculver – was built on a bluff at the northern end of the Wantsum channel.

The evening before our visit, I had read an account of Reculver in the late eighteenth century written by a vicar and antiquary from Norfolk called Sir John Cullum. He reported that the crumbling of the cliffs regularly deposited Roman coins on the beach, where local kids picked them up and tried to sell them to suckers like him. He was offered a handful for a reasonable price but they were 'not worth purchafing' being 'all fo corroded' and all 'fmall, fome extremely fo.' (Fpit it out, Revd – they were grotf!)

Now – a little late in the day, perhaps – the beaches below the towers and to either side are designated a scheduled monument where metal detecting is prohibited. We were going to walk east, beyond the towers, till we hit the first permissible beach and continue from there.

As we were kitting ourselves up in the car park, Kris sidled over to me and said softly, 'I need to talk to you about something.'

'Oh yeah?'

He looked around him. The others were within earshot.

'I'll tell you on the beach.'

As we walked towards the towers, I took up the rear, feeling glum. What was Kris going to tell me? I hardly noticed the tourists and cyclists, who were looking with both bemusement and amusement at our waders and wellies, our shovels and absurd electronic sticks. I decided he was going to admit to being a nighthawk. The van must be part of it. The whole horrible scenario was falling into place.

Beyond the second breakwater after the towers, we dropped on to the beach. Up by the concrete sea wall, two huge dumper trucks were ferrying shingle around, trying to redistribute whole sections of beach that had been moved by winter storms and longshore drift. A bulldozer was on hand to ram the shingle into place. We made for the water's edge. It was 3.30pm, an hour to low tide. Simon and Luke were immediately in the zone, headphones on, heads bowed.

Kris turned back and creaked up to me in his waders.

'After our conversation in the pub last night I was thinking about what I'd said, and I haven't been completely straight with you.'

Here we go, I thought.

'That stuff I said about not wanting to do an office job because it kills something inside you – that wasn't the real reason . . .'

In his twenties, said Kris, he was diagnosed with ulcerative colitis. The fear of being unable to control his bowels in public made him withdraw from the world and he became agoraphobic and 'highly anxious'. This image of being a free-spirited soul, a tousled troubadour of weald and beach, was part of the picture he constructed to rationalise his decisions and disguise their motives. Having to break up the band was not so easily explained: 'We were going places. Had to cancel a gig in Brixton. John Peel was going to be there. It broke me.'

YouTube put him plausibly in his bedroom where he has stayed, teaching bass guitar, teaching metal detecting, with forays into farmer's fields for his metal-detecting gigs that carry none of the danger of public transport, music venues or office blocks – for he can always become that ursine yardstick of things being just the way they should be, the bear who shits in the woods. And the van?

He brought it up, not me. Like a travel bag packed and ready by the door, the van has an emergency bucket on permanent standby below the bed platform, next to the space where the metal detectors slot. The van is the final frontier between him and his fear.

'There's a reason I am who I am,' he said to me now. 'A reason we all are who we are. In my case it's bad stuff. And I thought you ought to know.'

For the first ever time, I used the 'Wet sand' setting on my detector. Didn't get on with it at all. The signals were faint, and whenever I dug, the hole filled immediately with seawater. Waking up that morning, I'd had high hopes of a grot or two at Reculver. Now I could hardly concentrate as I mulled over what Kris had just told me. It made me think back to something Michael Lewis had said in the British Museum.

Trying to convey to me the significance of find spots to the professional archaeologist, how they add meaning to otherwise meaningless objects, he came up with a resonant analogy: 'It's a bit like identity. All of us reflect on where we've come from and where we grew up . . .' If you removed from your memory all the experiences that have made you – including or especially the 'bad stuff' – you wouldn't be you, you wouldn't have a clue who you are.

Kris was just coming to terms with who he was. Whether we realise it or not, it's what all of us are trying to do when you see us on our solitary, shuffling, head-down journeys across the fields. We're finding who we are. In my case, I'd been to the ends of the earth first, but this citizen of nowhere had been coming home for a while now. All the journeys – the scarcely believable quantity of travel I'd done – for what? A living for sure, a good one compared to most. But also a running away. A losing myself in places where no one could possibly know or judge me. Places to float and be invisible in. The pandemic had pinned me down, compelled me to touch base on England's clouded hills, and they were teaching me to see patterns and find belonging in them. The permissions we go on about – they're also permission to be ourselves.

Luke veered towards me.

'Found much?' I said before he could say the same thing to me.

'Fishing weights. This.' He produced a faceted copper ring. 'I think it's ordnance – or could be a Viking bracelet! You?'

'Nothing.'

'At all?'

I shook my head. I had found a big iron ring, blistered with rust, and it weighed a ton. I didn't want it in my bag, so I'd covered it back up with sand. (They might not admit it, but detectorists sometimes re-bury the junk they have found rather than having to lug it around.) Statistically this was to be my worst outing to date. No finds of any merit and no junk, apart from that iron ring. But I was fine with that. As the guvnor said, a find is a bonus.

At 4.10pm a little island began to appear out in the small grey waves. By 4.20pm an isthmus of shingle had been revealed. I walked it, halfheartedly sweeping the coil, treading on shells. On the island, I turned and looked back at the beach. Up on the promontory the towers of Reculver looked, in the flat light, like a shape of crêpe paper cut out with sharp scissors. Kris, Simon and Luke were small stick figures, detecting companionably close to one another by the water's edge. Watching them, I felt a twinge of envy, then remembered I was one of the crew now.

In this pop-up spot of loneliness, I pulled the gold bullet, the novelty reliquary, from my bag and hurled it as far as I could into the sea. It entered the water like an Olympic diver, making hardly a splash, and I felt a release in my soul.

The beach was suddenly empty, the others had called it a day and gone back to the car park. As I trudged after them along the sea wall, the sun pierced the sea mist and the ghosts of urchins clamoured towards me with grots in their outstretched hands. Next to the bulldozer, a man in hi-vis overalls was weighing me up – the kit, my weary gait, the lopsided smile on my face.

'You didn't find no gold then,' he said as I walked past. It was a statement, not a question; he thought he knew the score. But we're not always fools, looking for stuff we never find. Sometimes the light bends and the voices we tune into are sweet and true.

USEFUL NOTES

For those wishing to take up the hobby, the National Council for Metal Detecting (NCMD) is probably your first port of call. Its website, ncmd.co.uk, has lots of information and advice, including a Beginner's Guide (with specimen permission agreement form), a Code of Conduct and details of the treasure laws. Annual membership, which gives you insurance cover against mishaps in the field, costs peanuts. As I mention in the text, other bodies are available for joining.

The website of the Portable Antiquities Scheme (PAS), finds.org. uk, with its superb and ever-growing database (featuring 1,591,883 objects, including 5 recorded by me, at the time of writing and considerably more by the time of reading), will have you hooked. Besides the database (warning: you can fritter away whole days inside it), there are comprehensive guides to different objects and eras.

Greenlight Publishing (greenlightpublishing.com) has a list of reference books on finds as well as beginner's guides for detectorists. For background and news on archaeology, the Council for British Archaeology (archaeologyuk.org) is 'the voice of archaeology in the

UK'. See also *Current Archaeology* magazine (archaeology.co.uk) and websites thepipeline.info and bajrfed.co.uk.

The Historic Environment Record (HER) detailing the Historic England research records for your area can be found at heritagegateway. org.uk. There is no longer free online access to old, e.g. early Ordnance Survey (OS), maps. Resources such as archiuk.com, which has a database of old maps, require a subscription.

Old-school sleuthing – checking out local libraries (often brilliant but little-visited places that need all the support they can get), picking the brains of local historians and people who have lived in a place for donkey's years – is good fun and can be very rewarding. Use Google Earth to search areas and study your detecting sites in advance. You never know what ghostly traces you might spot.

So what metal detector should you buy? No idea! The choice is an invidious one, as there are so many good machines out there, in different price ranges, and people have their favourite makes and models. Best thing is to seek advice from old hands and read/watch reviews in *Treasure Hunting* (treasurehunting.co.uk) and *The Searcher* (thesearcher.co.uk) magazines and online.

There is no definitive list of metal-detecting clubs in the UK but plenty of information online and they all have their own Facebook groups. As a non-member, you can dip your toe in the water by going along on organised digs. In the end, it is all about the detecting community. They are a welcoming bunch and you will quickly find what you're looking for. As I did.

ACKNOWLEDGEMENTS

This book was only remotely feasible because so many detectorists showed such generosity in allowing me into their world, to the point where it became mine too. I'm unable to name them all because many were encountered casually in fields and meadows, but here are some: Sally and Rob; Andy and Paddy; Dean, Louise and Alex; Dawn Chipchase; Alastair Hacket, Linda Adams and Anthea Skea; Sergio and Víctor; Mike Clark and Jon Dixon; Rich and Si Finds; Steve, Billy, Simon and Luke. I reserve special mention for: Pete Welch, Christopher Holmes, Mark Vine, Dave Crisp, Gary Cook and Manni Kirchner. For his kindness and openness, Kris Rodgers is in a category of his own.

The worlds of archaeology, history and heritage preservation have also been generous in sharing their time and expertise with me. Thanks are due to Mark Harrison (of Historic England) and Daryl Holter; to archaeologists Dot Boughton, Sophie Hawke, Helen Geake, James Sainsbury, Neil Wilkin and Matthew Knight; and to local historian Jane Hurst. I am especially indebted to Jenny Durrant, Simon Maslin, Michael Lewis and, last but not least, Katie Hinds, who did a brilliant job of combing the text for stupidities and providing invaluable context.

My permissions were courtesy of David and Vanessa, Mr and Mrs Smith, Sheridan and Louise (sorry about the lawn), Liz, and Sam Ross-Skinner. Thanks to all.

On the writing side, I am grateful to Ben Ross at the *Telegraph* for the original commission; to Stuart Cooper, my agent, for finding the right home for the book and guiding me through so deftly; to Trevor Davies at Cassell/Octopus Books for getting it straightaway and having the vision to really lift it; to Sarah Hulbert for her meticulous copy-editing and Jo Richardson for her thorough proofreading; and to Leanne Bryan for bringing it all together so smartly. The evocative cover and lovely illustrations are the work of Mel Four, and I'm indebted to David Mossman for the photographs, which elevate the old objects I found to things of beauty.

On a personal note, cheers to Dave and to James Peto for indulging my rambling metal-detecting anecdotes in the Zoom Bar. Thanks to Michael Kerr for the best line in the book. And, finally, my amazed gratitude goes to my partner Miren for her smart feedback and meticulous editing – and for putting up with a stranger in the house and a funny machine in the porch.

INDEX